SYNTACTIC THEORY

Accession no.
360

D0487083

WITHDRAWN

WITHDRAWN

MODERN LINGUISTICS SERIES

Series Editors

Professor Noël Burton-Roberts
University of Newcastle upon Tyne

Professor Andrew Spencer
University of Essex

Each textbook in the **Modern Linguistics** series is designed to provide a carefully graded introduction to a topic in contemporary linguistics and allied disciplines, presented in a manner that is accessible and attractive to readers with no previous experience of the topic, but leading them to some understanding of current issues. The texts are designed to engage the active participation of the reader, favouring a problem-solving approach and including liberal and varied exercise material.

Noël Burton-Roberts founded the **Modern Linguistics** series and acted as Series Editor for the first three volumes in the series. Andrew Spencer has since joined Noël Burton-Roberts as Series Editor.

Titles published in the series

English Syntax and Argumentation (second edition)   Bas Aarts
Phonology   Philip Carr
Linguistics and Second Language Acquisition   Vivian Cook
Sociolinguistics: A Reader and Coursebook
Nikolas Coupland and Adam Jaworski
Morphology   Francis Katamba
Semantics   Kate Kearns
Syntactic Theory   Geoffrey Poole
Contact Languages: Pidgins and Creoles   Mark Sebba

Further titles in preparation

Modern Linguistics Series
Series Standing Order
ISBN 0–333–71701–5 hardcover
ISBN 0–333–69344–2 paperback
(*outside North America only*)

You can receive future titles in this series as they are published by placing a standing order. Please contact your bookseller or, in the case of difficulty, write to us at the address below with your name and address, the title of the series and the ISBN quoted above.

Customer Services Department, Palgrave Distribution Ltd
Houndmills, Basingstoke, Hampshire RG21 6XS, England

Syntactic Theory

Geoffrey Poole

LIS LIBRARY

Date	Fund
13/7/0a	La

Order No
2044080

| University of Chester |

palgrave
macmillan

© Geoffrey Poole 2002

All rights reserved. No reproduction, copy or transmission of
this publication may be made without written permission.

No paragraph of this publication may be reproduced, copied or
transmitted save with written permission or in accordance with
the provisions of the Copyright, Designs and Patents Act 1988,
or under the terms of any licence permitting limited copying
issued by the Copyright Licensing Agency, 90 Tottenham Court
Road, London W1T 4LP.

Any person who does any unauthorised act in relation to this
publication may be liable to criminal prosecution and civil
claims for damages.

The author has asserted his right to be identified
as the author of this work in accordance with the
Copyright, Designs and Patents Act 1988.

First published 2002 by
PALGRAVE
Houndmills, Basingstoke, Hampshire RG21 6XS and
175 Fifth Avenue, New York, N.Y. 10010
Companies and representatives throughout the world

PALGRAVE is the new global academic imprint of
St. Martin's Press LLC Scholarly and Reference Division and
Palgrave Publishers Ltd (formerly Macmillan Press Ltd).

ISBN-10: 0–333–77096–X hardback
ISBN-10: 0–333–77097–8 paperback
ISBN-13: 978-0-333-77096-2 hardback
ISBN-13: 978-0-333-77097-9 paperback

This book is printed on paper suitable for recycling and made
from fully managed and sustained forest sources. Logging, pulping
and manufacturing processes are expected to conform to the
environmental regulations of the country of origin.

A catalogue record for this book is available
from the British Library.

Library of Congress Cataloging-in-Publication Data

Poole, Geoffrey, 1969–
    Syntactic theory / (Geoffrey Poole)
        p. cm. – (Modern linguistics series)
    Includes bibliographical references and index.
    ISBN 0–333–77096–X – ISBN 0–333-77097-8 (pbk.)
        1. Grammar, Comparative and general – Syntax. 2. Government-binding
theory (Linguistics) I. Title. II. Modern linguistics series (Palgrave (Firm))

P291 .P64 2001
415–dc21   2001036097

Typeset in Great Britain by
Aarontype Ltd, Easton, Bristol

Printed and bound in Great Britain by
Biddles Ltd,. King's Lynn, Norfolk

for my parents, Lynn and Barbara,
and for María, my best friend ever

Contents

Figures and Tables

Figures

Tables

Preface

This may sound like an odd thing to say about a book entitled *Syntactic Theory*, but the fact that this book is about syntactic theory is, in certain respects, incidental. I've written a book about syntax, and not quantum hydrodynamics, simply because I happen to know a little more about the former than the latter. (At least that's what my degree parchment says.) What this book is really about is theory-building: how to examine data, formulate and test hypotheses, and evaluate the results. We'll be building towards a generic version of Government and Binding Theory, which was first outlined in a 1981 book by Noam Chomsky called *Lectures on Government and Binding*. Government and Binding Theory is what I grew up with, and, crucially for my purposes, the theory is generally explicit enough and detailed enough to have deductive structure. (This is unlike a lot of more recent Chomskyian work in the so-called 'Minimalist Program'.) Because of this detail and structure, we can see clearly how the parts of the theory interrelate and test the predictions that it makes.

This is important because linguistics in general, and syntactic theory in particular, offers an opportunity that you don't get in a lot of academic subjects: to really, honestly learn how to think. Even in a lot of natural sciences, like physics or chemistry, you really only learn a little about that. At the initial/undergraduate level, it's mostly about solving ready-made problems. You memorize various tools and methods that are pretty well fixed in stone and the only real challenge involves figuring out which equation is the one you need to solve the problem. There's no real suspense or sense of discovery because you're looking at problems that have had known solutions for 2000 years.

That's not the case in linguistics. It's still very much a process of feeling our way forward. Sure, some things are more secure than others, but there's still a lot of unexplored territory and lot of open questions. It's perfectly possible as an undergraduate to make a real discovery because you've had that flash of inspiration which nobody's had before, or because you got interested in looking at some aspect of a more exotic language that nobody's ever investigated. For that reason, I can't (and wouldn't want to) claim that the information and analyses in this book are The Truth, perfectly secure and immutable for all time. If that's what you're looking for, I'm sorry. I can't help you. (Do get in touch if you find it, however!) Even the most elegant or most sensible answers sometimes have problems, and I'll try not to just brush them under the rug, or to trick you into not seeing them. Also, for people who are interested in doing this, they can be interesting topics for independent study projects under your teacher's supervision.

For those people who will be going on to do syntactic theory in more detail, I've tried to cover most of the 'big' issues that underlie a lot of work that's done and that get talked about a lot. That way, when you go to read a real article on Chomskyian syntax, you should at least have some basic idea what the article's about and know some of the background. However, even for those people who never think about syntax ever again, I hope you'll be a better thinker and problem-solver at the end of the book than you were at the beginning. That'll be a useful skill no matter what you end up doing.

G.P.
University of Newcastle-upon-Tyne

Acknowledgements

I must first and foremost thank my editor and colleague Noel Burton-Roberts. I can't imagine what he must have thought when, less than six months after my arrival in Newcastle to take up my first job, I said to him 'I wanna write a syntax textbook. How do I go about it?' To my amazement, he said 'Well, here's how to write a proposal.' And, as a result, here we are. His help over the last couple of years in banging this into shape has been absolutely invaluable and I can assure you with 100 percent certainty that any errors or problems herein are a result of my not taking his advice about something. Chalk it up to a combination of piss and vinegar and the folly of youth.

I also must convey the now traditional thanks to Samuel D. Epstein, my old PhD supervisor, 'for trying to teach me to do linguistics right'. His training and supervision are reflected in just about every sentence. I also want to thank all my other teachers at Harvard and MIT, especially Höski Thráinsson, Jill Carrier, and Mark Hale.

It's amazing how the linguistics literature doesn't ever provide exactly the example that you need in order to make a point clearly, and so thanks to John Stonham, Ikuyo Kawanishi, and Fiona Lockett for help with data from Chinese and Japanese. And thanks also to all the students in my Spring 2001 class in Topics in the Structure of English for listening patiently to my early-morning attempts to make this stuff sound plausible.

Finally, a salty salute to absent friends (and former linguists), especially Erich, John, Scott, and Steve.

1 Introduction

Topics: the scientific study of language, the competence/performance distinction, studying a cognitive system, the principles and parameters of Universal Grammar.

1.0 INTRODUCTION

Language has been an object of interest and investigation for thousands of years. The dialogues of Plato, which form the starting point for most of Western philosophy and science almost 2500 years ago, contain speculations about language, particularly in the dialogue *The Cratylus*. One of the most interesting things about language is that, despite what you may have been led to believe by the popular literature, linguistic capacities of the sort that humans have don't seem to be possessed by other animals. Furthermore, every human being exposed to a language as an infant will grow into a competent speaker of a human language. In other words, language appears to be a species-specific property – something possessed by all human beings and only human beings. Our language plays a central role in human thought, society, and action. Therefore, in studying language, we're exploring in a fundamental way what it means to be human.

1.1 THE SCIENTIFIC STUDY OF LANGUAGE

The first question we need to ask ourselves is how we want to study language. The approach that we'll be taking in this book is most strongly influenced by the American linguist Noam Chomsky, one of the most important figures in twentieth-century linguistics. We'll see constant references to his work both in the broad outlines of the theory and in the details of particular analyses.

At the most general level, Chomsky suggests that we should investigate language by using the methods of the natural sciences – formulating hypotheses, testing those hypotheses against data, making our theory as simple as possible (as long as we make the right predictions), etc. That's not to say that this approach is guaranteed to succeed. It could turn out that using the methods of the natural sciences doesn't get us anywhere, in which case we'd need to try something else. But it seems right to say that this is where we should start.

On Chomsky's view, it's just a fact about the world that people speak and understand one another, on a par with any other fact about the natural world. I expel air from my lungs which sets air molecules in motion. Those molecules hit your eardrum and that causes thoughts to arise in your mind which roughly correspond to the content of what I said. This is just another fact about the world, like the fact that things fall down and not up. We want to try and formulate theories which explain why the world is the way it is, and not some other way.

Implicit in this approach is also the assumption that there's a right answer and there's a wrong answer, what philosophers call a 'fact of the matter'. Human beings have some way of speaking and understanding their language. We're constructing a theory about that ability, and that theory is either right or wrong. It either correctly describes the way that human beings *actually* speak and understand their language, or it doesn't. For this reason, it's important for us to be as explicit and clear as possible in constructing our theory. That way, we can more easily check to see whether our theory makes the right prediction or not.

This isn't the only possible approach to language, though. For example, the linguist Zelig Harris (who was Chomsky's PhD supervisor) believed that the study of language was more akin to the study of literature. It was a question of illuminating a subject from different points of view, with no one view being 'right' or 'better' than another. However, I'm inclined to agree with Chomsky that we should begin our investigation of language using the methods of the natural sciences, and at least see how far we can get with it.

1.1.1 What Are We Studying?

So if we're agreed that we want to approach language using the methods of the natural sciences, where should we begin? First, our ability to speak and understand our language must reside somewhere in the body. But where? The brain seems like a good bet. Certain kinds of brain injuries, such as strokes, can impair one's ability to speak and understand one's language. Similarly, if electrical activity in the brain is temporarily disrupted, this can also create language impairments. (This is commonly done during brain operations to map out which exact areas of a person's brain are used for language, in order to ensure that the surgeon minimizes the removal of tissue from those areas.) By contrast, if we look at the foot or the heart, there doesn't seem to be any injury to those areas which can impair our linguistic abilities in the same way. Therefore, at its most basic level, in doing linguistics we're studying the human brain. Whatever our linguistic capacities are and however they're organized, they're part of the human brain.

Having established that we're studying the brain, and that we want to study the brain scientifically, you might wonder we don't start talking in this book about various kinds of complicated brain-imaging scanners. Whenever you see a science documentary about the brain, the focus is almost exclusively on CAT scans, PET scans, MRI scans, EEGs, and the like. Society seems to create the impression that, in order to do 'Science' (with a capital S), you need to be wearing a white lab coat and use lots of expensive equipment. However, as we mentioned in the last section, doing science is really just about having a certain attitude and approach toward what you're studying. As long as you're constructing and testing theories with the goal of discovering something about the natural world, you're doing science.

In linguistics, it's not that we *couldn't* do brain scans. The problem is that not really enough is understood about the brain at that level for it to be a useful thing to do at this stage. At the low, 'nitty-gritty' level, we're not 100 percent certain what's responsible for our ability to speak and understand a language. Many people argue that neurons are relevant, but there could also be a role to play for electrical configurations, chemical activity, some combination of these things, or maybe even something else that we have yet to discover. Nobody is really sure what to look at. So, while complicated experiments with brain scans are part of the popular idea of 'studying the brain', there's no point in doing them if you don't really understand what the results mean.

Well, if we want to study the linguistic system of the brain scientifically, and we're not going to be doing brain scans, how should we approach it? What we have to do is treat the linguistic system of the brain like a 'black box'. We'll try to put things into one side of the black box and see what comes out the other side. From careful observation about what goes in and what comes out, we can begin to theorize about what has to be inside the black box in order to explain the results that we're getting. Eventually, we'll get to the stage where we can make predictions: if X goes into the black box, then Y should come out. If Y doesn't come out then our theory is wrong somewhere, and we'll need to change it. In fact, many philosophers see this process of 'falsification' as the litmus test for science. If you're being explicit enough to know that what you're saying is false, and then you try to correct your theory, you're doing science.

1.2 THE COMPETENCE/PERFORMANCE DISTINCTION

In this book, we'll be focusing on a particular aspect of the linguistic system, namely syntax. That is, we'll be focusing on sentence structure and 'grammar'. What sort of experiments should we run in order to investigate our grammatical capacities? How do we investigate this grammatical 'black box'? As Chomsky has noted on many occasions, there seems to be a distinction between what people *know* and what they *do*. Put another way, what we actually say during the course of ordinary conversation isn't always an accurate reflection of our linguistic capacities. We can make mistakes, such as slips of the tongue, for example. Chomsky refers to this distinction as the *competence/performance* distinction. Therefore, we don't want to focus our attention on what comes out of our mouths. We want to focus on the *underlying system*.

1.2.1 Studying Behavior

In earlier parts of the twentieth century, though, it was common for linguists to study 'linguistic behavior'. They would record as many speakers and as much natural conversation as they could, and then analyze these recordings and construct a theory based on what was found. This approach would seem to be perfectly in keeping with our goal of investigating language using the methods of the natural sciences. If we were studying, say, dominance hierarchies in ape groups, we would probably spend a lot of time observing and recording their behavior in different situations and then constructing a theory from that data.

However, there a number of reasons why that approach isn't the best way to investigate the syntactic capacities of human beings. When you're actually producing speech in real time, there are all sorts of factors which come into play – how tired you are, whether you're paying attention, etc. As a result, *actual* speech is full of 'mistakes', like false starts, slips of the tongue, and times when you start a sentence and then don't know how to finish it. I have myself on occasion produced sentences like (1) in conversation:

(1)   This is the film that you said that was good.

Now despite having produced this sentence in conversation, I would admit, if it were pointed out to me, that the sentence in (1) is *not* part of my language. Intuitively, I know there's something wrong with (1), and, more specifically, the problem occurs in the phrase 'said that was good'. In order for the sentence to be well-formed, the *that* must be deleted, creating (2). (This is true for most dialects of British and American English, although not all.)

(2)   This is the film that you said ( ) was good.

Thus, there is a competence/performance distinction. What I *do* with my language doesn't always accurately reflect what I *know* about my language because of the additional burdens involved in actually producing speech in real time.

This means that we could run into problems if we were to simply record a large amount of natural speech. It would presumably contain 'errors' of the sort we've just seen. But we would have no principled way of deciding what was an error and what wasn't without reference to the speaker's *knowledge* of what is an error and what isn't. In real life, you know whether a person has been interrupted, or broken off a sentence and started a new one, but that's because you're filtering the data through your own knowledge of the language system.

Another problem is that there are sentences which are perfectly grammatical, but which come up rarely, if at all, in ordinary conversation. In illustrating this point, Gregg (1989) discusses the following sentence:

(3)   Mary ate an apple, and Sue a pear.

He says of this sentence (p. 22): 'I do not produce [sentences of this type] because they sound incredibly affected, and I have enough problems of that sort already.' Nonetheless, if you're a native speaker of English, you know that (3) forms a part of your language. We would want our theory to explain why English speakers accept (3). However, it's not clear that we'd be able to do that if we just go out into the world and record people, since it might not come up very often in our sample. In fact, from a purely statistical point of view, sentences like this probably occur even less frequently than 'errors'.

Related to some of the points we've been making above, you also know that certain strings of words do *not* form a part of your language. When we were discussing 'errors' just a moment ago, I mentioned that (1) was ungrammatical in my dialect of English. However, this aspect of your linguistic knowledge isn't something that you'd discover if you were to just record people. People make mistakes, but that's different from getting systematic evidence that certain strings of words are ungrammatical.

For all of these reasons, it seems as though simply recording speakers has problems as a method for discovering how the 'black box' that constitutes our linguistic capacities works.

1.2.2   An Alternative to Studying Behavior: Studying Knowledge

Recall above the distinction between *competence* and *performance* which Chomsky draws our attention to. If studying performance (linguistic behavior) has the problems that we've seen, perhaps there's a way that we can focus on competence (linguistic knowledge) directly; that is to say, focusing on the cognitive system in the brain that *underlies* our linguistic behavior, rather than looking at the behavior itself (see Figure 1.1).

To do this, the standard experimental task is to solicit judgements from native speakers about the sentences of their language. Part of what you know about your language is that certain strings of words are part of that language and certain other strings are not. For example, the following string of words forms part of my language, a fairly standard dialect of American English:

(4)   I haven't read the book yet, but I will tomorrow.

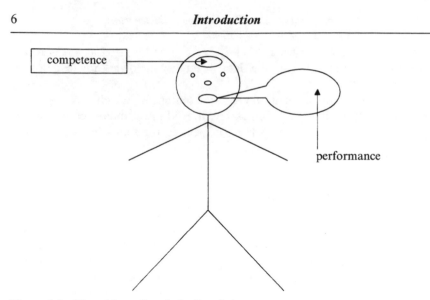

Figure 1.1   The object of study in linguistics

However, the words in a different order create a sentence which is not a part of my language:

(5)   *I yet the read book haven't, but will tomorrow I.

For a native speaker of many dialects of British English, on the other hand, neither (4) nor (5) forms a part of their language. They are both ungrammatical. The grammatical version of (4) in their dialects is (6), which to me sounds very strange.

(6)   I haven't read the book yet, but I will do tomorrow.

By feeding test sentences to native speakers of a language, and asking for their intuitive judgements/reactions, we can begin to understand what's inside the 'black box'. We can begin to understand how their linguistic system is set up.

Consulting native speaker intuitions in this way would seem to avoid, or at least minimize, the problems that we saw above when we considered simply recording speakers. There is still the problem of error due to interfering factors (which we'll discuss below). However, the burdens associated with what you're asking them to do are at least reduced. If you just have to provide your intuitive judgements, that's easier than having a 'real' conversation, with all of the distractions that that entails. You also are able to test both less frequently occurring structures and structures which you expect to be ungrammatical. Although people may not use sentences like (3) or (1) in ordinary conversation, you can still get judgements regarding them.

1.2.3 Grammaticality vs. Acceptability

As we mentioned just a moment ago, the grammaticality judgement task, which focuses on linguistic competence rather than linguistic performance, would seem to minimize errors due to interfering factors. However, it's important to see that, even when you're using grammaticality judgements, one must still consider whether the data is 'reliable'. There are things which can influence native-speaker intuitions which are not due to the linguistic system proper, but which are intimately related, including affectedness (which we mentioned above in discussing example (3)) and stylistics. For this reason, in addition to a competence/performance distinction, we also have a distinction between grammaticality and acceptability.

For example, sentences which themselves have sentences as their subjects can often be somewhat awkward stylistically.

(7) ?Once [that John was leaving] became clear, we abandoned the project.

In (7), the underlined adverbial clause contains a sentence *that John was leaving* which is itself in the subject position of the sentence *that John was leaving became clear*. This can result in a sentence which doesn't flow and which is difficult to understand. To make the sentence easier to understand, the sentential subject is often put at the end and a dummy pronoun *it* placed in subject position:

(8) Once *it* became clear *that John was leaving*, we abandoned the project.

Unlike the somewhat awkward (7), (8) is perfect. However, despite the fact that (7) and (8) differ in *acceptability*, they are both *grammatical*, in the sense that our grammar (theory) should generate them. Our judgements in (7) are being influenced by extra-grammatical factors. In this case, stylistics and difficulty of processing.

This point is also illustrated by a story that Professor Jill Carrier, one of my old teachers, related to me about some fieldwork that she was doing with a native speaker of Tagalog, a language of the Philippines. She had a list of sentences that she was checking with the informant, and they were all confirmed as grammatical in Tagalog as expected. However, there was one particular sentence where the informant said 'Oh, no. Nobody would ever say that. That's impossible.' This was deeply puzzling, as from a structural point of view it seemed to be identical to various other sentences which were all reported to be perfectly fine. After much thought and further questioning, she discovered that the problem was that the example sentence happened to involve children swimming in the ocean. The informant had objected to the sentence because the ocean was full of sharks and no children would ever be swimming in the ocean. It was too dangerous. Clearly, in that instance, it wasn't that the informant's *grammar* didn't generate the sentence in question. Instead, non-linguistic factors – knowledge of the real world – were influencing his judgement. What we are trying to do is isolate purely linguistic capacities.

Thus, whenever we're discussing grammaticality judgements or consulting with informants, we need to make sure that we keep this distinction between acceptability and grammaticality in mind. There may be plenty of sentences that our mental grammar generates. There are some, like (3), which are said quite infrequently, but there are also sentences which we would *never* say for one reason or another. If we want to correctly characterize how the 'black box' of our linguistic capacities works, we want to be sure that our theory captures *all* of the sentences that it allows.

1.3   SOME SIMPLE APPROACHES TO GRAMMATICALITY JUDGEMENTS

In the previous sections, we've argued that we should focus in on a particular aspect of your linguistic knowledge: grammaticality judgements. You know instantly and without prior instruction that certain sentences of your language are grammatical and certain other ones are ungrammatical. But how do you know what you know? Where do these grammaticality judgements come from?

To start with, let's take some first guesses at what might be going on. Just to be methodical, we'll start with some simple possibilities and work through to more complicated ones. Hopefully, you'll be convinced that these various simplified accounts aren't plausible.

1.3.1   The 'Parrot' Theory

The first, most naïve account of how you come to have grammaticality judgements would be that you judge a sentence grammatical if you've heard it before, and judge it ungrammatical if you haven't heard it before. Call this the 'parrot theory'. This is pretty obviously wrong, I think. One of the most striking features of language is its unbounded capacity for innovation. It's quite likely that a large number of the sentences in this paragraph, not to mention the book so far, will be sentences that you've personally never come across before (unless you've heard me lecture). However, none of these sentences strikes you as strange or unfamiliar. I can even make up a sentence which I'm 100 percent sure is new in the history of the English language (at least at the time of writing):

(9)   Although Huxley's *The Doors of Perception* was never intended to be taken internally, there were many people in the late 1960s who failed to heed the warnings of prominent scholars and critics.

I'd bet a lot of money that (9) has never been produced ever in the entire history of the English language, yet you see it as a well-formed sentence of English without any effort whatsoever. I take that as fairly conclusive proof that one's grammaticality judgements aren't based on simply whether you've heard the sentence before. Otherwise, you ought to judge (9) as ungrammatical, and you don't.

1.3.2 Other Seemingly Plausible Suggestions

It also appears as though various other seemingly simple and plausible ideas don't play a role in our grammaticality judgements. For example, judgements about grammaticality are totally independent of what, if anything, the sentence means. (10) is a famous example sentence from Chomsky (1957):

(10) Colorless green ideas sleep furiously.

Personally, I don't have the first clue what this sentence means. Ideas don't normally have colors, but even if they could, they certainly couldn't be colorless and green simultaneously. I'm also hard pressed to understand what sleeping furiously might entail. However, one thing I do know is that (10) is different from (11), where the words are in the reverse order:

(11) *Furiously sleep ideas green colorless.

The difference is that (10), despite its bizarre non-meaning, is syntactically well-formed. (11), on the other hand, is not syntactically well-formed.

The reverse situation can be found as well – that is, sentences which *do* make sense, but which we instantly judge to be ungrammatical. Consider (12):

(12) *The child seems sleeping.

Unlike (10) or (11), we have no problem assigning a meaning to the sentence in (12). If a foreigner had produced it, we would have no difficulty understanding what he or she intended to convey. However, we all know instantly that (12) is not a grammatical sentence of English, even though its meaning is clear.

In a similar way, ease of use doesn't seem to have any implications for grammaticality. There are plenty of sentences which are grammatically well-formed but which are not easy to use for one reason or another. Consider tongue-twisters, for example:

(13) She sells seashells by the seashore.

The fact that they're difficult to use (difficult to pronounce, in this case) is precisely why they're of interest. But crucially, they're not ungrammatical.

Sentences can also be difficult to use because they're difficult to parse. So-called 'garden path' sentences are ones in which your parser is 'tricked' into assuming that a sentence has a structure which needs to be revised when you get to the end of the sentence. (14) is a famous example:

(14)   The horse raced past the barn fell.

The effect when reading a garden-path sentence is usually lessened, but they can be quite startling when you hear one spoken to you. That's because when you're parsing the spoken sentence in real time, your parser is usually fooled into thinking that the past participle *raced* is in fact the main verb of the sentence. You don't realize you've made a mistake until you hear *fell*, and you're suddenly left with a word that you don't know what to do with. You've then frantically got to go back and figure out where you went wrong, which is harder to do when the sentence is spoken as opposed to read. You then realize that *raced* is supposed to be a past participle rather than the main verb. It's the horse *which was raced past the barn*. In spite of all this though, when the intended reading is pointed out to you, you realize that the sentence is in fact grammatical.

1.3.3   Analogy

A slightly more sophisticated version of the 'heard it before' theory is less obviously stupid. It could be that you judge a sentence as grammatical if it's 'similar to' or 'analogous to' a sentence that you've heard before or that you know is grammatical. Call this the 'analogy' theory. The essential problem is that, as an explanation of your linguistic abilities, the whole concept just looks wrong. Consider the following pair of sentences:

(15)a.   It is likely that John is here.
    b.   It is probable that John is here.

Likely and *probable* mean almost exactly the same thing, and so it's perhaps not surprising that they can both appear in the 'it is X that John is here' frame, as we see in (15). However, consider (16):

(16)a.   John is likely to be here.
    b.   *John is probable to be here.

If analogy or similarity were the main factor in explaining why we have the grammaticality judgements that we have, it's not clear at all how or why (16b) is ungrammatical. *Likely* and *probable* are synonyms, they behave identically in (15), yet you know instantly and without prior instruction that (15b) is grammatical and (16b) is ungrammatical. Why does analogy fail here?

An even more telling example, I think, can be seen in the sentences that we were looking at earlier in the context of the competence/performance distinction in section 1.2.1 above, having to do with the presence or absence of *that*. In virtually all situations, *that* can be either present or omitted with no change in grammaticality:

(17)a. I know *that* Mary is here.
    b. I know Mary is here.

This optionality seems to remain when there is a question, rather than a statement:

(18)a. Who knows that Mary is here?
    b. Who knows Mary is here?

(19)a. Who do you think that Mary saw?
    b. Who do you think Mary saw?

However, there is one exception to this otherwise entirely regular pattern. When the *subject* of the embedded clause is questioned, the presence of complementizer *that* is no longer optional. It is obligatorily absent. (Again, this is true for *almost* all dialects of British and American English.)

(20)a. *Who did you say that left the room?
    b. Who did you say left the room?

Immediately, and without any prior instruction, you know that there's something wrong with (20a), even if you can't put your finger on what it is.

This is totally unexpected if something like analogy or similarity is relevant for understanding our intuitions about grammaticality. What we have is a paradigm which is absolutely and utterly regular, except for the one exception in (20a). If analogy were relevant, then (20a) should be grammatical, on analogy with (17a), (18a), and (19a). This really makes it look as though analogy or similarity isn't relevant for grammaticality.

1.3.4 Conclusion

What seems to be going on is that our intuitions about grammaticality stem from the fact that the brain contains a system for analyzing sentences. When presented with a sentence of English, it's analyzed by the cognitive system that you possess, providing you with a judgement about its acceptability. You have internalized a 'grammar' of your language.

What we're really doing in syntax, then, is something that you won't find in any other subject. In exploring this mental computational system and how it works, what we're doing is, in a sense, nothing more than telling you things that you already know. We are attempting to develop a theory about what's already in your head. However, that doesn't mean that you can put down the book and run away. Although you do, in an important sense, already know everything that we'll be talking about, the problem is that you don't *know* that you know it. It's knowledge, but unconscious knowledge. Syntactic theory is about making this knowledge explicit.

1.4   LANGUAGE ACQUISITION AND UNIVERSAL GRAMMAR

We've come to a pretty radical conclusion. Part of your linguistic abilities consists of having judgements about whether sentences are grammatical in your language or not. We concluded that this was because your brain contains a cognitive system which analyzes (or 'generates') sentences. In this section, we're going to ask a simple question, which turns out to have a complicated answer: how did this cognitive system get there? How did you acquire this ability to judge the grammaticality of sentences? The answer to this acquisition question will turn out to have a huge influence on the way we conduct our inquiry into syntax.

With respect to this issue, the linguist Noam Chomsky has observed what he calls 'the logical problem of language acquisition'. In a nutshell, what adults come to know about their language goes far beyond anything they were actually exposed to as children. The examples that we mentioned back in Section 1.3.3 are prime examples. *Likely* and *probable* are about as close synonyms as you can get. Yet you know instantly that *John is likely to be here* is grammatical but *John is probable to be here* isn't. However possible it might be that *one particular* speaker's experience enabled him or her to figure these facts out, it can't possibly be that *everyone's* experience was enough. Yet this is something that *every* speaker of English knows.

Here's another example, which we'll be looking at in the next chapter. (21) is a perfectly well-formed sentence of English:

(21)   Jack met the student from England and I met the one from France.

The element *one* here seems to be filling in for *student*. (21) means *Jack met the student from England and I met the student from France*. However, if we change the prepositional phrase, things change radically:

(22)   *Jack met the student of physics and I met the one of chemistry.

For some reason, although *one* can substitute for *student* in (21), it can't in (22).

So the question is: How did you come to know these facts? It certainly couldn't have come from any explicit instruction by teachers. It's unlikely that any of them would have noticed these facts. It's equally unlikely that the data you were exposed to when you were acquiring your native language was itself detailed enough for you to be able to figure out these facts. And, even more to the point, these facts are again something that *every* speaker of English knows. No matter how likely it is that you somehow managed to get exactly the right data, it's unlikely that *every* speaker of English got exactly the right data. Our experiences as children were all radically different. It looks like what we have is a case of knowledge being manufactured from nothing, not just in you, but in every speaker of English. How is this possible? This, as Chomsky sees it, is the logical problem of language acquisition.

Chomsky has a logical yet radical suggestion in order to solve this problem: if we have knowledge that couldn't have come from the data we were exposed to, it must have come from somewhere else. Chomsky proposes that this 'somewhere else' is an inborn language acquisition device specific to the human species. (This is what we mean by 'species-specific'.) Just as it is genetically predetermined that a human being will grow arms and not wings, it is genetically predetermined that a human being will acquire a human language. Children come pre-equipped to the task of language acquisition with a device that is designed to take certain kinds of acoustic disturbances ('sounds') as its input, and as its output creates a cognitive system for understanding and using language. If we assume that being exposed to a language acts as a trigger for the unfolding of a genetic program, on a par with development of limbs and organs, this would seem to solve the questions about language that we've just raised. You end up with a linguistic system that goes well beyond the particular input data you were exposed to, in precisely the same way that organ development 'goes beyond' the particular 'nutritional inputs' (i.e., food) that you were exposed to as a child.

Chomsky's hypothesis is that this 'language acquisition device', more commonly known as Universal Grammar (UG), has two central parts to it which aid in the task of language acquisition: *principles* and *parameters*. In fact, the general approach to syntax that we'll be arguing for in this book gets its name from these parts of Universal Grammar. It's called the 'Principles and Parameters' approach.

1.4.1 An Introduction to Principles and Parameters

The idea is that the *principles* of Universal Grammar account for the respects in which all human languages are the same. Most of the topics that we'll be discussing in this book concern principles of UG, and we'll be drawing data from English and many other languages in order to argue that principles of UG are at work.

Parameters, on the other hand, are intended to capture certain ways in which languages differ. Now, obviously, one way that languages differ is that they have different words for different concepts. So dog is *dog* in English, *hund* in German, *perro* in Spanish, etc. These are differences that simply have to be memorized by the child, and it's only when the child is exposed to the language that he or she will know what the words are going to be.

However, there are other ways in which languages differ. For example, the languages of the world seem to divide up into *null subject languages* and *non-null subject languages*. English is a non-null subject language. That is to say, English sentences must *always* have a subject, even when that subject appears to contribute nothing to the meaning of the sentence. Consider (23):

(23)a.   It is raining.
    b.   It seems that John is here.

The subject of the sentences in (23) is *it*, but this pronoun is totally meaningless. You're not pointing to something when you say (23a) or (23b). The pronoun doesn't refer to anything. However, because English requires a pronounced subject at all times, these 'dummy' pronouns must be inserted. By contrast, in a null subject language like Spanish, these dummy pronouns are omitted. The subject is simply not pronounced.

(24)a.   Llueve.
    rains
    'It's raining.'
    b.   Parece que Juan está aquí.
    seems that Juan is here
    'It seems that Juan is here.'

The hypothesis is that Universal Grammar contains a parameter called the Null Subject Parameter. Therefore, in some sense, the child already knows from birth that the language that he or she will be exposed to will either be a null subject language or a non-null subject language. Once the child begins to hear data, it is a relatively simple matter to set the parameter one way or the other. A parameter is like a question. Setting the parameter is a matter of answering that question in light of the evidence from the particular language.

1.5 DESCRIPTION AND EXPLANATION – THE CASE OF STRUCTURE-DEPENDENT RULES

One important benefit that our postulation of an inborn Universal Grammar also gives us is the ability to go beyond merely describing individual languages. It puts us in a position to *explain* why particular languages are the way they are. For example, one of the things which seems to characterize all languages that have been studied so far is that they form yes/no questions (and, in fact, all questions) in a *structure-dependent* fashion.

By way of illustrating the structure-dependence of yes/no questions in English, consider the following examples:

(25)a.　The agent has left the building.
　　b.　Has the agent left the building?

In (25a) we have a declarative statement. In (25b), we have the corresponding yes/no question; that is to say, a question which asks for a yes or no answer. Imagine you're a Martian scientist trying to discover what the rule is for English yes/no question formation. (Since you're a Martian, you're not familiar with English or any other human language.) On the basis of the pair in (25), a simple rule that looks like it accounts for the data is (26):

(26)　Move the third word to the front of the sentence.

This rule not only accounts for the pair in (25), but also an infinite number of other sentences, including pairs like those in (27) and (28):

(27)a.　The man is here.
　　b.　Is the man here?

(28)a.　My friend will go to the store.
　　b.　Will my friend go to the store?

The rule in (26) does not require analyzing the sentence in terms of its structure. You just go along the words one by one until you hit the third word, and you move that word to the front of the sentence. It is therefore a *structure-independent* rule.

Interestingly, although the structure-independent rule in (26) is very simple to apply, you quickly discover that it isn't right. Consider the (declarative) sentence in (29):

(29)　The man from the bank will remember nothing.

If we were to apply the structure-independent rule in (26), we would scan along from left to right until we encountered the third word, which in this case is *from*. We move *from* to the front of the sentence, and we get (30):

(30)　*From the man the bank will remember nothing?

This is clearly not a grammatical sentence of English. If we want to make the declarative sentence in (29) into a question which asks for a yes or no answer, we need to move *will* to the front of the sentence:

(31)   Will the man from the bank remember nothing?

So clearly our rule for yes/no question formation in (26) isn't right. But what is?

One thing to notice about (30) is that our rule in (26), which just counted words from left to right, ended up moving a preposition (*from*) to the front of the sentence. However, we know that in order to form a yes/no question, what we need to do is move an *auxiliary verb* to the front of the sentence. (Let's put aside the cases where we have no auxiliary, in which case you'd have to insert the 'dummy' auxiliary *do*.)

(32)a.   *Should* John have gone to the store?
      b.   *Will* the book arrive on time?
      c.   *Has* Mary defeated her opponents?

It's possible that we can save a structure-independent approach by modifying our rule in (26) to something like (33):

(33)   Move the first auxiliary verb to the front of the sentence.

That rule *does* correctly get us (31), and all of the other cases that we've seen so far, but it's still structure-independent. It doesn't require that we know anything about the *structure* of the sentence. We just scan from left to right until we hit the first auxiliary verb, and then move it to the front of the sentence.

However, (33) isn't the English rule either. Consider (34):

(34)   The man who has written the book will be followed.

Using that rule, we'd predict that the yes/no question corresponding to (34) should be (35):

(35)   *Has the man who written the book will be followed?

If this isn't the right rule either, then what is it?

Since you're a speaker of English, a human language, and not really a Martian scientist, it'll probably seem obvious what the 'right' answer is. But it's important to see how unexpected that answer is. The 'right' answer is something like (36):

(36)   Move the first auxiliary verb *in the predicate* to the front of the sentence.

You don't just move along and pick the third word or the first auxiliary in a structure-*independent* way. The rule that you've internalized requires treating the sentence not just as a string of words coming one after the other. Instead, you treat the sentence as if it has structure. The English rule for yes/no question formation is structure-*dependent*. In this case, at the very least you have to divide the sentence up into a subject and a predicate:

(37)a.   Subject: The man who has seen the book
    b.   Predicate: will be followed

Having identified the predicate, you can then find the first auxiliary in the predicate and move it to the front of the sentence. This rule will also account for the other sentences that we've seen:

(38)a.   Subject: The agent
    b.   Predicate: has left the building

(39)a.   Subject: The man
    b.   Predicate: is here

(40)a.   Subject: My friend
    b.   Predicate: will go to the store

(41)a.   Subject: The man from the bank
    b.   Predicate: will remember nothing

So it seems that even a simple thing like turning a declarative sentence into a yes/no question requires an analysis that is, from a computational point of view, somewhat complicated. You don't just scan across and pick the first auxiliary, or the tenth word or something. You need to analyze the sentence into a subject and a predicate in order to find the main verb phrase.

Now the reason for this long discussion about structure-dependent vs. structure-independent rules is to make a point about Universal Grammar. If we look at all the languages of the world that have so far been studied, the number of languages which use structure-independent rules is exactly none. There seems to be no language in the world which uses structure-independent rules for anything. No language, for example, forms questions by moving the third word to the front of the sentence, or by taking the words in the declarative and reading them in reverse order.

As we mentioned above, if we were just looking at language after language in a descriptive way, we'd have no explanation for this fact. It would just be a coincidence. We'd look at English and say, 'Wow, no structure-independent rules'. We'd then move on to Swahili and say, 'Wow, no structure-independent rules'. And so on and so forth. On the other hand, if we as humans possess a genetically determined Universal Grammar, then we can explain why we find what we find. There's something about Universal Grammar which doesn't allow for structure-independent rules.

We can even go further than this, however. If we're right to say that Universal Grammar doesn't allow for structure-independent rules, and that's what accounts for the fact that no language has them, then we make a further prediction that we can check. Assuming that the language acquisition process consists of language data interacting with Universal Grammar, then we should predict that no child should ever hypothesize a structure-independent rule during the course of language acquisition. If Universal Grammar is always there in the background, helping the child process the input data, then the child should never use structure-independent rules at any stage. Universal Grammar doesn't allow them.

Interestingly, this prediction also seems to be verified. No child is ever exposed to sentence pairs like (27) and (28) above and hypothesizes a computationally simple structure-independent rule like (26) or (33). They always and automatically make a structure-dependent choice. It might be the wrong structure-dependent choice, but it's still a structure-dependent choice. Thus, it would seem that they never hypothesize a structure-independent rule for anything because it's never an option. Children come pre-equipped to the task of language learning knowing that all grammatical rules have to be structure-dependent.

1.5.1   Other Sources of Evidence

There's some interesting corroborating evidence as well from studies of an autistic patient, who's called Christopher in the literature. Christopher has some fairly severe cognitive deficits and has to be looked after in an institution, but like some autistic patients, he also has a talent. That is, there is one area where he seems to perform much better than ordinary people. Christopher's particular talent is languages. He enjoys learning new ones and does so effortlessly and at a tremendously rapid pace. He can translate back and forth between them perfectly, getting all the grammatical endings right, etc. If Universal Grammar is implicated in Christopher's talent, then we would expect to see that reflected in the way he acquires his languages.

Structure-dependency is actually one of the things that Christopher has been tested on, and the results seem to support the existence of Universal Grammar. Christopher and a control group of normal people were presented with two languages to learn. One was Berber, a North African language, which has incredibly complex rules and constructions. The other was a made-up language which crucially contained structure-*independent* rules. Although Christopher mastered Berber without difficulty just as he had other languages, he struggled with the made-up language, and was never able to master it. The control group struggled with Berber, and also struggled initially with the made-up language, although they eventually did better than Christopher on the made-up language.

This would seem to provide strong corroborating evidence for the claim that Universal Grammar exists, and that it prohibits structure-independent rules. By hypothesis, Christopher's considerable linguistic resources come from Universal Grammar. His general problem-solving abilities are not very good. By contrast, the control group may not have the access to Universal Grammar that Christopher has (being adults), but they do have good general problem-solving skills. This would explain why the control group had difficulties with Berber which Christopher did not, and why they had more success with the made-up language. Since the made-up language contained rules which were prohibited by Universal Grammar, the control group could switch gears and treat it as though it were a puzzle, calling on their general problem-solving abilities. Since Christopher has very little resources in this area, he was unable to succeed with it.

1.5.2 Description and Explanation

So, ultimately, while we're interested in individual languages, we're also interested in discovering what we can about Universal Grammar, the initial state of the language faculty in the mind/brain. As a result, we have a constant flow of ideas back and forth between individual languages and Universal Grammar. In order to account for some particular fact about English, we might hypothesize that Universal Grammar is implicated. But a hypothesis about the make-up of Universal Grammar makes a prediction about other languages. We therefore then need to check those other languages to see if the prediction is verified.

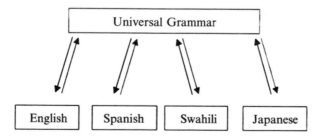

Figure 1.2 The relationship between languages and Universal Grammar

In this way, we can make a distinction between two kinds of arguments: *conceptual* and *empirical*. Roughly speaking, when we're making an argument that goes *from* Universal Grammar *to* a particular language, we're dealing with a conceptual argument. Our theory about how Universal

Grammar works says X, and so therefore we expect that we'll find X when we look at individual languages. When we're going *from* individual languages *to* Universal Grammar, then we're making an *empirical* argument. We've got some fact X about a language, and so we need to work that fact X into our theory about Universal Grammar.

We'll try as much as possible to make arguments of both types. Rather like a pair of scissors, we'll work best when we come from both directions at once. In that way, we can be as secure about our conclusions as possible.

1.6   INTRODUCTION TO THE BOOK

Now that we've discussed some general things about the study of language, I want to turn to a specific introduction to the subsequent chapters. Each chapter covers a specific topic, from sentence structure to transformations and beyond. Several of the later chapters, however, return at a more advanced level to issues raised in earlier chapters. This way, you can get an introduction to a topic in an earlier chapter, and then come back in a later chapter to more recent proposals. If you work all the way through to the end of the book, you should be well prepared, with a little bit of coaching, to take the next step – reading actual articles in the linguistics literature.

In the individual chapters, one of the things you'll find is that there are in-text exercises scattered throughout. There are two kinds. The first kind is labeled 'Exercise'. These are just like the exercises at the end of the chapter, but placed right after the relevant point of the discussion in the chapter. These are there to give you a chance to practice using the theory while the relevant concepts are fresh in your mind, and answers can be found at the end of the chapter. The second kind of exercise is labeled 'Before Continuing'. These exercises will usually come at a point where we've encountered a problem with the theory. The reader is encouraged to stop for a minute before reading on and give some thought to how to solve the problem or address the question. The immediately following discussion will then provide an answer to the question. Just like anything else, the easiest way to get comfortable with the theory is to practice it. Pretty soon the whole thing will be second nature. As I mentioned, the end of each chapter also contains exercises for you work on to practice the things that you've learned.

Each chapter also has an annotated bibliography of readings and references, if you're interested in reading more about some of the ideas discussed in a particular chapter. In many cases, the references will be to articles that we've actually discussed in the chapter. Sometimes in the chapter I will have omitted complexities that aren't relevant for the argument, or translated an argument from a slightly different framework into the one we're using, so the bibliography gives me a place to let you know that.

One of the things that's slightly different about this book is that each chapter will conclude with a section entitled 'Open Issue'. These sections are designed to take something from the chapter a step further, or into a controversial direction. I thought it was important to include things like this to show you that we're not dealing with a theory that's fixed in stone, with all problems solved and nothing new to think about. They're meant to be starting points for your own thinking, and to provide suggestions for research projects. You might try to find evidence from a different language for an Open Issue proposal or perhaps look for counter-examples and discuss whether or not they represent real problems.

1.7 SUMMARY

In this chapter, I've tried to sketch out some of the basic assumptions which underlie the more technical parts of the rest of the book. As a native speaker of a language, one aspect of your linguistic abilities is the ability to judge whether a given string of words forms a part of the language you speak or not. In other words, you have judgements about grammaticality and ungrammaticality. This ability stems from the grammar of your language which you unconsciously 'constructed' based on the language acquisition data that you were exposed to in childhood. However, what your grammar contains seems to go well beyond the data you were exposed to. Additionally, speakers of a language all converge more or less on the same grammar despite the wide variation in particular data they happened to have been exposed to. For these reasons, it's hypothesized that there is a language acquisition device, or Universal Grammar, which is part of our common genetic endowment as humans. In trying to develop a theory about 'English', by which we mean the internalized grammar of a speaker of English, we also need to construct a theory of Universal Grammar.

BIBLIOGRAPHY

Probably the most accessible work by Chomsky himself on these general topics is Chomsky (1988). It's a transcription of a series of lectures given at the University of Managua for a general audience; that is, for people who didn't know anything particularly about linguistics. One caveat, though: since the audience were native Spanish speakers, the examples he picks, though not complex, are taken from Spanish rather than English. There are translations of everything, though, and it's actually good practice for getting used to non-English examples. Most standard Chomskyan linguistics text-books don't devote much discussion to general, 'nature of linguistics' questions, but a notable exception is Haegeman (1994). Chapter 1 of that book has some very good discussion of general issues and the setting out of the Chomskyian linguistic program. For people interested in reading more about the autistic patient, Christopher, and what he can tell us about the Chomskyian approach to language, you can check out Smith and Tsimpli (1995).

2   Phrase Structure

Topics: arguments for constituent structure, motivation for X′-Theory.

Open Issue: the structure of the double object construction.

2.0   INTRODUCTION

Now that you have some idea what our general approach to 'language' is going to be and seen some reasons why studying language and languages in the manner of the natural sciences might be an interesting way to proceed, it's now time to get on with the theory-building part of things. We'll start by looking at some very simple sentences, and exploring what you already know about them in virtue of being a native speaker of a language, English in this case.

One of the things that you know about the sentences of your language is that they're made up of words, and that certain of those words go together to create larger units. Since you don't always know *consciously* what you know about your language, we'll look at various traditional tests which can tease out what you know about the structure of sentences.

We'll then introduce *phrase-structure rules* and *phrase-structure trees*. Phrase-structure trees are used to graphically illustrate the structure of a given sentence. We'll then refine our phrase-structure rules and trees in order to better account for what you know about the different ways words are organized in the structure of sentences. What we'll conclude by the end of the chapter is that Universal Grammar provides you with a general format for phrase-structure rules and trees, called X′-Theory.

2.1   A SIMPLE STARTING POINT

Let's start by taking a look at an ordinary English sentence like (1), with a view toward exploring some of the things that you know about it:

(1)   The student will meet her friend at the station.

The first observation to make with respect to (1) will strike you as the most blindingly obvious thing I could possibly say. I claim that part of what you know when you know your language is that a sentence like (1) is made up of words.

I know what you're thinking: 'Of course (1) is made up of words! How could it possibly be otherwise?' However, if we were to look at a sound spectrograph of (1), a visual representation of the sound energy created when (1) is produced, you would see that there are no breaks in the sound energy corresponding to where the word breaks are. It's all one continuous flow. Therefore, even something as simple as the fact that you perceive (1) as having words is due to the cognitive system that you have for processing language. You might be inclined to think that you know about word breaks just because the breaks are there in the writing. However, this is just an accident of English. Plenty of other writing systems (like Japanese *katakana*) put breaks after every syllable rather than every word. Word breaks are also easily perceived by speakers who are illiterate, nor do you have any problem 'hearing' word breaks in sentences with new words or words that you've never seen written.

However, you know more than just that the sentence in (1) is made up of words. You also know intuitively that certain words in (1) belong, in traditional terminology, to the same part of speech. That is, *student, friend*, and *station* are all nouns, *at* is a preposition, *meet* is a verb, and so on. You might again think that this is something that you've been taught explicitly at school, but in fact all you're doing at school is being given labels for things you already know about.

We'll take those intuitions over fairly directly, although we'll refer not to 'parts of speech', but rather to a word's *syntactic category*. Here are some examples of elements from various syntactic categories. As you can see, the correspondence between syntactic category and traditional 'part of speech' is pretty straightforward:

Table 2.1 Syntactic Categories

Noun	table, sincerity, station
Preposition	at, on, in, by, over
Adjective	green, intelligent, generous
Verb	give, put, run, sleep, disturb
Auxiliary	can, should, must, will
Determiner	the, a, this, those, several, my

The only one that might be slightly unfamiliar is *determiner*. It's kind of a catch-all category which includes what are traditionally called articles (*the, a*), demonstrative adjectives (*this, that, many, several*), and the like. However, don't worry now about memorizing the syntactic category of every word. It'll become second nature in no time.

Now, not only do you know that each of the words in (1) belongs to a certain syntactic category. You also know that certain strings of words in (1) go together to form larger units and that other strings of words don't. For example, the two words at the beginning of the sentence *the student* go together to form a *noun phrase* (NP). On the other hand, the string of words *student will meet* does not form any kind of unit. *Her friend* and *the station* are also examples of noun phrases in (1). The nouns *student, friend,* and *station* are the heads of these three noun phrases respectively. They are the most important elements – the pivots around which the entire phrase turns. Phrases can also be parts of larger phrases. For example, the noun phrase *the station* combines with the preposition *at* to form the *prepositional phrase* (PP) *at the station.* In this case, the preposition *at* is the head of the prepositional phrase.

EXERCISE 1

Give the syntactic category of each word in the following phrases. What is the syntactic category of the entire phrase (e.g., noun phrase, adjective phrase, etc.)? Which word is the head of the phrase?

(a) the book about linguistics,
(b) at the end of the platform,
(c) see the answer,
(d) aware of the problem

2.1.1   Phrase-Structure Trees and Phrase-Structure Rules

So it seems as though part of what you know when you know English is that there are two 'levels' of organization. There's the word or 'head' level and the phrase level. Each phrase has a head, although not every word in the sentence will be the head of a phrase.

In order to express your knowledge about the structure of phrases, we could simply list the information:

(2) *at the station* (Prepositional Phrase)
    a.   at: preposition (head of phrase)
    b.   the station: Noun Phrase
        i.   the: determiner
        ii. station: noun (head of phrase)

However, a more compact way of illustrating this organization is to use a phrase-structure tree:

(3)

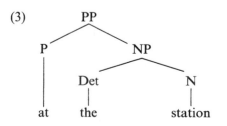

(3) indicates precisely the same information as (2). The entire phrase *at the station* is a preposition phrase, which is itself made up of a preposition combining with a noun phrase. This particular noun phrase consists of a determiner and a noun. Therefore, the phrase-structure tree makes a specific claim about what you know about your language. To draw the tree in (3) for the phrase *at the station* is to claim that your cognitive system assigns that structure to it.

However, in fact you know more about your language than this. It's not just that this particular prepositional phrase is made up of a P and an NP (and perhaps there are others which aren't). Rather, you know that *all* prepositional phrases are made up of a P and an NP. What your cognitive system seems to possess is the following phrase-structure *rule*:

(4)   PP → P NP

(4) doesn't just make a claim about a particular prepositional phrase, it says that all well-formed prepositional phrases are composed of a preposition followed by a noun phrase. If we claim that this rule forms part of what you know when you know your language, then we can account for not just the prepositional phrase in (3), but an infinite number of other PPs as well:

(5)   to the store, at the bank, from John, toward the future, etc.

Similarly, the tree in (3) claims that you know something about the particular noun phrase *the station*. However, we can account for more by assuming that you know the following phrase-structure rule:

(6)   NP → Det N

This rule accounts for your knowledge of *the station* as well as an infinite number of other NPs:

(7)   the book, that airplane, a review, several decisions, etc.

Unlike PPs, however, if we wanted to account for what you know about all possible NPs, we'd need to add to the rule in (6). For example, nouns in the plural can appear without a determiner:

(8)   Books are helpful on occasion.

Therefore, we'd need to enclose the *Det* portion of the rule in parenthesis, to indicate its optionality:

(9)   NP → (Det) N

In addition to the determiner being optional, a well-formed NP can also have an optional preceding adjective phrase, as well as an optional following prepositional phrase:

(10) (The) (bright green) books (about magic potions) are helpful on occasion.

Therefore, the rule in (9) should really be at least (11):

(11) NP → (Det) (AP) N (PP)

Having looked a little bit at the individual phrases from the sentence in (1), let's now see if we can draw the phrase-structure tree for the entire sentence. My personal feeling is that it's easier to work from the bottom up when first learning to draw phrase-structure trees, so let's start with the words and their syntactic categories:

(12) Det   N   Aux   V   Det   N   P   Det   N
      | | | | | | | | |
      The   student will meet   her   friend at   the   station

As we mentioned above, *the student, her friend,* and *the station* are all noun phrases, so let's put those in:

(13)   NP   NP   NP

      Det   N   Aux   V   Det   N   P   Det   N
      | | | | | | | | |
      The   student will meet   her   friend at   the   station

We also know that Ps go together with NPs to form PPs, so let's hook *at* and *the station* together:

(14)   PP

            NP   NP   /   NP

      Det   N   Aux   V   Det   N   P   Det   N
      | | | | | | | | |
      The   student will meet   her   friend at   the   station

Now *meet* is a verb, and is therefore the head of a verb phrase. *Her friend* is the direct object of the verb, and so therefore must be in the verb phase. The PP *at the station* gives the location where the meeting action took place, and so therefore is also in the verb phrase. You might think the auxiliary should also go in the verb phrase, but it doesn't, for reasons we'll discuss in Chapter 10.

(15)

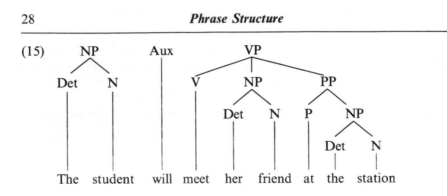

The student   will meet   her   friend at   the   station

We're now just left with the subject NP, the auxiliary, and the VP. These
things go together to form the sentence as a whole:

(16)

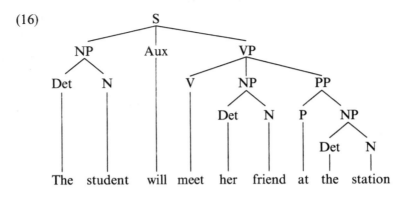

The student   will meet   her   friend at   the   station

So now we have a phrase-structure tree associated with the sentence in (1).
However, as before, we want to make claims about not just the sentence in
(1) but an infinite number of other sentences. What we therefore want to do
is take what we've done so far and generalize it. If we do that, we have the
phrase-structure rules in (17):

(17) a. S → NP Aux VP
     b. NP → (Det) (AP) N (PP)
     c. VP → V NP PP
     d. PP → P NP

Just as with our NP rule, though, we're going to need more rules for well-
formed VPs. In (17), we have only one rule for VP expansion, VP → V NP
PP. However, there are many more possible VPs than just this one. Consider
the VPs in (18):

(18) a. John *slept* (VP → V)
     b. Mary *gave Bill the book* (VP → V NP NP)
     c. Ivan *went to the museum* (VP → V PP)

If we were going to try to account for a substantial fragment of English using phrase-structure rules, we'd need a lot more rules of the sort in (18). However, we won't be pursuing this at any length here because we're going to see in Section 2.6 that the phrase-structure rules (in the form that we've seen so far) need to be substantially modified anyway. However, we'll keep using them for the moment so that you can get a feel for how phrase-structure rules work in general.

EXERCISE 2

Using (16) as a model, draw the trees for (18a) to (c), using the changes to the VP rule which are indicated in the parentheses.

2.2 CONSTITUENCY

So far, we've been leaving things on a somewhat intuitive level when it comes to the details of sentence structure. We all share the feeling that, for example, *at the station* forms some kind of a unit, a PP in fact, whereas other strings of words don't form a unit. Let's call these units *constituents. Student will meet*, for example, doesn't feel like a unit of any kind.

Feelings and intuitions are all well and good, and it's true that they do play an important starting role in just about any scientific project. However, it's also true that intuitions can be wrong. For example, I have the intuition that every morning the sun rises in the sky while the Earth remains perfectly still. Despite the fact that there's a part of my brain somewhere that knows that that intuition is wrong, that doesn't alter the fact that the intuition is very strong indeed. Therefore, it would be nice if we could devise some tests to back up our intuitions as to which groups of words do or do not form constituents. To that end, we'll take a look at some traditional tests which are used to indicate constituency: the Substitution test, the Coordination test and the Movement test. Some are a little bit more reliable than others for reasons which we'll see in later chapters.

2.2.1 The Substitution Test

The first test that we'll look at is called the *Substitution Test*. This constituency test relies on the fact that groups of words which function as constituents in the sentence can generally be replaced in a sentence by a single word. This confirms that the group of words forms a constituent. Depending on exactly the single substitution word you choose, you can even identify the syntactic category of the constituent you're dealing with.

Pronouns, for example, can be used to tell whether a given string of words constitutes an NP constituent. If a given group of words can be replaced by a pronoun, then that group of words is not only a constituent, but is specifically an NP. Consider the contrasts between the sentences in (19):

(19)a.　　The Belgian scientist who won the Nobel Prize at the age of 22 retired today.
　　　b.　　She retired today.
　　　c.　　*The Belgian scientist who she today.

The pronoun *she* is able to replace the entire string of words *the Belgian scientist who won the Nobel Prize at the age of 22*. On the other hand, as (19c) indicates, *she* cannot replace the string of words *won the Nobel Prize at the age of 22 retired*. This suggests that the string of words does not form an NP constituent.

The Belgian scientist who won the Nobel Prize at the age of 22 is not the only string of words in (19a) which can be replaced by a pronoun. For example, we could take *the Nobel Prize* and replace it by the pronoun *it*, creating (20):

(20)　　The Belgian scientist who won it at the age of 22 retired today.

You'd have to have been talking about the Nobel Prize during a previous part of the conversation in order for (20) to be an appropriate thing to say, of course. Compare (20) with (21) for example:

(21)　　*The she won the Nobel Prize at the age of 22 retired today.

Unlike (20), (21) is just an unintelligible jumble. This is because *she* has replaced *Belgian scientist who* in (19a), and these words do *not* form a NP constituent.

EXERCISE 3

Using pronouns such as *he/she*, *it*, *them* etc. identify all of the NPs in the following sentences:

(a)　The new gorilla's attendant put a tasty banana on the purple table.
(b)　The person responsible for security left the visiting dignitaries in a miniscule antechamber.

Just to have a general term to refer to these single words that can substitute for others, let's refer to them as 'proforms'. Pro*nouns* substitute for NPs, but there are other proforms which can substitute for other syntactic categories.

For example, words such as *here, there,* or *then* can substitute for certain kinds of PPs. Consider the contrasts in (22):

(22)a.   Bill's book about economics in the eighteenth century was found in the dining room.
 b.   Bill's book about economics then was found in the dining room.
 c.   Bill's book about economics in the eighteenth century was found there.
 d.   *Bill's book about there century was found in the dining room.

Again, we see that the proforms *then* and *there* can only substitute for a constituent which is a PP. A group of words which is not a constituent, like *economics in the eighteenth* cannot be substituted for.

EXERCISE 4

Use PP proforms to identify the PPs in the following sentences:

(a)   Mary put the book in Sue's jacket on Thursday.
(b)   The agent who left the computer on the table at lunchtime was dismissed on the very day he was hired.

2.2.2   The Coordination Test

Conjunctions, elements like *and, or,* and *but,* can serve as a very useful aid in determining the constituent structure of a sentence, since only constituents can be conjoined. Furthermore, both elements to be conjoined must be of the same syntactic category (i.e., two Ns, two APs, etc.). Sequences of words which are not constituents cannot be conjoined. Consider the following sentence:

(23)   John's exposé in *The Guardian* gave new hope to the government's opponents.

We could use the Substitution test from the previous section to identify several strings of words as constituents. For example, *John's exposé in The Guardian* is a constituent, as it can be replaced by the proform *it*.

(24)   It gave new hope to the government's opponents.

We could, however, also use the Coordination test to confirm this result by attempting to coordinate *John's exposé in The Guardian* with another NP.

If the result is grammatical, than this would confirm that *John's exposé in The Guardian* is indeed a constituent:

(25) [John's exposé in *The Guardian* and the subsequent revelations] gave new hope to the government's opponents.

In (25), *John's exposé in The Guardian* has been coordinated with another NP *the subsequent revelations*, indicating that it is indeed a constituent.

We get the same results if we try to coordinate other constituents. For example, we can also have coordinations like (26a) (VP-coordination) and (26b) (PP-coordination):

(26)a. John's exposé in *The Guardian* [gave new hope to the government's opponents and put fear into ministers' hearts].
   b. John's exposé in *The Guardian* gave new hope [to the government's opponents and to seekers of justice throughout the world].

On the other hand, if we were to take a string of words which does not form a constituent, the resulting coordination would be ungrammatical:

(27) *John's exposé in *The Guardian* [gave new and renewed old] hope to the government's opponents.

EXERCISE 5

Use the coordination test to identify three constituents in the following sentence:

John's predilection for original thinking placed his family in dire peril.

2.2.3 The Movement Test

In addition to substitution and conjunction, it's also possible to use Movement as a test for constituency. We'll talk about movement in greater detail in Chapter 6. For the moment, all that's really important to notice is that certain groups of words seem able to be moved around as a unit in the sentence whereas others cannot. For example, consider (28):

(28) John will leave a book on the table.

It is possible to take various constituents in (28) and move them to the front of the sentence, giving it an emphatic or contrastive interpretation. This is called *Topicalization*:

(29)a. On the table John will leave a book, but on the chair he will leave some paper.

b. The book John will leave on the table, but the letter he will put in the bin.

On the other hand, if we try to take a string of words which does not form a constituent and topicalize it, the result is ungrammatical:

(30)a. *Book on, John will leave the table.
   b. *On the, John will leave the book table.

Unfortunately, the Movement test is probably the least reliable of the three tests that we've mentioned because movement in general, and Topicalization in particular, are subject to a number of constraints which have nothing to do with constituent structure. For example, topicalization of a VP is rather odd in most dialects of English:

(31) Leave the book on the table, John will.

Probably the most well known 'speaker' of a dialect in which this is possible is the character Yoda from the *Star Wars* films. However, there *is* a serious point we can make. In writing dialogue for that character, the writers never topicalize non-constituents, so even if Yoda's topicalization is a little freer than most dialects of English, he would never produce sentences like those in (30).

    Because of these 'outside' influences on movement, the Movement test can only be used in a 'positive' way. That is to say, if something passes the Movement test, then it definitely is a constituent. If it *doesn't* pass the Movement test, then you can't conclude anything. It might be a constituent, or it might not. As an example of this, notice that *the table* in (28) is clearly a constituent (being an NP). It passes the Substitution and Coordination tests with flying colors (32).

(32)a. John left a book on it.
   b. John left a book on the table and the chair.

However, if we use the Movement test, (33) is rather odd:

(33) *The table, John will leave a book on, but the box, John will put a record in.

By contrast, the phrase *left a* fails the Substitution and the Coordination tests, and is definitely not a constituent. It also fails the Movement test:

(34)a. *John it/there book on the table.
   b. *John left a and threw the book on the table.
   c. *Left a, John book on the table (but put a, John record in the box).

So the Movement test should be used with a little caution. Only constituents pass the Movement test, but both constituents and non-constituents can fail it. A quick confirmation with the other tests is often a good idea if there is any doubt.

EXERCISE 6

Use the movement test to identify two constituents in the following sentence:

Mary can see her friends on Thursday in Birmingham.

2.4 THE ELEMENTS OF A PHRASE-STRUCTURE TREE AND THEIR RELATIONS

Having seen a few elementary phrase-structure rules and phrase-structure trees in the previous section, we need to introduce some terms for talking about phrase-structure trees and the relations between the elements in them, which are called 'nodes'. We'll be using these terms so frequently throughout the book that they'll become second nature in no time.

We'll start off in a seemingly aggressive vein with the term *dominate*. One node *dominates* another when you can trace a path from the first node to the second one moving only downward through the tree. Take a look at the sentence in (35), and the phrase-structure tree representation for it in (36):

(35)   The agent will go to Madrid.

(36)

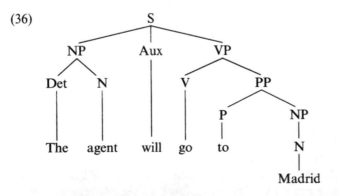

Notice that the S node dominates *every* other node in the tree. Starting from S, you can get to any of the other nodes in the tree by moving only downward. On the other hand, the PP node dominates only the P node and NP node associated with *Madrid*. The PP node does not, for example, dominate the NP node associated with *the agent*. You can't get from the PP node to that NP node by only going down.

A more specific type of domination is *immediate domination*. A node *immediately dominates* every node which you can get to by moving down exactly *one* level. So while S dominates every other node in the tree, it immediately dominates only the NP *the agent*, Aux *will*, and the VP *go to Madrid*. Similarly, the VP node dominates five nodes (V, PP, P, NP, and N), but it only *immediately* dominates V and PP.

As a point of cultural interest, nodes in a phrase-structure tree are always female rather than male. It's not uncommon to see the nodes which something immediately dominates referred to as its *daughter* nodes. Less often, you'll see a node which immediately dominates something referred to as its *mother* node. One place, however, where the matriarchal term is used very frequently is for *sister* nodes, that is, daughters of the same mother, as in (37) or (38):

(37)

(38)

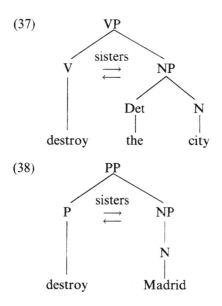

Notice that these relational terms can give us a way of defining a constituent. Any group of heads which are exhaustively dominated by a given node (i.e., there is a node which dominates every one of those heads and no others) is a constituent. For example, we know that the group of words *to Madrid* is a constituent, and that's represented in the tree in (36). The PP node dominates the P *to* and the N *Madrid*, and no other heads.

The last relation between nodes that we'll look at in this section will play a major role in the chapters to come: c-command. C-command was first formulated by a linguist named Tanya Reinhart (1976), and has since come to play a fundamental role in syntactic theory. The notion of c-command seems relevant to almost every phenomenon. (We'll see most of the common ones at some point in this book.)

C-command is usually defined in the following way:

(39)   A node α c-commands another node β if and only if the first branching node which dominates α dominates β.

In the tree in (36), for example, the subject NP node (dominating *the agent*) c-commands every other node in the sentence apart from S itself. The first branching node which dominates the subject NP node is the S node, and that S node dominates every other node in the sentence. However, the NP *Madrid* c-commands only the preposition *to*. The first branching node dominating *Madrid* is the PP node, and that dominates only the preposition. (Just as a side note, even though it technically satisfies the definition, nodes don't c-command themselves or any nodes that they themselves dominate.) Using the relational terms of this section, we could put (39) another way by saying that a node c-commands (1) its sisters and (2) every node that its sisters dominate.

EXERCISE 7

Draw the tree for 'The man will see the book'. Indicate three pairs of nodes which are sisters. What nodes does Aux c-command?

2.5 ARE TWO LEVELS ENOUGH?

So far, we've seen that knowing your language entails not only knowing that individual words belong to a syntactic category, such as Noun or Verb, but also that certain words go together to form larger phrases, such as Noun Phrases and Verb Phrases.

However, there's some evidence to indicate that two levels, the word/head level and the phrase level, isn't enough. The cognitive system that you possess seems to analyze phrases in terms of *three* levels, not two. The idea that there are *heads* (things like nouns, prepositions, adjectives, etc.) and *phrases* (noun *phrases*, adjective *phrases*, etc.) may well be familiar to you from somewhere, whether it's traditional English grammar instruction or maybe a foreign language that you studied. However, probably nobody's ever tried to convince you that there is a level of organization *between* the head (word) level and the phrase level.

In order to show that there are constituents which are intermediate between the head level and the full phrase level, we can use exactly the same arguments that we used in the previous section to show that phrases existed.

2.5.1 The Structure of NPs

To start off with, consider (40), focusing in on *one*:

(40)   Jack met the student from England, and I met the one from France.

Clearly, *one* in (40) is some kind of proform. The question is what it's substituting for. Given (40) the answer looks fairly straightforward. *One* appears to be substituting for N, so we have a structure like (41):

(41)

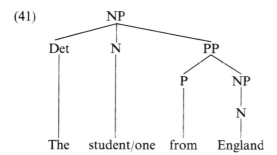

However, consider (42):

(42)   *Jack met the student of philosophy, and I met the one of Greek.

(42) presents a problem. On the basis of (40), it looks like we just established that *one* substituted for N. If *one* can substitute for the N *student* in (40), why can't it substitute for the N *student* in (42)?

One way to approach the problem is to question the assumption that there are only two levels of phrase structure (N and NP). At the moment we only have the head level and the full phrase level. Therefore, there are only two things that *one* could be substituting for: N or NP. But if we say that *one* substitutes for N, then there's no explanation for why (42) is ungrammatical. On the other hand, if *one* substitutes for NP, then (42) is predicted to be ungrammatical, but so is (41). That's also wrong.

However, if there's a *third* level, between the head level and the full phrase level, and *one* is a substitute for this *intermediate* category, we can explain the difference between (41) and (42). Following standard usage, we'll call this intermediate level the N' level (read 'N-bar').

Let's start with (41). Under this new three-level hypothesis, if *one* can substitute for *student* to the exclusion of the prepositional phrase *from England*, then *student* must be *both* an N *and* and N' at the same time. In other words, the structure of *student from England* is really (43):

(43)

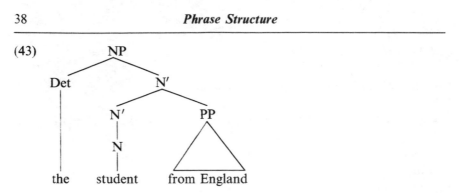

The prepositional phrase *from England* is not a sister to N, but rather is a sister to N'.

Turning now to (42), if *one* can't substitute for *student* in (42), that must mean that *student* is *not* both an N and an N' in (42). *One* appears only able to substitute for the entire phrase *student of philosophy*:

(44) Jack met this student of philosophy, but I met that one.

That would be consistent with the following analysis of the NP *the student of philosophy*:

(45)

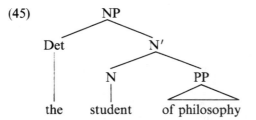

Here, rather than *student* being both an N and an N', the only N' is the phrase *student of philosophy*. *Student* by itself is not an N'.

If we look at what happens when we have *both* an *of* PP and a *from* PP, we can see that it looks like our analysis in (43), and (45) is on the right track. Consider the following NP:

(46) the student of philosophy from England

If we apply the *one* substitution test to (46), this seems to confirm our analysis:

(47)a.   Jack met the student of philosophy from England and I met the one from France.
  b. *Jack met the student of philosophy from England and I met the one of Greek from France.

Once again, this data suggests that only *student of philosophy/Greek* is an N' and that *student* by itself is not.

Having introduced this third level of organization, the N' level, as a solution to the *one* substitution problem, we now need to look around to see if there is any independent supporting evidence to back this analysis up. Do the other tests for constituent structure that we introduced in the previous section confirm the N'-analysis?

The Movement test doesn't seem to. If we attempt to topicalize our hypothesized N', the result is ungrammatical:

(48)   *Student of philosophy, I met the yesterday, but student of Greek I met the today.

However, bear in mind what we said about the Movement test. If a string of words can be moved as a unit, then it definitely is a constituent. If the string of words can't be moved as a unit, then it might or might not be a constituent. So the ungrammaticality of (48) is, in the end, inconclusive.

However, we still have the Coordination test. In order for two things to be coordinated, they must be the same syntactic category and the same level. That is to say, you can only coordinate two NPs, for example, not an NP and an N. Also, the combined phrase as a whole has the syntactic category of its two conjuncts. So two conjoined NPs together form an NP, and can appear anywhere a 'normal' NP can.

Looking at (45), this structure claims that *student of philosophy* is an N' to the exclusion of the determiner *the*. Can we coordinate two N's to the exclusion of the determiner? It appears as though we can. Consider the NP in (49):

(49)   The student of philosophy and advisor to the stars

In (49), we've conjoined *student of philosophy* and *advisor to the stars*. Clearly, *advisor to the stars* is not an N. Neither is it an NP. It has no determiner, and can't appear as the subject of a sentence:

(50)   *Advisor to the stars predicted disaster for Brad and Jennifer.

Therefore, it seems as though *advisor to the stars* must be N'. That would seem to show that *student of philosophy* is also an N'. Therefore, the structure of (49) must be (51):

(51)

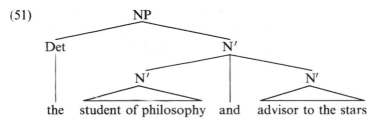

Notice that the N' level, unlike NP or N, can be repeated or *iterated*, as many times as necessary. For example, we could have an NP like (52), which would have the structure in (53), as shown by (54):

(52)   The book about linguistics in my pocket

(53)

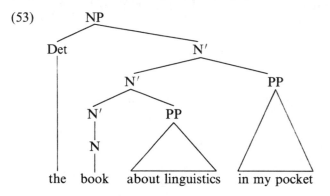

(54)a.   I like the book about linguistics in my pocket more than the one about physics on the table.   (*one = book*)
  b.   I like the book about linguistics in my pocket more than the one on the table.   (*one = book about linguistics*)

Since both *book* and *book about linguistics* are substitutable by *one*, they must both be N's.

So, with the addition of (iterable) N's, we'll need to modify our phrase-structure rules for NPs. In Section 2.1.1, we had the following rule for NP:

(55)   NP → (Det) (AP) N (PP)

But this phrase-structure rule has only two levels, NP and N. We need to split this rule into two parts in order to introduce the N' level:

(56)a.   NP → (Det) N'
  b.   N' → (AP) N (PP)

(56) claims that every NP immediately dominates at least an N' and every N' immediately dominates at least an N. However, because N's can be iterated, we have to leave open the possibility of N's immediately dominating other N's, as in (53). So we need three rules instead of two:

(57)a.   NP → (Det) N'
  b.   N' → (AP) N' (PP)
  c.   N' → (AP) N (PP)

By the addition of the phrase-structure rule in (57b), we can create structures like the one in (53). Therefore, if (57) constitutes part of what you know when you know English, we explain how you know that (53) has the structure it does. We can therefore explain how you know facts about *one* substitution in sentences like (41), (42), and (54).

2.5.2   The Structure of VPs

We can give a parallel argument for the existence of an intermediate level between the head and the phrase level for verbs, using the substitutor *do so*. Consider (58):

(58)   Joe will buy a book on Tuesday, and Sam will do so on Friday.

Just as with *one* above, the question is what *do so* is substituting for in (58). In (58a) it is substituting for the sequence of words *buy a book*. Therefore, *do so* must be substituting for more than just V. To confirm this, if we try to use *do so* to substitute for just V, the result is ungrammatical:

(59)   *Joe will buy a book, but Sam will do so a newspaper.

However, under a two-level system, our only other choice is that *do so* is substituting for VP, but that doesn't look right either. If *do so* were substituting for VP, we'd expect (58) to be ungrammatical. The prepositional phrase *on Friday* is clearly part of the VP. It's indicating the time at which the buying of the book took place.

Do so in (58) is substituting for *part*, but not *all*, of the VP. If the Substitution test is genuine, and only sequences of words which are constituents can be substituted, then there must be some intermediate level of constituency that's *between* V and VP which *do so* is substituting for. If we have a three-level system, incorporating a V' level between VP and V, we would seem to be able to capture the contrast. *Do so* is an element which substitutes for V', rather than V or VP. Then, if the PP *on Friday* is a sister to the V' *bought the book*, then we explain why *do so* can replace *bought the book* to the exclusion of the PP *on Friday*:

(60)

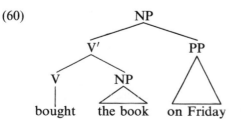

We can also explain why (59) is ungrammatical. Just as *of* PPs must be sisters to N and cannot be sisters to N', direct objects must be sisters to V. They cannot be sisters to V'. Therefore, the only V' is the entire string of words *bought the book*.

We can see this even more clearly with verbs which take more than one object. Consider the verb *put*, as illustrated in (61):

(61)a.   Mary put a book on the table.
   b.   *Mary put a book.
   c.   *Mary put on the table.

Put requires both an NP and a PP object. Neither one may be omitted. If that's the case, we expect that the structure of the VP should be (62):

(62)

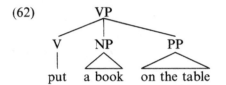

If (62) is the correct structure, and what we've been saying so far about *do so* is right, then we predict that, unlike (58), *do so* should not be able to substitute for the string of words *put the book*. That string of words is not a V', and in fact is not even a constituent. That prediction looks to be correct:

(63)   *Mary put a book on the table and Bill did so on the chair.

Just as with the NPs that we saw in the previous section, the intermediate level in VPs is iterable as well. So, for instance, we could have a sentence like (64):

(64)   John gave a speech at 3 o'clock on the 30th of June in Madrid.

Before Continuing: Use the *do so* test to show that there must be 3 V's in (64).

Do so can replace *gave the speech, gave the speech at 3 o' clock*, or *gave the speech at 3 o'clock on the 30th of June*.

(65)   John gave a speech at 3 o'clock on the 30th of June in Madrid ...
   a. ... and Mary did so at 5 o'clock on the 27th of September in Valencia.
   b. ... and Mary did so on the 27th of September in Valencia.
   c. ... and Mary did so in Valencia.

Notice too that, as we'd predict, *do so* cannot substitute for *gave* to the exclusion of *the speech*, since *gave* is not by itself a V'. It's only a V.

(66) *John gave a speech at 3 o'clock on the 30th of June in Madrid, and Bill did so a statement later that day.

Before we leave this topic, though, I want to mention a sentence which may have occurred to you:

(67) John gave a speech at 3 o'clock on the 30th of June in Madrid, and Mary did so as well.

Here *do so* seems to be substituting for the entire VP *gave a speech at 3 o'clock on the 30th of June in Madrid*. There are a number of ways of dealing with this problem which are all essentially identical. What we'll say here is that *do so* may actually substitute for *either V' or VP*.

However, this doesn't in any way threaten the three-level analysis that we've proposed here. Under the simple two-level analysis, there are no sub-constituents within VP. A phrase-structure rule like (68) would give you the 'flat' tree in (69):

(68) VP → V NP PP PP PP

(69)

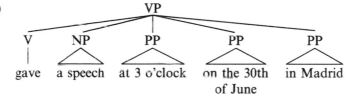

Remember that trees make claims about knowledge–specifically, your knowledge of English. (68) and (69) make the claim that there's a VP *gave a speech at 3 o'clock on the 30th of June in Madrid* and no other constituents. And that seems to be a wrong claim about your knowledge of English. As we've seen, the Substitution test indicates that you know that *gave a speech, gave a speech at 3 o'clock*, and *gave a speech at 3 o'clock on the 30th of June*, are all sub-constituents of VP. Put another way, you know that the sentences in (65a) to (65c) are grammatical. Therefore, the structure of the VP in (67) must be (70):

(70)

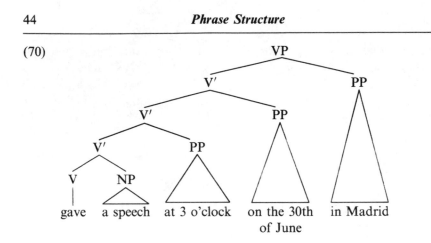

In addition to the Substitution test, we can also call on the Coordination test to verify the need for an intermediate level between V and VP. Consider the following sentence:

(71)   John cleaned windows and painted doors for three hours.

(71) is actually ambiguous between two possible conjunctions. One is a conjunction of VPs, in which John cleaned windows for some unspecified amount of time and then painted doors for three hours. That interpretation would be associated with the tree in (72):

(72)

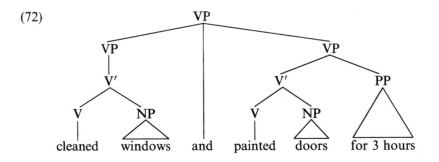

However, of more interest to us is the fact that there is a second interpretation for (71) in which John was engaged during a three-hour period in window-cleaning and door-painting. That interpretation is only possible if *cleaned windows and painted doors* forms a constituent within the VP to the exclusion of the PP *for three hours*. But if the VP itself has no internal structure, as is the case under the two-level analysis, then there's no way to explain this. Under a three-level analysis, however, we can explain this second interpretation as arising from a conjunction of V's, as illustrated in (73):

(73)

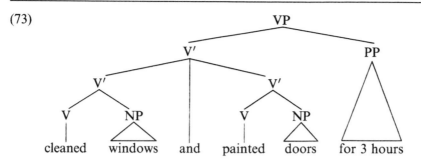

This would seem to confirm the three-level analysis for VPs.

On the basis of all this, we'll have to modify our phrase-structure rules for VP in the same way we did for NP. Instead of having two levels, as in (74), we need three levels, as in (75):

(74)   VP → V (and various other things)

(75)a.   VP → V' (XP)
   b.   V' → V' (XP)
   c.   V' → V (XP)

Again just as with NPs, (75b) is for when V' iterates and (75c) is for when we finally get to the head. 'XP' in (75) is just a placeholder to indicate that any kind of phrase is possible (PPs, NPs, etc.)

2.5.3   Intermediate Levels and Other Categories

We've now seen two categories, NP and VP, where we can construct arguments from substitution for a three-level system. Is there anything to be said about the other major syntactic categories, AP and PP? Well, yes. Consider the following AP and PP:

(76)   very nervous of exams

(77)   nearly in the hole

It's true that we don't have the same Substitution tests that we saw for NP and VP because there don't seem to be any appropriate proforms for A' and P'. However, we can still use the Coordination test.

(78)   very [nervous of exams and anxious about the result]

(79)   nearly [over the water hazard and into the hole]

LIBRARY, UNIVERSITY OF CHESTER

The fact that *nervous of exams* and *anxious about the result* can be conjoined to the exclusion of the adverb *very* suggests that A's are being conjoined. Similarly, (79) seems to show a conjunction of P's. Representing (76) and (77) using intermediate bar-level categories, we have the following:

(80a)

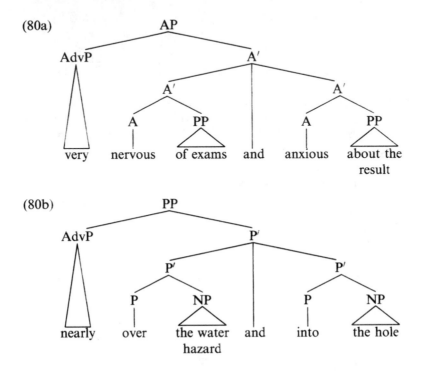

(80b)

We would, of course, need to then modify our phrase-structure rules for APs and PPs in the same way as we have for NPs and VPs to add in the third level.

2.6   INTRODUCTION TO X'-THEORY

So far we've done pretty well getting our phrase-structure rules in order, but you may have noticed a problem creeping into things, particularly when we introduced the X' level. The problem is redundancy. The changes we made to the NP phrase-structure rules look an awful lot like the modifications that we later made to the VP phrase-structure rules. Comparing (75) and (44) above should make that quite clear.

And this is not just a problem with VP and NP. In fact it's a general problem with phrase-structure rules of the sort that we've been looking at so far. For example, every NP that we've seen so far has a head N. Every AP has had an A head. Every PP has had a P head, and so on. We've never seen cases where a VP has an A head, for example, nor do there seem to be any cases like that in languages of the world. This might seem like a completely trivial point. I can hear you saying 'Well, it's obvious. You couldn't have a verb phrase if it didn't have a verb in it somewhere!' However, it's important to be surprised by 'obvious' things, and to distinguish what's obvious from what the theory allows you to do.

If the cognitive system that you possess as a native speaker of a language can be correctly described as having rules of the form 'V' → V (XP)', why aren't there rules of the form 'V' → A (XP)'? Or perhaps 'NP → P' (XP)'? From a formalism point of view, there's nothing to distinguish rules like (44) and (75) from countless other possible rules which we never find. And our theory at this point doesn't explain why.

We've also got a related problem with redundancy. It looks as though our phrase-structure rules are missing a generalization. All NPs immediately dominate an N'. All VPs immediately dominate a V'. All PPs immediately dominate a P'. It looks as though we've got a pattern here.

As first suggested by Chomsky (1970) (a paper termed 'monumentally important' by Webelhuth (1995b: 18)), we might be able to eliminate the redundancy and increase our explanatory power by generalizing the phrase-structure rules. Put another way, Chomsky proposed that what you have as part of your cognitive system is a *general* format for phrase-structure rules which are independent of any syntactic category (N, A, V, etc.). So, instead of having rules like (44) and (75), we have the general schema in (81). This approach is known as X'-Theory (where X, Y, and Z are just variables standing for any syntactic category):

(81)a.   XP → (Spec) X'
   b.   X' → X' (YP)
   c.   X' → X (ZP)

Although the X can stand for N, V, A, or P, you must fill in the X's on both sides of the arrow with the same choice in any given instance of (81a), (b) or (c), so VP must dominate a V', an A' can only immediately dominate another A' or an A, and so on.

If (81) is part of the cognitive system which enables you to speak and understand your language, then we explain why many potential rules (like VP → A' PP) aren't found. With the schema in (81), they can't be created. Every phrase, whether it be NP, VP, AP, or PP, must by the rules in (81) ultimately end up with an N, V, A, or P head.

Also, using the general format in (81) eliminates the redundancy among categories. The reason why all VPs immediately dominate a V' is because they're following the general schema in (81).

2.7 INSIDE THE XP (TERMINOLOGY PART II)

Having looked at some general terms which are used to describe relations
between nodes in a tree in Section 2.4, let's take a look at some
configurational terms relating to the structure of phrases now that we've
introduced the X'-system. Again, these terms will become second nature in
no time, so don't worry if they seem a little complicated at first.

(82)

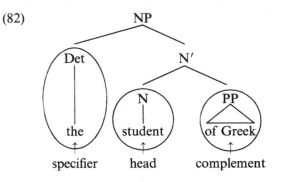

The most important part of the phrase is the *head*, which we've mentioned
before in discussing the two-level system. Within the X'-system, it's common
to see the head X of an XP written as 'X°', which is read as 'X-zero'. (The
idea is that the single-bar level is level 1, so one level below that is level zero.)

Another very common configurational term when discussing XPs is the
complement. Looking at rule (81c) of the general X' schema, the complement
is the optional sister ZP to the head X. A complement is always defined
relative to a head. So in the NP that we drew the tree for in (82), the complement is the PP *of Greek*. That PP is the sister to the head N of the NP.
As you can see, the complement can often be what would traditionally be
called the 'object' of the head, particularly with verbs and prepositions.

EXERCISE 8

Identify the head and the complement of the head within the following XPs:

(a) the book about linguistics,
(b) jealous of Federico's achievements,
(c) into the fray,
(d) buy the record

The third and final important configurational term within the XP is the
specifier. Like the complement, the specifier is defined in a purely relational
fashion. It often gives more information about the head or makes it more
specific, but for our purposes it is simply the element which is immediately

dominated by XP and is a sister to X' which we saw in rule (81a) of the X' schema. So in the tree for the NP in (82), the determiner *the* is the specifier of the NP. It's important that you remember the 'immediately dominated by XP' part of the definition though, because you can have more than one X', and therefore more than one element which is a sister to X'. But only one of them can be the specifier of the XP. Consider (83), with the tree in (84):

(83)   the book about linguistics on the table

(84)

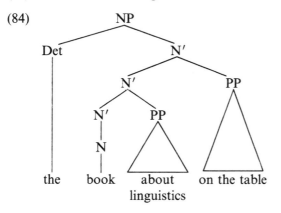

Notice that both the determiner *the* and the PP *on the table* are sisters to N'. However, only one of them is the sister to N' which is immediately dominated by NP. That's the determiner. Therefore, *the* is the specifier of the NP in (83).

EXERCISE 9

Identify the specifiers in the following XPs:

(a)   **Brian's recordings of whales,**
(b)   **three miles down the road,**
(c)   **rather appalled by the situation**

2.8   SUMMARY

In this chapter, we've made a start at characterizing some of the things that you know when you know a language. Sentences are not perceived as one big blur, even if that's exactly what they are from an acoustic point of view. The language faculty which you were born with breaks the acoustic blur into words, which are then organized into larger constituents. We saw that various tests, such as Substitution, Coordination, and Movement, seem to operate only on constituents, thereby providing evidence for their existence.

In exploring pro forms in more detail, we discovered that your language faculty appears to structure phrases into three levels: the maximal projection or XP level, the intermediate X′ level, and the head or X° level. However. rather than having a large number of different phrase-structure rules which encoded a lot of the same information, we hypothesized that what the language faculty provides is a single general format for phrase-structure rules, X′-Theory:

(81)a.　XP → (Spec) X′
　　b.　X′ → X′ (YP)
　　c.　X′ → X (ZP)

OPEN ISSUE: THE STRUCTURE OF THE DOUBLE OBJECT CONSTRUCTION

One area of sentence structure which has been something of a thorn in linguists' sides has to do with the phrase-structure representation of what is called the *Double Object* construction. Certain verbs, such as *give*, *show*, and *send*, have alternations like the one seen in (85):

(85)a.　I showed a book to John.
　　b.　I showed John a book.

In both cases, *show* is taking both a direct object (*a book*) and an indirect object (*John*). In (85a), the direct object appears in a standard direct object position following the verb and the indirect object appears in a prepositional phrase. Nothing particularly weird there. In (85b), on the other hand, we have the 'double object' version. The indirect object has shifted in front of the direct object, and neither NP has a preposition.

We need to figure out what the structure is in (85a) and (85b). The way to do that is run the sentences through various tests which we know depend on structure and see how they come out. As mentioned in Section 2.4, a lot of syntactic processes seem to depend on c-command. If we can get a handle on what the c-command relationships are within the VPs in (85a) and (85b), we can figure out what the right structure is. We'll have much more to say in later chapters about these sorts of tests, but for now you'll have to just trust me that c-command is relevant for these things.

First of all, as we'll see in Chapter 5, it turns out that reflexives like *herself* and *ourselves*, as well as reciprocals like *each other* need to be c-commanded by their antecedents. Just to give a quick example, *John likes himself* is grammatical because *John*, the subject (and the antecedent of *himself*), c-commands the direct object reflexive *himself*. On the other hand, *himself likes John* is ungrammatical because *John* fails to c-command *himself*. With that in mind, consider (86):

(86)a. I showed Mary to herself.
   b. *I showed herself to Mary.

The fact that (86a) is grammatical while (86b) is not suggests that the direct object (immediately following the verb) c-commands the NP object of the preposition, but not vice versa.

Other tests which also require a c-command relationship between two elements also seem to give the same result. In structures of the form *each . . . the other*, the NP containing *each* must c-command the NP containing *the other*. Additionally, so called *negative polarity items* must always be c-commanded by a negative expression. Testing these in a double object environment, we have (87) and (88):

(87)a. I showed each partner to the other.
   b. *I showed the other to each partner.

(88)a. I told nothing to anyone.
   b. *I told anything to nobody.

Taking into account the results of this experiment, it already looks like we have a bit of a problem. The first object must c-command the second object, but the first object must also be a sister to the verb because it's the direct object. What we'd want would be something like (89):

(89)

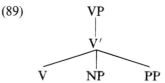

Unfortunately, this structure isn't technically generable by our X′-Theoretic phrase structure rules in (81), because they only allow X′ to have *two* daughters. However, if we put that to one side, the facts do fall into place. Since the second object is introduced by a preposition, it won't be able to c-command anything outside of the PP, and we therefore expect that the direct object CP will c-command the object of the preposition, but not vice versa.

However, the real problem comes when we look at the double object version in (85b). Neither the direct object nor the indirect object is introduced by a preposition, so, thinking about what we've seen so far, we might expect that something like (90) would be the right structure, again allowing for triple branching (this was the structure for double object constructions originally proposed by Oehrle (1976)):

(90)

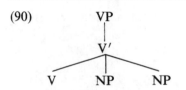

Since the two objects are sisters, they c-command each other, and we predict that, in the double object versions of (86)–(88), both the (a) and (b) sentences should be grammatical.

The problem is that this isn't what we find. Oddly enough, as observed by Barss and Lasnik (1986), we *still* see an asymmetry. It looks like the first object still c-commands the second object.

(91)a.   I showed Mary herself.
   b.   *I showed herself Mary.

(92)a.   I showed each partner the other.
   b.   *I showed the other each partner.

(93)a.   I told nobody anything.
   b.   *I told anyone nothing.

Therefore, it would seem that the structure in (90) proposed by Oehrle isn't right.

(94) represents another structure which has been proposed for the double object construction. This one comes from Chomsky (1981).

(94)

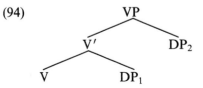

(94) does have the virtue of conforming to X'-Theory. Each node has only two daughters. However, the problem is that this doesn't get you the facts that we've seen in (91)–(93) either. In the tree in (94), the second object DP_2 asymmetrically c-commands the first one DP_1. Therefore, we'd predict the opposite pattern of grammaticality judgements. It should be the (a) sentences which are ungrammatical.

Unfortunately, there's no really appealing way to resolve this problem. It looks like the only way out would be to simply deny that c-command was relevant to these phenomena, and so the sentences in (86)–(88) and (91)–(93) really tell us nothing about the structure whatsoever. That would be really unpleasant, though, as well as running counter to a ton of work that says that c-command *is* relevant.

For the moment, we'll have to leave the problem there. For illustration purposes in the next few chapters, we'll just use Chomsky's structure in (94) on those couple of occasions when we need to draw the tree for a double object structure to illustrate something else. However, Larson (1988) has proposed a really neat way of solving the problem of double objects, which will be accessible after Chapter 10.

BIBLIOGRAPHY

The book which probably deals most extensively with X'-Theory is Jackendoff (1977). I think this is a terrific book, with lots of interesting data and arguments. He's assuming an even more complicated system than we are though (4 levels, not 3), so some of the trees and sentences will need 'translation'. However, it's worth checking out to see X'-Theory applied to examples beyond the basic data that we've discussed here. Chapter 1 of Webelhuth (1995a) also has a pretty good discussion of X'-Theory. It's not a textbook *per se* – more like a handbook of Government and Binding Theory, but the core of Chapter 1 is pretty accessible. Of the 'real' textbooks, Haegeman (1994) has probably the most extensive discussion of X'-Theory.

ANSWERS TO IN-TEXT EXERCISES

Exercise 1

Give the syntactic category of each word in the following phrases. What is the syntactic category of the entire phrase (e.g., noun phrase, adjective phrase, etc.)? Which word is the head of the phrase?

(a) the book about linguistics,
(b) at the end of the platform,
(c) see the answer,
(d) aware of the problem

(a) the: determiner; book: noun; about: preposition; linguistics: noun. The whole phrase is a noun phrase, with *book* as its head.

(b) at: preposition; the: determiner; end: noun; of: preposition; the: determiner; platform: noun. The whole phrase is a prepositional phrase with *at* as its head.

(c) see: verb; the: determiner; answer: noun. The whole phrase is a verb phrase with *see* as its head.

(d) aware: adjective; of: preposition; the: determiner; answer: noun. The whole phrase is an adjective phrase with *aware* as its head.

Exercise 2

Using (16) as a model, draw the trees for (18a) to (c), using the changes to the VP rule which are indicated in the parentheses.

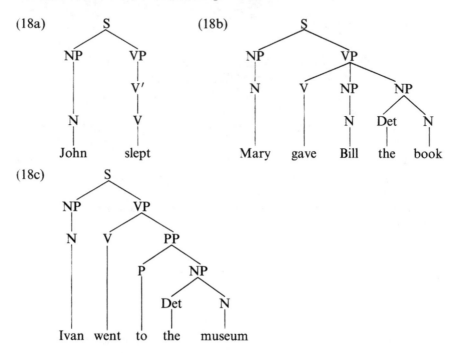

(18a)

S
NP   VP
       V′
N   V
John   slept

(18b)

S
NP   VP
N   V   NP   NP
           N   Det   N
Mary gave Bill the book

(18c)

S
NP   VP
N   V   PP
            P   NP
                 Det   N
Ivan went   to   the   museum

Exercise 3

Using pronouns such as *he/she*, *it*, *them* etc. identify all of the NPs in the following sentences:

(a)   The new gorilla's attendant put a tasty banana on the purple table.
(b)   The person responsible for security left the visiting dignitaries in a miniscule antechamber.

(a) The NPs are *the new gorilla*, *the new gorilla's attendant*, *a tasty banana*, and *the purple table*.

His attendant put a tasty banana on the purple table.
He put a tasty banana on the purple table.
The new gorilla's attendant put it on the purple table.
The new gorilla's attendant put a tasty banana on it.

(b) The NPs are *the person responsible for security, the visiting dignitaries,* and *a miniscule antechamber.*

He left the visiting dignitaries in a miniscule antechamber.
The person responsible for security left them in a miniscule antechamber.
The person responsible for security left them in it.

Exercise 4

Use PP proforms to identify the PPs in the following sentences:

(a) Mary put the book in Sue's jacket on Thursday.
(b) The agent who left the computer on the table at lunchtime was dismissed on the very day he was hired.

(a) The PPs are *in Sue's jacket* and *on Thursday.*

Mary put the book there on Thursday.
Mary put the book in Sue's jacket then.

(b) The PPs are *on the table, at lunchtime,* and *on the very day he was hired.*

The agent who left the computer there at lunchtime was dismissed on the very day he was hired.
The agent who left the computer on the table then was dismissed on the very day he was hired.
The agent who left the computer on the table at lunchtime was dismissed then.

Exercise 5

Use the coordination test to identify three constituents in the following sentence:

John's predilection for original thinking placed his family in dire peril.

There are several possible constituents one can identify:

John's predilection for original thinking
[John predilection for original thinking and his reckless disregard for his safety] placed his family in dire peril.

original thinking
John's predilection for [original thinking and direct action] placed his family in dire peril.

his family
John's predilection for original thinking placed [his family and his many friends] in dire peril.

dire peril
John's predilection for original thinking placed his family in [dire peril and mortal danger].

Exercise 6

Use the movement test to identify two constituents in the following sentence:

Mary can see her friends on Thursday in Birmingham.

There are several possible constituents one can identify:

her friends
Her friends, Mary can see on Thursday in Birmingham, but her enemies, she can see anytime.

on Thursday
On Thursday, Mary can see see her friends in Birmingham, but on Friday, she has to go to the conference.

in Birmingham
In Birmingham, Mary can see her friends on Thursday, but in Newcastle, she has to see her business partners.

Exercise 7

Draw the tree for 'The man will see the book'. Indicate three pairs of nodes which are sisters. What nodes does Aux c-command?

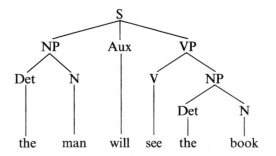

There are several pairs of nodes which are sisters: {NP, Aux}, {Aux, VP}, the two instances of {Det, N} and {V, NP}

Aux c-commands: {NP, Det, N, VP, V, NP, Det, N}

Exercise 8

Identify the head and the complement of the head within the following XPs:

(a) the book about linguistics,
(b) jealous of Federico's achievements,
(c) into the fray,
(d) buy the record

(a)   head: book; complement: about linguistics
(b)   head: jealous; complement: of Federico's achievements
(c)   head: into; complement: the fray
(d)   head: buy; complement: the record

Exercise 9

Identify the specifiers in the following XPs:

(a) Brian's recordings of whales,
(b) three miles down the road,
(c) rather appalled by the situation

(a)   Brian's
(b)   three
(c)   rather

ADDITIONAL EXERCISES

Exercise 1

Consider the following phrase-structure tree:

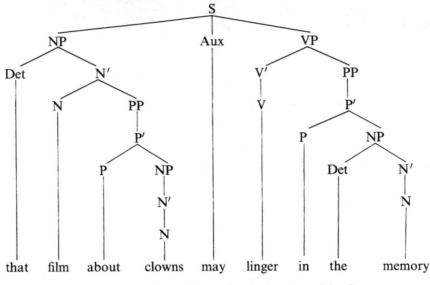

(a) Give two nodes which are immediately dominated by S.
(b) Give two others which are dominated, but not immediately dominated, by S.
(c) What nodes does V c-command?
(d) What is the sister of V'?
(e) What is in the specifier of NP?
(f) What is the complement of P?

Exercise 2

For each of the following XPs, identify the head, complement, and specifier (if any). Draw them using the phrase-structure rules of this chapter.

1. Phil's album of 40 big-band hits
2. quite cognizant of the dangers to life and limb
3. over by the temple to the frog-god
4. receive the package from Toledo
5. books on the hall table
6. John might see the picture
7. right on the ceiling
8. rather disappointed with the outcome

Exercise 3

Draw the trees for the following sentences

1. The elderly clerk can issue the ticket.
2. The player from London will see his agent.
3. John has taken a nap this afternoon.
4. I liked the book about linguistics in the market.
5. I liked the book about linguistics in the twentieth century.
6. The test of time will reveal the true winners.
7. A green shirt is a big advantage in certain situations.

Exercise 4

We've seen in Section 2.5.1 how the 'one-substitution' test can be used to give arguments for a three-level X'-system. In particular, we saw that *of* PPs are sisters to N and not sisters to N'.

(1)   *Jack met the student of philosophy, and I met the one of Greek.

However, consider the following sentence:

(2)   Bill has two quarts of wine and one of water.

Does this represent a problem for the theory we've proposed? Does the following contrast have any relevance to this issue?

(3)a.   I met the ones from France.
   b.   *The quarts of wine and the ones of water were left behind.

3 Functional Categories

Topics: introduction to IP, CP, DP, the structure of conjunction, head-initial and head-final languages.

Open Issue: problems with coordination.

3.0 INTRODUCTION

In the previous chapter we gave arguments for adopting the X'-system in (1) as a description of what you know about your language:

(1)a. XP → (Spec) X'
   b. X' → X' (YP)
   c. X' → X (ZP)

However, in doing so, we focused on phrases like NPs and VPs. The majority of the categories that we've seen so far, specifically N, V, A, and P, are usually referred to as *lexical* categories. These contrast with the so-called *functional* categories I, C, and Det. In this section, we're going to argue that functional categories like C and Det, just like their lexical counterparts, also have structure fully consistent with the X' schema just outlined. We'll also argue that X'-Theory is just as valid for seemingly more exotic languages like Turkish and Japanese.

3.1 FROM AUX AND S TO IP

When we were discussing X'-Theory in the last chapter, you may have been wondering what happened to the following phrase-structure rule:

(2) S → NP Aux VP

This phrase-structure rule really looks like a problem. If we're right to say that (1) is the general format that all phrase-structure rules have to follow, then we'll have to change (2). It doesn't fit the X' format at all. Within the X' system, there's always a one-to-one relationship between heads and phrases. Every NP has a head N in it and every head N is the head of some NP and so on. However, in (2), we've got an S on the left side, but it doesn't appear to dominate anything of category S. On the right side, all we've got are NP, Aux, and VP. Going the other way, the Aux category would seem to be a head also, but there's no Aux′ or AuxP anywhere to be found.

We can kill two birds with one stone if we say that what's really going on is that S is essentially an 'Aux-phrase' which has Aux as its head. Also, just to make a terminological change to bring us into line with the way linguists talk, we'll also need to change the name of the Aux node to 'Inflection', which is usually abbreviated to 'I' or 'Infl'. With the addition of an intermediate I′ category, we can replace (2) with something much neater and consistent with X′-Theory:

(3)a.　IP → NP I′
　　b.　I′ → I VP

The subject of the sentence is now the specifier of IP (Inflection Phrase) and the VP is the complement of I.

Although there is no element which can act as a proform for I′, we can use the Coordination test to show that IP needs three levels of structure.

(4)　John will read the book but may become confused.

What we have in (4) is a conjunction that includes the auxiliary and the VP. That suggests that these elements form a constituent to the exclusion of the subject. However, the phrase-structure rule in (2) claims that these elements do *not* form a constituent. For that reason, (2) seems to be an incorrect characterization of what you know when you know English. On the other hand, the X′-consistent phrase-structure rules in (3) *do* predict that the auxiliary (in I) and the VP *do* form a constituent, namely I′.

EXERCISE 1

Using IP, draw the tree for the following sentence:

Mary will read several newspapers.

In those instances where there is no auxiliary, we'll assume that the I head of IP contains two pieces of information: the tense of the sentence (e.g., past or present, since future tense is indicated by the auxiliary *will*) and the subject-verb agreement information, as in (5). It is because tense and subject-verb agreement are marked by inflectional endings on the verb that the whole sentence is called 'IP'.

(5)   John went to the store

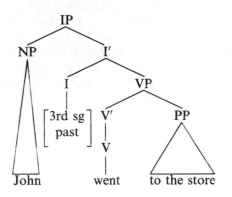

To see concretely why I needs to have tense and agreement information, let's examine a construction called 'VP-ellipsis'. Under certain circumstances, when two sentences are conjoined, the second VP can be deleted:

(6)   Mary can't go to the store but John can.

In (6), the VP in the second conjunct is identical to the VP in the first conjunct (*go to the store*), but it remains unpronounced, leaving behind the auxiliary *can*. But consider what happens when there is no overt auxiliary:

(7)   I buy books every day but John doesn't.

Because there is no auxiliary, the dummy verb *do* must be inserted in the second conjunct. However, notice that the dummy verb shows up in specifically the present tense (*doesn't* vs. *didn't*) and third person singular form (*doesn't* vs. *don't*). Therefore, it must be the case that the tense and subject-verb agreement information are (inflectionally) present in I even when there is no auxiliary to 'spell them out'.

   In order to remember this, when drawing a phrase-structure tree with no auxiliary, be sure to indicate the tense and agreement information in I. Thus the sentence in (8) has the tree in (9):

(8)   You buy books every day.

(9)

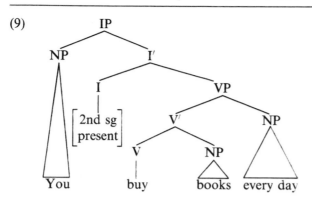

3.2 COMPLEMENTIZERS AND CPS

Consider the following sentences in light of the discussion in the previous section:

(10) Mary will meet her friend at the station.
(11) I was wondering whether *Mary will meet her friend at the station.*

Clearly (10) is a sentence, so it must be an IP. It seems equally clear that the italicized string in (11) is also. The question is what to do about *whether*. Clearly, we can't just say that the V *wonder* takes an IP complement, as in (12):

(12)

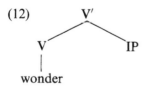

That would predict that (13) should be grammatical, and it isn't:

(13) *I wonder Mary will meet her friend at the station.

In order to account for (11), while not allowing (13), what we need to say is that the IP *Mary will meet her friend at the station* combines with some other category, whose head is *whether*.

  Elements like *whether* or *that* (as in *I know that Bill is here*) are traditionally referred to as *complementizers*. They get that name because they are added to the beginning of an IP in order to help the IP fit in as the complement of a verb. If the complementizer C (*whether* in this case) is the head of

CP, then X′-Theory tells us that it must have a specifier and a complement in a three-level structure:

(14)

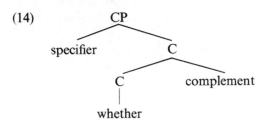

In this case, the IP *Mary will meet her friend at the station* is the complement of C. It has no specifier, although we'll come to some examples later which do.

Putting all of this together, we would draw the tree for (11) as (15):

(15)

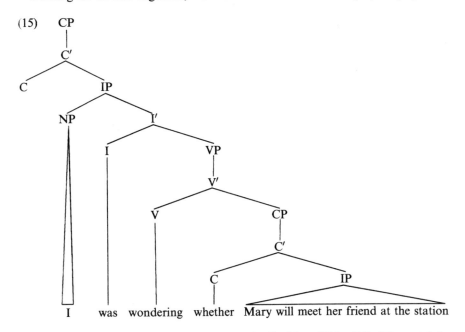

You may be wondering why we've started off with a CP in (15). It's certainly true that sentences don't start with complementizers:

(16)   *That I was wondering whether Mary will meet her friend at the station.

However, we'll see in cases in later chapters that there are some sentences which do start with complementizers, so it's a good habit to get into to start with them even if, at this stage, they don't look necessary.

3.3 GETTING INTO DET: THE DP HYPOTHESIS

In the previous sections we started trying to tighten up our phrase-structure assumptions a bit to bring them into line with the X' system, eliminating heads like Aux that had no associated phrases and eliminating 'phrases' like S which didn't seem to immediately dominate an element of the same category.

Continuing this exercise, let's examine the element Det, which is still outside the X' system. Determiners are clearly heads, not phrases, but we've just been sticking them in the specifier of NP position without saying anything more about them. In this section, we'll examine some arguments that Dets, in fact, have associated D's and DPs. However, it will turn out that it's not as simple as sticking a DP in the specifier position, as in (17):

(17)

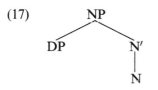

There have been various arguments given in the literature that what we've been calling *noun* phrases are actually *determiner* phrases. That is, the structure of *the book* actually has a determiner head which takes an NP as its complement:

(18)

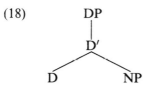

Abney (1987) pulls together some observations regarding gerundive 'Poss-ing' constructions in English to argue for the existence of determiner phrases. An example of the gerundive 'Poss-ing' construction in English is (19):

(19) [John's building a spaceship] caused a huge commotion.

There's a simple question about phrases like *John's building a spaceship* which turns out not to have an obvious answer: what syntactic category is it? Is it a noun phrase? Or is it something sentential, like an IP or a CP?

On the one hand, (19) as a whole looks like it must be a noun phrase. It can turn up in noun phrase positions where CPs are usually excluded. In (20), we see that a 'Poss-ing' phrase can be a subject, and in (21) the object of a preposition:

(20)a. *I wondered if [$_{CP}$ that John built a spaceship] had upset you.
   b. I wondered if [John's building a spaceship] had upset you.
   c. I wondered if [$_{NP}$ the book] had upset you.

(21)a. *I told you about [$_{CP}$ that John built a spaceship].
   b. I told you about [John's building a spaceship].
   c. I told you about [$_{NP}$ the book].

However, it also seems clear that *building a spaceship* represents a VP. In particular, the '-ing' element of the gerundive 'Poss-ing' is not a noun which has been derived from a verb, like *destruction* or *referral* (from *destroy* and *refer* respectively), but instead has all the characteristics of a verb. It takes direct objects, for example, without requiring any kind of preposition, such as *of*:

(22)a. John destroyed the spaceship.
   b. John's destroying the spaceship (caused a panic).
   c. *John's destruction the spaceship (caused a panic).
   d. John's destruction of the spaceship (caused a panic).

The '-ing' element also takes so-called 'verbal particles', which can shift position just as they would with a 'real' verb:

(23)a. John explained away the problem/John explained the problem away.
   b. John's explaining away the problem/John's explaining the problem away ...
   c. *John's explanation away of the problem/*John's explanation of the problem away ...

What we seem to be stuck with are two pieces of a puzzle that don't fit together. If we just bolt together what we've got so far in a Frankenstein's monster-like fashion, it's this:

(24)

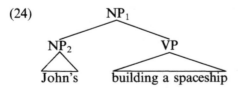

Unfortunately, this is not a structure which is allowed by X'-Theory.

Before Continuing: Explain why (24) is not allowed by X'-Theory.

The problem is that NP$_1$ is a noun phrase, but it fails to immediately dominate an N'. NP$_1$ doesn't seem to have an N head either.

However, perhaps the sentence-like nature of 'Poss-ing' gerundives can offer a clue as to what to do. Consider the tree for (22a):

(25)

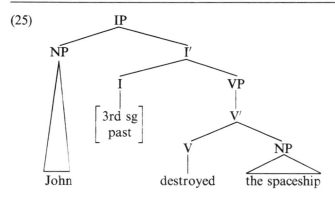

Here, we have a subject *John* and a VP *destroyed the spaceship*. A mediating role is played by the functional category I. It 'hooks up' the VP with its subject. It allows the two to get together. If we assume that there's some mediating category in the gerundive 'Poss-ing' construction, that would provide us a way out of the X′-Theoretic problem that we had in (24):

(26)

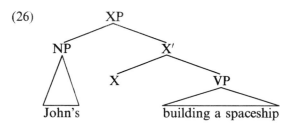

The only question now is 'What is "X", our noun phrase correlate of I?'. Well, there aren't really too many options. It's at least possible that X is some category which never has any overt words. However, that would be an unpleasant innovation to have to make. Even the other functional categories like I and C have at least *some* actual words which belong to them (modals like *can* and *will* for I and complementizers like *that*, *whether* and *if* for C), and it's not completely clear how a child learning English would even figure out that this category existed if there were no overt words of that category. It really looks like everything falls together nicely if we assume that that the mystery category is Det, the determiner, and what we've previously thought of as noun phrases are actually determiner phrases.

(27)

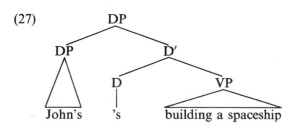

3.4 COORDINATION AND X′-THEORY

The final functional category which we'll consider in this chapter is conjunctions, as illustrated by (28):

(28) John and Bill went to the store.

In Chapter 2, when we were illustrating the 'Coordination test', we weren't explicit about what phrase-structure trees we were assuming for coordinated structures. Our hypothesis is that X′-Theory is provided by Universal Grammar and creates a general framework which all phrase structure conforms to. If that's correct, then we would hope to find an X′-consistent way of incorporating sentences like (28).

Various researchers have suggested (29) as a way of meeting our requirements:

(29)

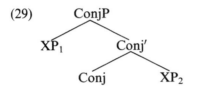

The conjunction *and*, in this case, is the head of an X′-consistent functional category ConjP. It takes the first conjunct as its specifier, and the second conjunct as its complement.

Now, it's all very well to say that we can *create* a structure for conjunctions which is X′-consistent, but the real question is whether there's any *evidence* that (29) is the right analysis. In other words, we have a *conceptual* reason for proposing the structure in (29), but we now need to find some *empirical* support for it.

One argument which has been advanced in support of the structure in (29) has to do with subject-verb agreement. There are various examples from languages of the world in which a verb shows subject-verb agreement only with the *first* of the two conjoined subjects. Consider the following example from Czech:

(30) Půjdu   tam [já   a ty].
      go-1sg.future there I   and you
      'I and you will go there.'

We haven't encountered any non-English data before, so a quick word is in order regarding how to read the examples. The first line is the sentence in the original language, converted to a Roman alphabetic script if necessary (as with, for example, Japanese or Russian). The second line is a morpheme-by-morpheme 'translation'. For example in (33), the Czech word *půjdu* contains two parts: the root *go* and the first person singular, future tense ending. The third line is a translation of the original example sentence into grammatical English.

In (30), the verb is marked with first person singular agreement marking. It seems as though it agrees with only the first conjunct *I* and not the second conjunct *you*. We see a similar situation in the following Palestinian Arabic example:

(31) Galaten   [?el-banat we-l-wlad] ?el-bisse.
     killed3pl.fem the-girls and-the-boy   the cat
     'The girls and the boy killed the cat.'

Again, the verb seems to agree with only the first conjunct, which is third person plural feminine.

The structure in (29) provides a natural way to accommodate these facts, through the mechanism of *specifier-head agreement*. There seems to be a special relationship that heads have with elements in their specifiers. Specifier-head agreement is a process by which information can be passed between the specifier of a functional category and the head.

The most common example of specifier-head agreement is subject-verb agreement within IP. As we discussed in Section 3.1, we can see from VP-ellipsis data that the I head of IP contains the verbal agreement information. When the subject is third person singular in English, for example, the verb takes its characteristic '-s' ending. It is because the subject is in the specifier of IP that I 'knows' what person and number the subject is.

The structure in (29) explains why we should see the facts in (30) and (31), where the entire conjoined phrase seems to have only the person, number, and gender features of the first conjunct. What we have is simply another case of specifier-head agreement. The first conjunct, under the analysis in (29), is the specifier of ConjP. Via specifier-head agreement, it and the Conj head will agree person, number, and gender features.

Now, because Conj is the head of ConjP, the features are said to 'percolate' up to ConjP, with the result that the entirety of the conjoined phrase has only the person, number, and gender features of the first con-junct. By specifier-head agreement again, ConjP and I agree in first person singular features. This process is illustrated in (32):

(32)

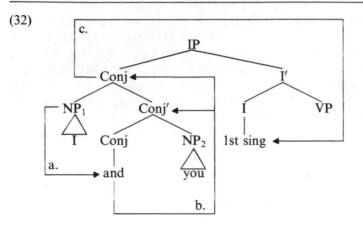

    a.   specifier-head agreement between Conj and its specifier
    b.   feature 'percolation' from Conj to ConjP
    c.   specifier-head agreement between ConjP and I

Thus, we see at least one piece of support for an X'-consistent approach to conjunction, and we seem to have a pleasing convergence between conceptual and empirical considerations.

3.5 HEAD-INITIAL AND HEAD-FINAL LANGUAGES

So far, it looks as though X'-Theory does at least a decent job of accounting for the data that we've looked at so far. However, what are we to make of the following data?

(33)   Ben Newcastleda otoruyorum.   (Turkish)
        I   Newcastle-in live-1st sg.pres.
        'I live in Newcastle.'

(34)   Watashi-wa Newcastle-ni sunde-iru.   (Japanese)
        I-subj   Newcastle-in live-present
        'I live in Newcastle.'

Even just looking at the PPs in Turkish and Japanese, it looks as though we're going to have to do some serious modification to the X'-system. These languages have what are called *post*positions as opposed to the *pre*positions which English has. That is to say, the head P of the PP comes *after* its complement instead of before. And the VP works the same way. PP *in Newcastle* is itself the complement of the verb *live*, and once again we see the complements of the VP coming *before* the head V. If you look at the X′ schema as illustrated in (1) at the beginning of this chapter, you'll see that they only allow for *pre*positions. The complement must *follow* the head. The schema in (1) does not allow for postpositions. But that's what we seem to have here.

How should we respond to this problem? We could simply say that Turkish and Japanese are different and leave it at that. We could then write another set of rules to account for Turkish and Japanese. The X′ system already does a lot of work for us in eliminating redundancies in English. Perhaps there's nothing more to be said about it than that. However, remember that as *linguists* we're interested not just in a theory about English, but also in a general theory of all human languages. In other words, we're interested in investigating Universal Grammar – in what all languages have in common. Ideally, then, we want a *single* set of very general rules covering all languages.

But how do we go about generalizing over the English rule for prepositions and the Japanese/Turkish rule for postpositions:

(35)a.   English: PP → P NP
    b.   Japanese/Turkish: PP → NP P

What the two rules in (35) have in common is that they both say that a PP consists of a P and an NP. The only difference seems to be the order which is imposed on the two sub-constituents. Therefore, all we need to do to generalize over the two is to say that linear order is *not* imposed. This can be indicated by the use of the 'comma' notation:

(36)   English/Turkish/Japanese: PP → P, NP

The phrase-structure rule in (36) is read as indicating that a PP is made up of a P and an NP, which can come in either order.

Therefore, if we remove the linear ordering from the X′-schema in (1), we have (37):

(37)a. XP → (Spec), X′
    b. X′ → X′, (YP)
    c. X′ → X, (ZP)

By doing this, and claiming that (37) is provided by Universal Grammar, we can account for the Turkish and Japanese examples in (33) and (34) by assuming that their structure represents the 'mirror-image' of English. So if we were to draw the trees for (33) and (34), they'd look like (38):

(38)

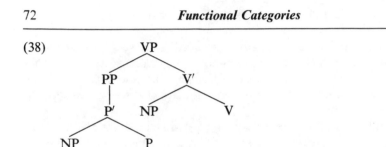

Languages like English, where the order of (22c) comes out as (35a), are referred to as *head-initial* languages because the head precedes its complements. Languages like Turkish and Japanese are referred to as *head-final* languages because the head follows its complements.

3.6 SUMMARY

In this chapter, our goal has been to extend X′ consistency throughout the phrase-structure system. We saw that some categories, like S, Aux, and Det, didn't fit easily into the X′ system. If our hypothesis is correct that the X′ system is provided by Universal Grammar as a general format for phrase-structure rules, then we want to recast any non-X′-consistent categories. We showed how an X′ consistent recasting of S and Aux into IP, Det into DP, and coordination into ConjP might be accomplished. We also saw some empirical evidence that an X′-consistent approach to these categories was the right one. In the final section, we saw that not only is X′-Theory independent of particular syntactic categories (i.e., it describes everything from DPs to PPs to VPs), but it is also independent of linear order. That is to say, the rules in (1) are intended to characterize not only *head-initial* languages, where the head X precedes the complement ZP, but also *head-final* languages, where the head X follows the complement ZP.

OPEN ISSUE: PROBLEMS WITH COORDINATE STRUCTURES

In Section 3.4, we presented the standard, X′-consistent approach to conjunction in (39):

(39)

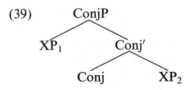

However, this view has not always been the standard one, and various authors have noted that certain facts about conjunction are hard to explain under the analysis in Section 3.4.

We noted in Section 3.4, for example, that (39) allows us to account for the fact that agreement is typically with the first conjunct, rather than with the second conjunct, or with some union of their features. Under specifier-head agreement, the grammatical features of XP₁ are shared with the Conj head, which then pass them up to ConjP. However, Borsley (1994) notes that there are problems with this approach.

Borsley, for example, casts doubt on whether we can account for the agreement facts of conjunction using the mechanism of specifier-head agreement. Looking at subject-verb agreement, it is clear that only person, number, and possibly gender features are shared via specifier-head agreement. Crucially, however, categorial features are *not* shared. In other words, the NP in the specifier of IP does not share its 'nouniness' with the head I of IP, turning the IP into an NP. If it did, we would have to allow complementizers to take NP complements, which is clearly not possible in general.

(40)a. *I said [CP that [NP the book]].
   b. *I asked [CP whether [NP the file]].

Therefore, it seems as though we must not allow specifier-head agreement to extend to copying the syntactic category of the specifier on to the functional category. However, this sharing of syntactic categorial features seems to be precisely what is needed in the case of conjunction. The conjoined entity has the same syntactic category as the two individual conjuncts.

Furthermore, there are also cases where we would want to say that feature sharing between the first conjunct and the head does not happen. This is exemplified by sentences such as (41) (from Borsley (1994)):

(41) You and I understand ourselves/*yourself well.

In (41) it would seem that the subject must be first person plural, in order to account for the appearance of *ourselves* rather than *yourself*. However, under the specifier-head agreement account in Section 3.4, we would expect the subject to be second-person singular.

(42)   ConjP

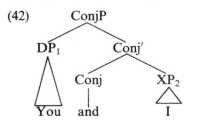

Since *you* and *and* agree via specifier-head agreement, ConjP must also therefore be second person singular, and we predict the opposite pattern of grammaticality to the one we see in (41).

A second problem noted has to do with the bar-level of the conjoined categories. The traditional structure in (39) claims that the conjoined elements together form a maximal projection, not an intermediate X′ projection or a head. However, there are cases where the conjoined constituent appears to be just such a thing. Consider (43) and (45):

(43)   John [may like Mary] and [must like Sue].

In Section 3.1, we gave sentences like (43) as evidence for the existence of I′. Both conjuncts contain an auxiliary verb, which means we must have two Infls. However, we have only one subject, *John*, which suggests that we have only one Spec IP. Unfortunately, though, the traditional structure in (39) doesn't give us a way to express (43). By X′-Theory, the daughters of IP must be an XP (the specifier) and I′. IP cannot have as its daughters a DP specifier and ConjP, another maximal projection.

(44)

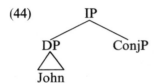

We run into a similar situation in (45):

(45)a.   We [handed] or [sent] a copy of the letter to every student.
   b.   He was there [before] and [after] the lecture.

In this case, however, what we appear to have is conjunction of heads, rather than intermediate projections. In (45a), we have two verbs *handed* and *sent*, but only one set of objects. In (45b), we have two prepositions sharing a single object.

Just as in the previous cases, however, the traditional structure for conjunction in (39) doesn't give us an X′-consistent way to express this. Consider the tree for (45b) for example:

(46)

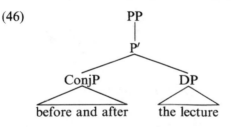

The structure in (46) seems to be a clear violation of X'-Theory. P' has two maximal projections as its daughters, ConjP and DP, rather than a head P and a DP complement.

In summary, it looks as though we may need to temper the initial enthusiasm we had back in Section 3.4 for the X'-consistent approach to conjunction. However, we will continue to assume it for the rest of the book, keeping in mind the problems that we've seen.

BIBLIOGRAPHY

Chomsky (1986) suggested the idea that the X' system could be extended from lexical categories to functional categories, and introduced CP and IP. The first person to bring together evidence that NPs could and should be reanalyzed as DPs was Abney (1987). The arguments that we gave for DPs in Section 3.4 are taken from the introductory chapter of that work, and some of that introductory material is reasonably accessible. Finally, an excellent overview of the status of ConjP is Borsley (1994). Some of his criticisms and observations about ConjP were discussed in the Open Issue.

ANSWERS TO IN-TEXT EXERCISES

Exercise 1

Using IP, draw the tree for the following sentence:

Mary will read several newspapers.

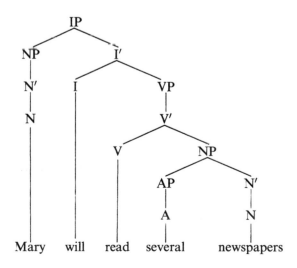

ADDITIONAL EXERCISE

Exercise 1

Draw trees for the following sentences using IP, CP, DP, and ConjP.
(Warning: some may be head-final!)

1. The report by the police will affect the community and its members.
2. John's friend and Bill's mother can send the letter.
3. I know that the cheque will arrive on time.
4. Mary performed the experiment and completed the report.
5. Lions in my garden are a source of irritation.
6. I was wondering whether Bob said that Mitch was leaving.
7. Maria's growing five hundred plants caused an overflow on the patio.
8. Jun-ka chinkwu eykey chayk-ul ilkessta.   (Korean)
    Jun   friend   to   book   read
    'Jun read the book to a friend.'
9. Juan dijo que María va   a Madrid.   (Spanish)
    Juan said that Maria is going to Madrid
    'Juan said that Maria is going to Madrid.'
10. Rajakah   kanyaya saha vadati.   (Sanskrit)
    The laundryman the girl   with speaks
    'The laundryman speaks with the girl.'

4 θ-Theory and Case Theory

Topics: argument structure, θ-roles, morphological vs. abstract Case, the Case Filter, the Visibility condition.

Open Issue: the Case Filter, Visibility, and degrees of ungrammaticality.

4.0 INTRODUCTION

The last chapter looked at how words and phrases are organized into larger groups. In this chapter, we will focus in on words and phrases in more detail. In particular, we'll be looking at the relationship between *predicates* and *arguments*. These are terms from formal logic which have been borrowed into linguistics, but what we're basically talking about are verbs, adjectives, and prepositions in the case of predicates, and DPs (and sometimes PPs) in the case of arguments.

By way of illustration, let's take a look at an example of a predicate that you'll be familiar with from mathematics: the 'equals' sign. The predicate has two arguments – that is, two required elements. You have to say what the two things are that are equal to each other. If you leave either one out, the (mathematical) expression is 'ungrammatical':

(1)a.　*x =
　　b.　* = y
　　c.　x = y

Verbs, adjectives, and prepositions can be thought of as predicates which take arguments in exactly the same way. For example, *destroy* can be thought of as a predicate which also takes two arguments (a destroyer and a destroyee). Leave either one out, and the (linguistic) expression is ungrammatical:

(2)a.　*John destroyed.
　　b.　*destroyed the building
　　c.　John destroyed the building.

We'll begin first by looking at what information from the lexical entry of a predicate is relevant for the syntax. We'll see that predicates in language have *argument structure*, which indicates what kinds of XPs the verbs require in order to complete their meaning. They assign *θ-roles* to these required XPs, which indicate the semantic role that they play in the syntax. The subpart of the theory which concerns these issues is called *θ-Theory*. Second, for those arguments of predicates which are DPs, we'll see that the predicate must assign *case* to the argument. Subjects get nominative case, direct objects get accusative case, etc. It's a traditional idea, and the idea of cases may be familiar to you if you've studied a language like Latin or German. This subpart of the theory, not too surprisingly, is called *Case Theory*.

4.1 AN INTRODUCTION TO ARGUMENT STRUCTURE

Let's begin the discussion by looking at a woefully inadequate grammar of English (i.e., a model of what you know when you know English). First, we have X'-Theory from Chapter 2. This gives us the general format for our phrase-structure trees:

(3)a. XP → (Spec) X'
   b. X' → X' (YP)
   c. X' → X (ZP)

However, in addition to what our phrase-structure trees can look like, we also need to have words to put in them. The place in the grammar where words and associated information are stored is called the *lexicon*, and the words themselves are usually referred to as *lexical items*. The lexicon is just the mental equivalent of a dictionary.

What we're interested in here is the information in the lexicon which is relevant for the syntax. Although we didn't talk about it in these terms, we've already seen one of the bits of associated information that will have to be stored in the lexicon: the syntactic category of a given lexical item. So, for example, part of the lexical entry for *sincerity* will indicate that it's a noun, as opposed to a verb or an adjective.

To account for what you know about English, we need the lexicon to specify more than just the syntactic category though. For example, *see* and *put* are both verbs. However, there is more to specify than that. Consider the contrast in (4):

(4)a.   John saw the book.
   b.   *John put the book.

If all you knew about *see* and *put* was that they were both verbs, we wouldn't be able to explain why you know that (4a) is grammatical and (4b) is ungrammatical.

What we need is some indication about the kinds of complements that a verb can have. *See*, for example, is able to take either a DP complement or a CP complement:

(5)a. John saw the book.
   b. John saw that the government was corrupt.

Other verbs, like *sleep* must not have a complement of any kind:

(6)a. John slept.
   b. *John slept the bed.
   c. *John slept that Bill left.

However, one thing that *sleep* and *see* do have in common is that they need a subject:

(7)a. John saw the book.
   b. John slept.

(8)a. *saw the book.
   b. *slept

So a verb like *sleep* is said to be a *one-argument* verb. It requires a subject, but may not have a direct object of any kind. A verb like *see* on the other hand is a *two-argument* verb (or, in logical terminology, a *two-place predicate*), with the second argument being either a DP or a CP. There are even *three-argument* verbs, like *put*:

(9)a. <u>John</u> put <u>the book on the table</u>.
   b. *John put the book.
   c. *John put on the table.
   d. *put on the table.

EXERCISE 1

Identify the following verbs as one-, two-, or three-argument verbs: confirm, show, fall.

It's more than just verbs that have arguments, though. For example, consider the preposition *at*. This preposition also has an argument:

(10)a. John left the book at the library.
    b. *John left the book at.

This information about the number and category of the arguments that a predicate takes is called the *argument structure* of the predicate.

4.2 θ-ROLES

Clearly, the argument structure of a predicate is related to its semantics. Whatever it is that makes *sleep* a one-argument predicate (i.e., intransitive) is related to what *sleep* means. Another addition to the lexical entry which we need to make, and which also seems connected to the semantics of the verb, concerns the *θ-roles* that a given element assigns. θ-roles encode the semantic roles possessed by the various DPs and PPs which are required by the predicate.

By way of illustration, consider (11):

(11)   Bob destroyed the statue.

Part of what you know about (11) is that *Bob*, the subject, is the voluntary agent of the 'destroying' action and *the statue* is the object affected by that action. This is expressed in the theory by saying that *destroy* is a predicate which assigns the *Agent* θ-role to its subject and the *Patient* θ-role to its object.

Now compare (11) with (12), where *destroy* has been replaced by *like*:

(12)   Bob liked the statue.

In (12) the subject of *like* isn't really an agent in the same way as (11). Bob's not really *doing* anything as the subject of (12) in the same way that he is in (11). Neither is Bob's action necessarily voluntary. Bob could, for example, like the statue in spite of himself. What's going on in (12) is that Bob is experiencing an emotion rather than performing an action. In order to encode the differences between sentences like (11) and (12), we say that *like* assigns the *Experiencer* θ-role to its subject rather than the Agent θ-role.

In the same way, the direct object *statue* in (12) isn't really an object affected by the action. In order to distinguish direct objects of verbs like *like* (where nothing is really happening to the statue) from direct objects of verbs like *destroy* (where something *is* happening to the statue), we say that the direct object of *like* is assigned the *Theme* θ-role.

Our main focus in this book is not lexical semantics or argument structure in themselves, so I won't go into tremendous detail about the nature of θ-roles. However, there are some aspects of θ-roles which do impinge on syntax. For example, part of your syntactic knowledge of English includes the fact that *destroy* and *like* behave differently with respect to the syntactic construction called 'wh-clefts':

(13)a.　What Bob did was destroy the statue.

　　b.　*What Bob did was like the statue.

It seems that the requirement for participating in this 'What X did was ...' frame is that X must be assigned the Agent θ-role by the verb.

We also can see contrasts like the one in (14):

(14)a.　What happened to the statue was Bob destroyed it.

　　b.　*What happened to the statue was Bob liked it.

Since the direct object of *like* is assigned the Theme θ-role as opposed to the Patient θ-role, and is therefore not affected by the action of the verb, it can't participate in alternations like the one in (14). Other θ-roles, primarily assigned by prepositions as opposed to verbs, include Goal, Source, and Location:

(15)a.　Mary gave the book to <u>John</u>.

　　　　　　　　　　　GOAL

　　b.　Alice checked the book out from <u>the library</u>.

　　　　　　　　　　　　　　SOURCE

　　c.　I saw the match in <u>Bilbao</u>.

　　　　　　　　LOCATION

4.2.1　Expletives and the θ-Criterion

In this section, we're going to look at so-called *expletive* elements. Now I know you'll be disappointed, but, in this context, we don't mean by 'expletive' things like '****' and '!(%"&'. When we speak of expletives in the context of syntax, we mean certain kinds of DPs which look like they must *not* be assigned a θ-role. Expletives tell us a lot of interesting things about what you know about your language.

Consider first (16):

(16)　It seems that John doesn't clean his house very often.

What would the θ-role that *seems* assigns to its subject *it*? Well, it doesn't look like there is one. Certainly *it* is not an agent, or an experiencer, or any of the other things that subjects normally represent. In fact, it appears as though *it* is contributing nothing to the semantic interpretation of the sentence whatsoever. For example, the following is completely nonsensical:[1]

(17)　What seems that John doesn't clean his house very often? (Answer: it.)

More importantly, notice what happens if we try to put a noun phrase like *the room* into the subject position of *seems*:

(18)   *The room seems that John doesn't clean his house very often.

It's not that there's no coherent interpretation for (18). Quite the contrary, (18) could perfectly well mean there's something about the room which gives you the impression that John doesn't clean his house very often. The room could be a complete mess, for example. However, despite (18) representing a perfectly meaningful thought, it is simply ungrammatical.

We can explain the contrast between (16) and (18) in terms of θ-roles. Let's suppose that there's a general requirement that says that all non-expletive DPs must be assigned a θ-role. This requirement is called the θ-Criterion:

(19)   *The θ-Criterion*
       All non-expletive DPs must be assigned a θ-role.

Now let's assume that the subject position of *seems* is not a position where a θ-role is assigned. That will account for the ungrammaticality of (18). The DP *the room* requires a θ-role, but is not in a position where it can get one. But what about (16), then? Well, if we assume that an element like expletive *it* cannot bear a θ-role, we account for the fact that (16) is grammatical. *Seems* is a one-place predicate. Its one argument is the CP. It therefore has no θ-role to assign to its subject, but that's OK because the expletive *it* doesn't require one.

It isn't the only element which appears able to function as an expletive. *There* can also do so as well when it appears as a subject:

(20)   There seems to be a problem here.

We can use expletives as a general test for whether a position is assigned a θ-role or not. For example, the subject of the predicate *be likely* is also not a position which is assigned a θ-role when it takes a CP complement:

(21)a.   *John is likely that he's a spy.
     b.   It is likely that John is a spy.
     c.   There is likely to be a spy in the room.

The fact that we can get expletive *it* and *there*, but not any other kind of DP shows that the subject position of *be likely* is not a position where a θ-role is assigned.[2]

A question arises, though, as to why English has expletives. They don't contribute anything to the semantics of the sentence. If *seems* and *be likely* don't assign θ-roles to their subjects, why can't the subjects just be left out? The fact of the matter is that they just can't be:

(22)a.   *Is likely that John is a spy.
   b.   *Is likely to be a spy in the room.

It's not clear what information is present in (21b) and (c) which is not present in (22), but the sentences are still ungrammatical. On the basis of facts like this, Chomsky (1981) proposed the *Extended Projection Principle* (EPP):

(23)   *The Extended Projection Principle*
   All clauses must have a subject.

(The EPP is an extension of an older principle, the Projection Principle, which said that all information in the argument structure of a lexical item had to be present in the syntax.) The EPP just appears to be one of those 'brute force' things. (23) doesn't explain why clauses have to have a subject, but it seems we need it on the basis of the ungrammaticality of sentences like (22a) and (b). All clauses must have a syntactically represented subject even if that means have a semantically empty (expletive) subject.

4.2.2   θ-Theory and PRO

Another impact that θ-Theory has on the syntax has to do with the analysis of infinitival tenseless constructions. Consider (24):

(24)   I hope to hit the target.

We've got two verbs here, *hope* and *hit*. *Hope* is pretty straightforward. It assigns the Experiencer θ-role to its subject and takes a clausal complement, either an infinitive (tenseless) clause, as in (24), or a finite (tensed) clause as in (25).

(25)   I hope that John will arrive tomorrow.

However, *hit* in (24) is more interesting. Under normal circumstances, *hit* takes two arguments – a subject, to which it assigns the Agent θ-role, and a direct object, to which it assigns the Patient θ-role.

(26)   John hit the target.

Both of these arguments are obligatory. (27a) can't mean 'John hit something or other' and (27b) can't mean 'Someone or other hit the ball':

(27)a.   *John hit.
    b.   *hit the ball.

But this is very strange given (24). In (24), *hit* has a direct object, *the target*, but it doesn't appear to have a subject. From what we've just seen in (27), it doesn't look plausible to say that a verb can just decide not to assign a θ-role that it has if it doesn't want to. In fact, it looks like we need to strengthen the θ-Criterion so that there's a one-to-one relationship between the θ-roles that a predicate has and DPs to which those θ-roles are assigned:

(28)   *The θ-Criterion (revised)*
       All non-expletive DPs must be assigned a θ-role and every θ-role must be assigned to a DP.

Additionally, in the case of subjects, we also have the Extended Projection Principle to worry about. So it looks like there's *two* principles being violated in (24). Not only does *hit* seem to have a θ-role that it's not assigning (even though the θ-Criterion says it has to), but the infinitive clause *to hit the target* also violates the Extended Projection Principle by having no subject.

These two problems have a single solution. If there were an *unpronounced* DP of some kind in the specifier position of the infinitival IP (i.e., in its subject position), we'd be all set. Rather than being different, *hit* would be exactly the same both in finite clauses and infinitives. It would have two obligatory θ-roles to assign. The only difference would be that in infinitives the subject remains unpronounced. Also, the Extended Projection Principle would be obeyed rather than violated. Let's refer to this unpronounced subject of infinitivals as *PRO*. The structure of (24) would therefore be (29):

(29)

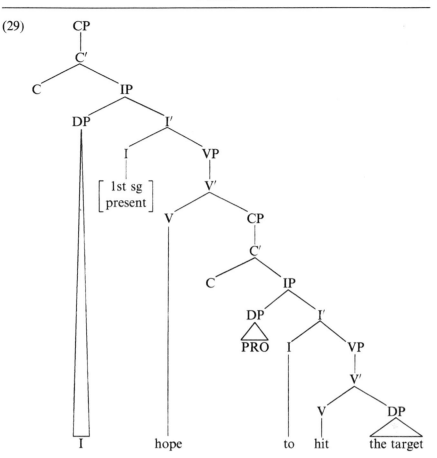

Notice that when we have PRO, the infinitival phrase is actually a CP, rather than an IP. In Chapter 8 we'll see why we need to say that. For the moment, though, you can just memorize it.

Assuming that there is an unpronounced PRO as the subject of infinitivals also explains another fact about their interpretation. (24) is not interpreted as something like 'I hope that somebody or other hits the target' or 'I hope that people in general hit the target'. What (24) means is 'I hope that *I* hit the target.' We can account for this fact by saying that the subject of *hope*, which is *I*, 'controls' PRO, and that *hope* is a *subject-control* verb. That is, PRO obligatorily refers back to the subject of *hope*. Many languages of the world have subject-control verbs, but English is somewhat exceptional in that it also has *object-control* verbs like *persuade*:

(30)   John persuaded Bill [CP PRO to go to college].

Here, it's not the subject *John* which is the controller of PRO. It's not John who's going to college in (30). Rather the controller of PRO is the object *Bill*.

In addition to 'controlled' PRO, there are also instances of what is called 'arbitrary' PRO:

(31)a. To return to the scene of the crime is never a good idea.
    b. PRO to return to the scene of the crime is never a good idea.

Just as in (24), *return* seems to be missing a subject in (31a). Again, though, we will analyze (31a) as having PRO as the subject of *return*, as illustrated in (31b). In this case, though, PRO does not have a controller and instead has a generic interpretation. What (31) means is 'for anyone to return ...' or 'for people in general to return ...'.

4.3 MORPHOLOGICAL CASE

Having introduced θ-Theory, and seen the implications that it has for our model of what speakers of English know, let's now turn to another area in which aspects of a word's lexical entry have an impact on the syntax: Case Theory. To begin our discussion of Case, let's take a look at the pronoun system of English. One of the interesting things about pronouns is that, as you know, they change form depending on their function in the sentence. So, for instance, when the first person singular pronoun is used as a subject, it is 'I'. However, when the same pronoun is the object of a verb or the object of a preposition, it takes the form 'me'. So we have contrasts like (32) and (33):

(32)a.   I like The Beatles.
    b.   *Me like The Beatles.

(33)a.   Mary gave the book to me.
    b.   *Mary gave the book to I.

This change of form in the pronoun is just about all that's left of a system which existed in older stages of English where not just pronouns, but also determiners and nouns in general, changed form depending on their grammatical function in the sentence. Also, the number of different roles which demanded a change was greater. So, for instance, in Old English we had contrasts like the following (from Freeborn (1992)):

(34)a. þæt   wif   andwyrde.
        The-NOM woman-NOM answered
        'The woman answered.'
    b. God   cwæþ to þam   wif-e
        God-NOM said   to the-DAT woman-DAT
        'God said to the woman ...'

In (34), the DP *the woman* changes form depending on its role in the sentence. When it is the subject, it appears as *þæt wif*. When it is an indirect object, it appears as *þam wife*. And there are languages of the world which are more complicated still. Nouns in Latin, for example, are in different forms depending on whether they are the subject or the object of the verb, or even depending on exactly which preposition they are the object of.

Taking over some traditional terminology from the study of Latin grammar, these changes in the form that the words take fall under the general heading of 'Case'. When a noun is in a certain form because it is the subject of a sentence, it is said to be in the *nominative case*. When it is in direct object position, it is said to be in the *accusative case*. When it is the object of a preposition, it is usually said to be in an *oblique case* (for example, the ablative case in Latin). The important point to note is that what case a DP is in depends on other elements in the structure, usually a verb or preposition. This information about Vs and Ps is going to have to be included in their lexical entry.

4.4   MORPHOLOGICAL CASE VS. ABSTRACT CASE

I want now to clarify something that we've so far been assuming regarding case assignment. We started the discussion by talking about pronouns in English, which actually change form depending on whether they are nominative or accusative case. However, we are now going to assume that *all* DPs, in English as well as in Latin, are actually assigned case, even when there's no change in form:

(35)a.   Brutus hit the ball.
    b.   The ball hit Brutus.

Even though the two *Brutus*'s look identical in (35), what we want to say is that the 'Brutus' in (35a) is really *Brutus-nominative* and the 'Brutus' in (35b) is really *Brutus-accusative*. It's just an accident of the morphology of English that the case marking in English is unpronounced. In Latin, the case marking would be pronounced (*Brutus* in (35a) and *Brutum* in (35b)). It's the same situation with *the ball*. It's really *the ball-accusative* in (35a) and *the ball-nominative* in (35b).

To formalize this distinction, when we're talking about *morphological* case, as in 'The ending for the instrumental case in Russian is -om', we'll use a lower-case 'c'. When we're talking about *abstract* case, we'll use a capital 'C'. The two (case and Case) are clearly related. Morphological case is the realization of abstract Case. So in *John hit him*, *him* is assigned (abstract) accusative Case. Because it's an English pronoun, that abstract accusative Case is realized as morphological accusative case (*him*). *John* on the other hand is assigned (abstract) nominative Case, but there's no realization of that with a visible (morphological) case-ending. For the most part, we'll be concerned in the rest of the book with abstract Case rather than morphological case.

4.4.1 Case assignment and M-Command

Let's move on now to examine in a little more detail where Case assignment comes from. Why is a given DP assigned nominative or accusative Case? We hinted just a moment ago that Case is assigned to DPs in certain structural configurations by certain other elements. Objects of verbs and prepositions are assigned accusative or oblique Case, and subjects are assigned nominative Case. In this section, we're going to examine the configurations under which Case assignment can take place. Put another way, we'll see that a particular structural/configurational relationship needs to obtain between the Case assignor and the assignee.

The canonical cases that we're interested in looking at are nominative and accusative Case assignment.

(36)

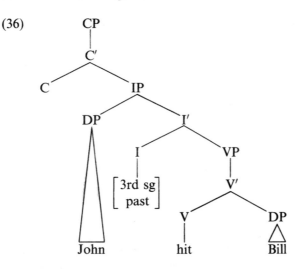

Nominative Case assignment is controlled by I. We'll say that I assigns nominative Case to its specifier (i.e., the subject) when it is finite (37a) but not when I is non-finite (as in infinitives (37b)). A Case-assigning preposition must be inserted in that instance (37c):

(37)a.   He hit the ball.
   b.   *He/Him to hit the ball would be amazing.
   c.   For him to hit the ball would be amazing.

The question is, though, what the precise relationship is which has to obtain between the Case assignor and the Case assignee. Let's start by considering the two standard cases that we have: nominative Case assignment by finite I and accusative Case assignment by V:

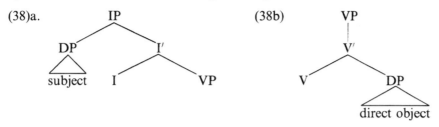

(38)a.   (38b)

If we were just looking at the VP case in (38b), you might think that c-command is the relevant relationship between Case assignor and Case assignee. The V does c-command its direct object. However, if we take a look at (38a), it's clear that c-command won't work. I doesn't c-command the subject in (38a).

There is one thing that (38a) and (38b) do have in common, though: the Case assignment is taking place *within* the maximal projection of the Case assignor. That is, the subject is in the specifier of IP position. It is within the IP which has the Case assignor I as its head. Similarly, in (38b), the direct object is also within the VP headed by V, which is the Case assignor.

We can formalize this notion of 'within the XP' by introducing the notion of m-command (where 'm' is after 'maximal', since XP is a maximal projection):

(39)   *m-command*
      A node α m-commands a node β if and only if the first maximal projection dominating α dominates β.

We can now define Case assignment in terms of m-command:

(40) α assigns Case to β if and only if
      (a) α is a Case assignor (i.e., V, finite I, or P), and
      (b) α m-commands β.

If the definition of m-command sounds a little familiar, it's because it's almost exactly the same as the definition of c-command from Chapter 2. The only difference is that for c-command you find the first branching node dominating α and for m-command you find the first maximal projection dominating α. This effectively ensures that it is the *head* of αP that assigns Case. They're two different relations, though. Notice in (38), for example, that while V c-commands the direct object DP, I does *not* c-command the subject DP. However, we'll see that we need both c-command and m-command.

4.4.2   The Need for Barriers

Although m-command seems to be the right relationship between Case assignor and assignee, we need to rein things in a bit. It's not that you can just assign Case to anything that you m-command. To see why consider (41):

(41)   I read the book in Moscow.

We want things to work out so that *read* (a verb) assigns accusative Case to *the book*, but, crucially, not to *Moscow*. *Moscow* must get oblique Case from the preposition *in*. We can see this even more clearly if we look at the equivalent of (41) in a language like Russian:

(42)a.   Ja pročital knigu   v Moskvje.
         I read   book-ACC in Moscow-LOC
         'I read the book in Moscow.'
     b.   *Ja pročital v Moskvu
         I read   in Moscow-ACC

Read's attempt to assign accusative Case to *Moscow* seems to be blocked by the preposition *in*.

   However, consider the tree for (41):

(43)

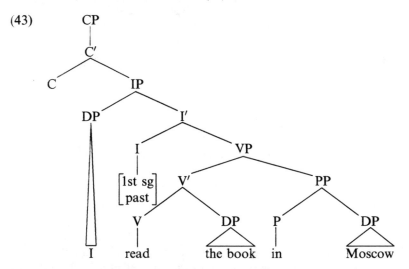

Read does m-command *Moscow*. (The first maximal projection dominating *read* is VP, and VP does dominate the NP *Moscow*.) Therefore, if Case assignment depends on m-command and nothing else, we have a problem.

   What we need is some way of 'protecting' objects of prepositions from being assigned Case by verbs. To do this, let's assume that heads exert a 'zone of control' within their maximal projections, preventing Case assignment by anything from outside. This idea is worked into the definition by adding a clause which says that maximal projections form barriers to Case assignment from outside the maximal projection.

(44) α assigns Case to β if and only if
   (a) α is a Case assignor (i.e., V, finite I, or P), and
   (b) α m-commands β, and
   (c) no barrier intervenes (where any maximal projection is a barrier).

With this definition of Case assignment, although the verb still m-commands the object of the preposition, it can't assign Case to it because of the intervening barrier PP.

EXERCISE 2

Which elements assign Case to the DPs in the following sentence:

John showed the book to Bill on Friday? Draw the tree.

4.5 EXCEPTIONAL CASE MARKING

Now that we have the standard Case assignment configurations under our belts, let's take a look at one configuration which has received a fair bit of attention over the years:

(45) I believe Mary to be the best candidate.

(45) is most commonly referred to as an Exceptional Case Marking (ECM) configuration. However, because *Mary* doesn't differ between *Mary-nominative* and *Mary-accusative*, (45) doesn't tell us as much as it could. By replacing *Mary* with a pronoun, we can use morphological case to tell us more about the abstract Case-assignment situation:

(46)a. I believe her to be the best candidate.
   b. *I believe she to be the best candidate.

On the evidence of *her* in (46a), Mary is receiving accusative Case in (45), not nominative Case. The lack of nominative Case is not surprising. We've seen that infinitival I (*to*) does not assign nominative Case. (Only finite I assigns nominative Case.) The accusative Case is surprising, though. The only potential source for accusative Case is the verb *believe* in the higher clause. However, unlike the cases of accusative Case marking that we've seen so far, *Mary* is not the direct object of the verb in (45). It's the subject of the lower infinitival clause. This is why it's called 'Exceptional' Case Marking.

If you think about what (45) means, you can see pretty clearly that *Mary* is the subject of the lower clause and not the direct object of *believe*. The object of my belief isn't actually Mary. Rather what I believe is that some situation or state of affairs is true, and that situation or state of affairs is represented by the IP *Mary to be the best candidate*. You can see this even more clearly by comparing two cases with *believe*: one where it takes a DP direct object and one where it takes an infinitival complement:

(47)a.   #I believe the politician, but I think he's lying.
    b.   I believe the politician to be lying.

The '#' symbol is used to indicate a sentence which is not syntactically ill-formed, but which is deviant for some other reason. In this case, it's because (47a) represents a contradiction. When *believe* takes a DP complement, the DP represents a true direct object. Therefore, in (47a) the object of belief is the politician, and it is contradictory to imply that you both believe and don't believe the politician. On the other hand, where *believe* is followed by an infinitival phrase, the complement of *believe* is the IP and it is the situation or state of affairs which represents the object of belief. Therefore, there's no implied contradiction in (47b) because you don't believe the politician. You believe a situation to be true, namely that the politician is lying.

Therefore, the structure for Exceptional Case Marking configurations will be (48), with the IP as the sister to the V:

(48)

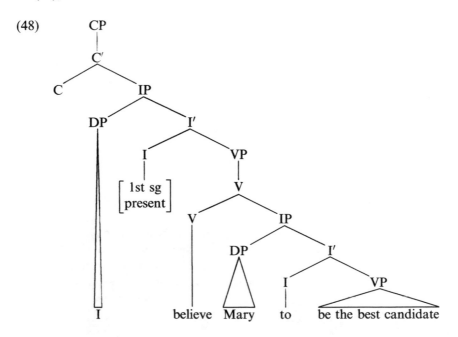

Other ECM verbs include *want* and *expect*.

Notice how an ECM verb like *believe* contrasts with a superficially similar verb like *persuade*, which we mentioned earlier:

(49)   I persuaded Mary to leave the room.

In this case, *Mary* is clearly the *object* of *persuade*. Unlike *believe*, you're not persuading a situation or a state of affairs. You're persuading *Mary*. *Believe* has one object, the clause, where the DP is the subject of that lower clause. *Persuade* has two objects, the persuadee, and what you persuaded them to do.

(50)a.   I believe [Mary to be the best candidate].
   b.   I persuaded [Mary] [PRO to leave the room].
        (cf. I persuaded Mary that Bill left the room.)

4.5.1   IP – It's Not a Barrier

However, it turns out that ECM configurations present a problem for what we've just said about Case assignment, and this is why they are called 'exceptional'. We argued just a minute ago that *Mary* is not the object of the verb *believe*, but rather is the subject of the IP *Mary to be the best candidate*. But if that's the case, how is it that *believe* is able to assign accusative Case to *Mary*? IP is a maximal projection just like any other, and therefore should present a barrier to government by *believe*. It doesn't seem to though. If it did then (45) should be ungrammatical. This, unfortunately, is just one of those situations like the Extended Projection Principle, where brute force is the order of the day. The response to this problem which is taken in the syntax literature (e.g., Chomsky (1986)) is to say that *infinitival* IP is 'defective'. Unlike other maximal projections, like PP, it is not a barrier to Case assignment.

At least there is a certain amount of initial plausibility to this idea. Infinitival I, which is realized as *to*, is quite different from other kinds of inflection. *To* has no person and number or tense information, for example. It doesn't assign nominative Case either; as we saw in (37) above. We therefore need the subject of the IP to be exceptionally Case marked with accusative Case from the matrix verb. We'll also see in Chapter 6 another case in which infinitival IP doesn't act as a barrier the way you'd expect it to, so at least the description seems right, even if it doesn't give any particular insight into what the ultimate explanation might be.

If, on the other hand, a CP is present, then Exceptional Case Marking is blocked by the barrier, just as you'd expect. This can be seen in the following contrast, adapted from Haegeman (1994):

(51)a.   I know [IP Mary/her to be an honest person].
   b.   *I know [CP whether [IP Mary/her to be an honest person].

In (51a) we see that *know* is an Exceptional Case Marking verb. However, when we insert the complementizer *whether*, we know that we must have a CP. The ungrammaticality of (51b) suggests that Case is genuinely coming from the higher verb *know*, rather than infinitival I assigning oblique Case. Furthermore, as our definition of Case assignment in (44) would predict, the CP barrier blocks Case assignment from *know*. Notice that it's not as though there's something incoherent about the thought expressed by (51b). If we replace the infinitival I with a finite I, the sentence becomes grammatical:

(52)   I know [CP whether [IP Mary/she is an honest person]].

Here *Mary* is assigned nominative Case by the finite I. This suggests that, after we make the stipulation that infinitival IP is 'defective', the general theory of barriers accounts for Case assignment in Exceptional Case Marking contexts.

4.6   THE CASE FILTER

In discussing ECM configurations as we have been, we've hinted at one of the central arguments for the existence of abstract Case assignment, which I now want to make explicit. This argument was first made by the linguist Jean-Roger Vergnaud in a famous letter to Noam Chomsky in the late 1970s. Vergnaud noted that it appears we need to say that *abstract* Case assignment is taking place in order explain certain contrasts in grammaticality. Consider (53):

(53)a.   I believe [IP John to be the best candidate].
   b.   *I hope [CP John to be the best candidate].
      (cf. I hope that John is the best candidate.)

In the previous section, we discovered *believe* is an Exceptional Case Marking verb, able to assign accusative Case to the specifier of its infinitival IP complement. *Hope* by contrast is not an ECM verb because *hope* takes a CP complement. If we have a rule which says that DPs must always be assigned Case, we can account for the contrast in (53). *Believe* can provide a source of Case, but *hope* cannot because CP (as a maximal projection) is a barrier to Case assignment. This requirement that DPs be assigned Case is usually referred to as the Case Filter:

(54)   *The Case Filter*
     A DP must be assigned Case.

The Case Filter can also account for a number of other contrasts. For example, consider (55), which we mentioned in passing earlier:

(55)a. *John to hit the ball would be amazing.
  b.   For John to hit the ball would be amazing.

As we saw in the previous section, one of the respects in which infinitival I is defective is that it does not assign nominative Case to its subject. Therefore, *John* in (55a) is in violation of the Case Filter. By contrast, when we insert the preposition *for*, as in (55b), it provides a source of Case for *John*. As a result, the sentence becomes grammatical.

However, having just reminded ourselves that infinitival *to* does not assign Case to the subject position, we do need to say something about PRO, as in (56):

(56)   John hoped PRO to win.

PRO must be a DP. It's DPs that turn up in subject position and it's DPs that verbs assign their θ-roles to. We need to say something about PRO because otherwise we incorrectly predict that (56) is ungrammatical. The usual way to account for (56) is to say that the Case Filter is restricted to *overt*, that is to say pronounced, DPs. Unpronounced DPs like PRO don't require Case. Viewed in this way, the Case Filter is essentially a morphological requirement.

One reason why this pronounced/unpronounced distinction might look like the right one is that the Case Filter applies to expletives just as it applies to other DPs:

(57)a.   I want it to seem that John died of natural causes.
  b. *I hope it to seem that John died of natural causes.

The DP *it* in (57) is an expletive, as *seem* does not assign a θ-role to its subject. However, the contrast suggests that expletive *it* does require Case. The only difference between (57a) and (57b) is that *want* can function as an Exceptional Case Marking verb but *hope* cannot. Therefore *it* can be assigned Case in (57a) but not (57b), thereby flouting the Case Filter.

The same contrast is observed with expletive *there*:

(58)a.   I want there to be six reports on my desk by noon.
  b. *I hope there to be six reports on my desk by noon.

If the Case Filter applies to all overt DPs, whether expletive or not, the contrasts in (57) and (58) are explained.

EXERCISE 3

Do the following sentences violate the θ-Criterion, the Case Filter or both?
Why?

(a)   *John seems that his wife left him.
(b)   *I promised it to seem that the arena was full.
(c)   *I decided the room to seem that John had left.
(d)   *I tried there to be three books on the table.

4.7   THE VISIBILITY CONDITION – AN IMPROVEMENT ON THE CASE FILTER?

So far the Case Filter looks like a reasonably plausible requirement.
Pronounced DPs need Case and unpronounced DPs don't need Case.
However, the Case Filter is not without its shortcomings. So let's take a look
at a popular replacement for the Case Filter, *the Visibility Condition*, which
proposes that there's an important relationship between the two topics
we've been looking at in this Chapter: θ-role assignment and Case.

Chomsky (1981) proposed a new way of looking at sentences involving
Case violations. He suggested that there wasn't really a separate Case Filter at
all. Instead, what it really all boiled down to was θ-role assignment. In order
for V, I or P to 'see' a DP and assign it a θ-role, it had to become 'visible' to the
θ-role assignor. The way to become 'visible' is to be assigned Case. This
requirement is referred to in the literature as the *Visibility Condition*.

Under this approach, Case assignment is now not a direct requirement. There's no principle that says 'you must have Case'. The grammar
couldn't care less whether you have Case or not. However, if you don't get
Case, you're going to run into trouble if you need a θ-role down the line.
You won't be 'visible' for θ-role assignment, and you'll end up violating the
θ-Criterion:

(28)   *The θ-Criterion*
       All DPs must be assigned a θ-role and every θ-role must be assigned
       to a DP.

So, unlike with the Case Filter, the division isn't between overt and non-
overt DPs, but rather between things that need θ-roles and things that don't.

Let's look at a couple of examples to see how the Visibility analysis differs
from the Case Filter analysis:

(59)a.   I believe [John to be the best candidate].
    b.   *I hope [John to be the best candidate].

The ECM verb *believe* assigns Case to *John* and it is therefore visible for θ-role assignment from *to be*. On the other hand, *John* in (59b) is not Case marked, and therefore not visible for θ-role assignment. As a result (59b) violates the θ-Criterion.

It's been argued that the Visibility analysis is conceptually superior to the Case Filter analysis. There's no question that we need the θ-Criterion in our theory. If we can get rid of the Case Filter, and reduce all Case-related violations to the θ-Criterion, then we have a simpler theory – only one principle and not two.

However, the Visibility approach to Case is in turn not without its problems, some of them rather serious. Since Case and θ-role assignment are explicitly tied together, it makes the prediction that wherever you have the need for a θ-role you should have Case and wherever you don't have a θ-role there should be no need for Case. There are potential counter-examples to this prediction in both directions.

Before Continuing: For each of these two predictions, we've seen something in this very chapter which would present a problem. What are they and why are they problematic?

On the one hand, there are elements which do receive a θ-role but which seem not to need Case. For example, PRO. Consider the contrast in (60):

(60)a. *I hope John to be here.
　　b. I hope PRO to be here.

The Case Filter analysis makes a correct prediction here, but the Visibility approach predicts that both should be ungrammatical. Both *John* and PRO need a θ-role as the subject of *to be*. There's no difference between them in this respect. This has led some researchers (e.g., Martin (1999)) to claim that PRO is assigned a form of Case called 'null Case', which overt DPs like *John* can't bear. However, this is still a reasonably controversial suggestion.

On the other hand, the Visibility approach also predicts that expletives shouldn't need Case. Since they are not assigned a θ-role, and in fact must never be assigned one, they should be free to be Case-less. This is not the case, however, as we can see in (61) and (62):

(61)a. I want it to seem that John died of natural causes.
　　b. *I hope it to seem that John died of natural causes.

(62)a. I want there to be six reports on my desk by noon.
　　b. *I hope there to be six reports on my desk by noon.

(61) and (62) seem to show clearly that expletive *it* and expletive *there* can only appear in Case marked positions. This is predicted by the Case Filter account, but not by the Visibility account. Visibility supporters do have a

potential reply for (62). It's been claimed that expletive *there* transmits Case to its 'associate' (*six reports* in (62)). Thus it might *appear* as though expletive *there* needs Case when it's actually the associate that needs it. However, the explanation for the behavior of expletive *it* is still unclear under Visibility.

For the rest of the book, what I'll do is retain the Case Filter and the θ-Criterion as separate principles, and not adopt the Visibility analysis. However, I've discussed it because it's very much the standard assumption in the literature. And there are lines of research that you might run into in your future reading, like the null Case for PRO idea, which seems like a weird suggestion unless you know the Visibility analysis and the problems that people have been trying to solve. I'd be negligent in my duties if I didn't prepare you for the wider syntax world that exists beyond this book, even if I don't always agree with it.

4.8 SUMMARY

In this Chapter, we focused on predicate/argument relations – that is, the relationship that DP subjects, direct objects, and so on have to their respective verb, adjective, or prepositional heads. The first area we looked at is called θ-Theory. It has to do with the way in which predicates assign semantic roles, called θ-roles, to their arguments. We discovered that every θ-role that a predicate has must be assigned to an argument, and that every argument must bear a θ-role. This is formalized in the principle called the θ-Criterion.

(28)   *The θ-Criterion*
        All DPs must be assigned a θ-role and every θ-role of a predicate must
        be assigned to an DP.

We also discussed elements called *expletives* which don't seem able to bear a θ-role, and saw how this led to the postulation of the *Extended Projection Principle*, the requirement that all IPs must have a subject. We then concluded that infinitival clauses must in fact contain an unpronounced subject, which we referred to as PRO.

The second area that we looked at was Case Theory. We argued that abstract Case assignment takes place even though most DPs in English don't show any reflection of it. This led to the postulation of the Case Filter:

(54)   *The Case Filter*
        A DP must be assigned Case.

There must also be a particular phrase-structure (configurational) relationship between the Case assignor and the Case assignee.

(44)   α assigns Case to β if and only if
    (a)   α is a Case assignor (i.e., V, finite I, or P), and
    (b)   α m-commands β, and
    (c)   no barrier intervenes (where any maximal projection is a barrier, except infinitival IP).

We then looked at a popular alternative to the Case Filter, the Visibility Condition, in which there is no direct requirement that DPs be assigned Case. Instead, Case plays an indirect role. Case assignment can take place or not. The grammar isn't bothered about it one way or the other, metaphorically speaking. However, if a DP doesn't have Case, then it is not 'visible' for θ-role assignment. If it later transpires that that DP needed a θ-role, then it will trigger a θ-Criterion violation.

OPEN ISSUE: THE CASE FILTER, VISIBILITY, AND DEGREES OF UNGRAMMATICALITY

In this Chapter, we've discussed Chomsky's (1981) suggestion that the Case Filter be eliminated and replaced by the Visibility Condition. However, Epstein (1990) argues for retaining the Case Filter as an independent principle of grammar. The core of Epstein's argument is that a theory in which the Case Filter is replaced by the θ-Criterion is incapable of correctly accounting for intuitions about different *degrees* and different *kinds* of ungrammaticality in certain cases. On the other hand, he argues, a theory which keeps the Case Filter and the θ-Criterion as separate principles explains those contrasts. I'll adapt and simplify what Epstein says a bit, but it's worth taking a look at as an example of how evidence that you wouldn't normally think of looking at can be relevant for the theory that we're developing.

Citing observations going back as early as Chomsky (1965), Epstein notes that differing *degrees* of ungrammaticality can be used as a fairly direct test for the existence of grammatical principles. We've been relying so far on the fact that you have intuitions about which sentences are grammatical and ungrammatical. However, it's not the case that all ungrammatical sentences feel the same. You also have intuitions about whether sentences are *more* ungrammatical than others, or are ungrammatical in different ways.

We can explain these kinds of judgements by saying that a sentence which feels *more* ungrammatical does so because it violates more principles, and sentences which feel ungrammatical *in a different way* do so because they violate different principles. By way of example, Epstein cites the following (from Chomsky (1965)):

(63)a.   *John compelled.
   b.   *Golf plays John.
   c.   John plays golf.

Here, Chomsky argues that there is a three-way contrast in grammaticality. (63c) is well-formed, but (63a) and (63b) are not. However, the ungrammaticality of (63a) and (63b) is not of the same kind. (63a) is a violation of the θ-Criterion. *Compel* is transitive, not intransitive, and a required argument is missing. On the other hand, in (63b) all of the arguments are present, but the DPs which are present in the subject and object positions are of the wrong semantic type. It's people that play games and not vice versa. (63b) satisfies the θ-Criterion, but assigning the agent θ-role to a game makes the sentence deviant.

With this in mind, let's consider the contrast in (64):

(64)a.   *I hope John to think that Bill left.
   b.   *I hope John to be likely that Bill left.

In both (64a) and (64b), the DP *John* is in a position which does not receive Case. However, in (64a) but not (64b), *John* is a position where, at least in principle, a θ-role could be assigned to it. The verb *think* has the Experiencer θ-role available to assign to its subject. The predicate *be likely* on the other hand, does not assign a θ-role to its subject.

What would the Case Filter and Visibility analyses have to say about (64)? Let's take the Case Filter analysis first. Under the Case Filter analysis, where the Case Filter and the θ-Criterion are separate, (64a) would violate only the Case Filter and not the θ-Criterion. Nothing prevents *John* from getting the Experiencer θ-role which *think* has to assign. It's just that *John* doesn't get Case because *hope* isn't an ECM verb. In (64b), on the other hand, *John* violates both the Case Filter and the θ-Criterion.

Under the Visibility analysis, in which Case assignment is merely a prerequisite for θ-role assignment, (64a) violates only the θ-Criterion. There is no Case Filter, but if *John* doesn't get Case then it can't get the θ-role it needs. Since *John* doesn't get Case, it's not visible to receive the Experiencer θ-role which *think* has to assign. The Visibility analysis of (64b) is exactly the same. *John* doesn't receive Case, and so is invisible for θ-role assignment. The fact that in (64b) there's no θ-role for *John* to get even if it were visible is irrelevant. We're still left with just a θ-Criterion violation and nothing else.

So, what do the Case Filter and the Visibility analyses predict with respect to *degrees* of ungrammaticality if, as Epstein and Chomsky suggest, judgements about degrees of ungrammaticality are relevant for our theory (in addition to judgements about straight grammaticality vs. ungrammaticality)? Well, under the Case Filter analysis, (64b) is predicted to be more ungrammatical than (64a). Both (64a) and (64b) violate the Case Filter, but (64b) violates the θ-Criterion in addition. On the other hand, the Visibility analysis says that there's no difference between (64a) and (64b). They both violate the same single principle: the θ-Criterion.

So that's the prediction about (64a) and (64b), now what's the judgement? This is admittedly a little tricky. Epstein's conclusion, after checking with both linguists and non-linguists is that (64b) is indeed worse than (64a). As he puts it (1990: 317) 'In both [(64a)] and [(64b)], there is "something wrong with" the lexical subject of the infinitive: the two cases are identical in this regard. However, [(64b)] differs from [(64a)] in that, in this example, "something else is wrong", namely something interpretive.'

However, notice that there's a slightly easier way we can ask the question if we turn things around. The Visibility analysis predicts that (64a) and (64b) should feel exactly the same. Both violate the θ-Criterion and nothing else. Does that seem right? I don't think so. Whatever's going on in (64a) and (64b), they certainly don't feel the same. The important point seems to be that you can kind of figure out what (64a) is trying to say. If a foreigner produced it, you could correct them with (65):

(65)   I hope that John *thinks* that Bill left.

On the other hand, (64b) just doesn't make any sense. Replacing the infinitival with a finite verb doesn't create a grammatical sentence:

(66)   *I hope that John is likely that Bill left.

Therefore, whatever the subtleties of judgement, (64a) and (64b) don't feel like they're ungrammatical in the same way. But that's what the Visibility analysis predicts. And that might be an argument that the Visibility analysis is on the wrong track.

What this Open Issue illustrates is the complex relationship between our intuitions and our theory. Because we've chosen to investigate our linguistic capacities using the scientific method, it is perfectly legitimate to try to reduce the complexity of the overall theory by eliminating principles and 'neatening things up'. However, we must make sure that at the end of the day our theory still makes the right predictions about the data.

BIBLIOGRAPHY

Ray Jackendoff is one author who has looked extensively at the relationship between the lexicon and the rest of the grammar. His (1984) book outlines a theory of 'lexical-conceptual structure' which is further elaborated in Jack-endoff (1990). Grimshaw (1990) is also a good general book on argument structure. On θ-Theory and Case, the standard reference is again Chomsky (1981), but again that book can be difficult. Textbooks such as Lasnik and Uriagereka (1988) and Haegeman (1994) contain more 'user-friendly' discussion. There is discussion as well in Webelhuth (1995a). Chapter 1 contains some relatively accessible discussion of Case Theory and and Chapter 2 discusses θ-Theory.

ANSWERS TO IN-TEXT EXERCISES

Exercise 1

Identify the following verbs as one-, two-, or three-argument verbs: confirm, show, fall.

Confirm is a two-argument verb. It requires a subject (*confirmed the result) and also a direct object DP or CP. ('John confirmed the result' or 'John confirmed that the match had taken place', but not *'John confirmed'.)

Show is a three-argument verb under normal usage. It again requires a subject (*'showed the book to John'), and both the direct object and the indirect object are required as well. ('Mary showed the book to John' and not *'Mary showed the book' or *'Mary showed to John'.) You can say 'Mary shows pure-bred dogs', but *show* has a special meaning here, something like 'to enter (animals/plants) in competitions'.

Fall is a one-argument verb. It requires only a subject ('John fell') and may not take any objects. (*'John falls the stairs every day'.)

Exercise 2

Which elements assign Case to the DPs in the following sentence: John showed the book to Bill on Friday. Draw the tree.

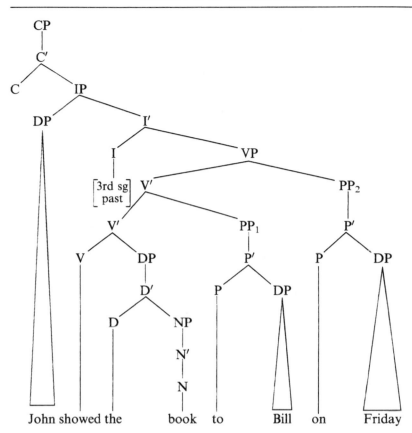

John showed the book to Bill on Friday

John is assigned Case by the finite I, which contains the tense and agreement information. The finite I m-commands *John* (the first maximal projection dominating *John* is IP and IP dominates *John*) and no barrier intervenes between I and the DP subject. Finite I is also a Case assignor.

The book is assigned Case by the verb. The verb m-commands *the book* (the first maximal projection dominating *gave* is VP, which dominates *the book*) and no barrier intervenes between V and DP. V is also a Case assignor.

Both *Bill* and *Friday* are assigned Case by their respective prepositions *to* and *on*. They both m-command their objects (with PP$_1$ and PP$_2$ being the first maximal projections dominating *to* and *on* respectively) and no barrier intervenes between P and DP. P is also a Case assignor.

Exercise 3

Do the following sentences violate the the Case Filter, the θ-Criterion or both? Why?

(a) *John seems that his wife left him.
(b) *I promised it to seem that the arena was full.
(c) *I decided the room to seem that John had left.
(d) *I tried there to be three books on the table.

(a) violates the θ-Criterion only. The subject position of *seems* is a position to which Case, but not a θ-role is assigned. Therefore, *John* never receives a θ-role and the sentence violates the θ-Criterion, but not the Case Filter.

(b) violates only the Case Filter. *It* is not assigned Case by non-finite (infinitival) I (since it is not a Case assignor) and the CP barrier blocks any potential Case from *promise* (which is not an Exceptional Case Marking verb in any case). The subject position of *seem* is not assigned a θ-role, but expletive *it* does not require one. Therefore only the Case Filter is violated.

(c) violates both the Case Filter and the θ-Criterion. *The room* requires both Case and a θ-role, but neither is available to the subject of a non-finite CP. Therefore both requirements are violated.

(d) violates the Case Filter. *Try* is not an ECM verb, and the CP barrier blocks Case in any event. However, since expletive *there* does not require a θ-role, there is no θ-Criterion violation.

ADDITIONAL EXERCISES

Exercise 1

(a) Draw the trees for the following sentences, being sure to indicate PROs where needed, and
(b) Identify the Case assignors for all DPs.

1. I hope that John will go to the store.
2. I want to read the book.
3. Mary persuaded John to run for political office.
4. I need to return John's video.
5. John thinks that it is likely that Mary has left.
6. To run from danger can be a sensible decision.

Exercise 2

In the following sentences, what θ-roles are assigned to the subject and object? Use the tests in the chapter ('What X did was ...'/'What happened to X was ...') to back up your intuitions.

1. Sue struck the ball cleanly.
2. John opened the door.
3. The book fell off the table.
4. Mary surprised Bill.
5. The court summons surprised Bill.

Exercise 3

Which of the following sentences involve Exceptional Case Marking and which involve PRO?

1. The police believe John to be in London.
2. I forced John to go to the audition.
3. I expect John to go to the audition.
4. I know Mary to be an honest person.

Exercise 4

Which of the following predicates assign a θ-role to their subject position? Give actual linguistic data (i.e., grammatical and ungrammatical sentences) to support your conclusions:

(a) appear (when it takes a finite clause CP complement)
(b) consider
(c) strike (in the metaphorical sense of 'consider' and when it takes a CP complement)

Exercise 5

Modern Icelandic seems to allow objects to be dropped in certain conjoined contexts:

(1) Ég tók bókina   og las.
     I took the book and read
     'I took the book and read (it).'

(a) Assuming that 'read' has the same argument structure in Icelandic and English, would you be suspicious if (1) were the only example of a 'dropped object'? Why? What other interpretation for (1) would there be?

(b)   Would the grammaticality of (2) lead you to reconsider your answer in (a)? Why or why not?

(2)   Ég elska þig og dái.
      I love you   and admire
      'I love you and admire (you).'

5 Introduction to Binding Theory

Topics: Principles A, B, C.

Open Issue: the non-complementarity of pronouns and anaphors.

5.0 INTRODUCTION

In this Chapter, we're going to look at one of the most investigated areas of syntax in the last 20 years or so, called Binding Theory. Binding Theory is concerned with the conditions under which two DPs in the sentence can be interpreted as referring to the same person or thing. Consider the sentences in (1), under the assumption that we're talking about our mutual friends John and Bill:

(1)a.   John likes himself.
  b.   John likes him.
  c.   John thinks that Bill likes him.

In (1a), *himself* can only refer back to *John*, and not to *Bill* or some third party. In other words, (1a) can only mean *John likes John*, and not *John likes Bill*. In (1b), on the other hand, we have the reverse situation. *Him* cannot refer to *John*. It must refer to *Bill* (or someone else). However, in (1c), the DP *him* can refer back to John. (1c) means *John thinks that Bill likes John* (again, or some third party). It can't mean *John thinks that Bill likes Bill*.

We'll see that we need to differentiate between three different kinds of DPs, which have three different syntactic requirements. The first kind of DPs are called *anaphors*. These are reflexives, such as *herself*, *ourselves*, and *themselves*, and reciprocals, such as *each other*. The second kind are *pronouns* – elements such as *them* and *you*. The third kind are called *R-expressions*, the most common of which are proper names like *Mary* and *Pat* or DPs like *the man*. The syntactic requirements of these three types of DPs are encoded in the three principles of Chomsky's (1981) Binding Theory: Principles A, B, and C. We'll spend most of the time looking at anaphors, actually, but only because we'll need to introduce all of the relevant concepts along the way. Once we have Principle A under our belts, it'll take about two seconds to explain Principles B and C.

5.1 ANAPHORS AND PRINCIPLE A

The first kind of DP that we'll be looking at are *anaphors*. There are two kinds of anaphors: reflexives, like *herself*, *themselves*, and so on, and *reciprocals*, like *each other*. What is special about these elements is that they require that an *antecedent* be present; that is, another DP somewhere in the sentence that tells you who or what the anaphor is supposed to be referring to. It turns out that the antecedent can't be just anywhere (even if 'antecedent' makes it sound as though it has to precede), and in this section, we'll try to discover what the constraints are.

5.1.1 The Minimal IP Requirement

Compare the sentences in (2), where subscripts are used to identify which person or entity the DPs in the sentence are intended to refer to:

(2)a.   *Himself$_i$ left.
  b.   John$_i$ likes himself$_i$.
  c.   *John$_i$ likes themselves$_j$.

In (2) we have reflexives, but reciprocals pattern exactly the same way:

(3)a.   *Each other$_i$ left.
  b.   They$_i$ like each other$_i$.
  c.   *John$_i$ likes each other$_j$.

(In fact, from now on we'll just use reflexives to illustrate the discussion. Everything that we say about reflexives is true of reciprocals, though.)

Let's see if we can start to draw up a theory to explain the distribution of anaphors based on (2) and (3). That is to say, under what circumstances do we expect that a sentence containing an anaphor will or will not be well formed? As always, we should start with the simplest hypothesis and work from there. On the basis of (2) and (3), it looks like the simplest thing we can say is (4).

(4)   An anaphor must have an antecedent which agrees with the anaphor in gender and number.

That would account for (2) and (3). In the (a) sentences, the anaphors *himself* and *each other* don't have any antecedent at all, and therefore (4) would predict that they are ungrammatical. By contrast, in the (b) sentences, the anaphor has an antecedent, and so our hypothesis in (4) would again make the correct prediction. The (c) sentences show that the antecedent must agree with the anaphor in person, number, and gender features. An anaphor with plural features cannot take a singular antecedent.

However, it's clear straight away that we need to modify our hypothesis in (4). It's not just that there has to be an antecedent floating around. The antecedent has to be in the same sentence as the anaphor. To see why, take a look at the sentences in (5):

(5)   I saw John$_i$ yesterday. *Himself$_i$ finally quit his job.

Here, we would say that *himself* has a **discourse antecedent**; that is, an antecedent which is not in the same sentence, but which exists elsewhere in the discourse. Discourse antecedents are perfectly OK for things like pronouns:

(6)   I saw John$_i$ yesterday. He$_i$ finally quit his job.

However, it seems that they're not good enough for anaphors.

EXERCISE 1

Show that reciprocals do not allow discourse antecedents.

So it looks like we'll have to be more specific about the kinds of antecedents that anaphors can have:

(7)   An anaphor must have an antecedent in the same sentence.

So far so good, but not for long. Consider the sentence in (8):

(8)   *Mary$_i$ thinks that Bill$_j$ likes herself$_i$.

In this case, the anaphor *herself* is in the same sentence as the only possible antecedent *Mary* (the whole thing is one big sentence), but (8) is still ungrammatical. (*Bill* is not a possible antecedent because it does not agree with the anaphor in gender.) It looks as though the antecedent must not only be in the same sentence as the anaphor, but also the antecedent must be sufficiently 'close' to the anaphor.

But what does 'close' mean here? Well, notice that in (8) we have a case of embedding. The sentence in (8) *Mary thinks that Bill likes herself* has within it a second sentence, namely *Bill likes herself*. On the other hand, in (2b) we have only the one sentence *John likes himself*. If we strengthened the requirement on antecedents, so that the antecedent had to be in the same *minimal* sentence as the reflexive, then that would account for the difference. Only in (2b) is the antecedent in the same *minimal* IP as the reflexive (i.e., in the same clause). To see that, let's draw the tree for (8) and (2b).

(9)

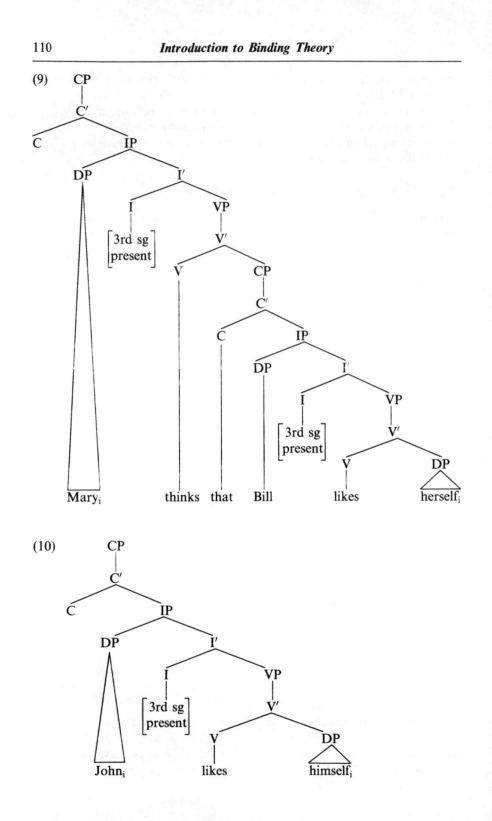

(10)

As you can see from the trees, the minimal or closest IP which dominates *herself* in (8) is the embedded IP *Bill likes herself*. Although the reflexive is within that IP, the antecedent is not. On the other hand, in (2b) there's only one IP, so the minimal IP dominating the reflexive *himself* is the IP *John likes himself*, and this time the antecedent *is* in the same minimal IP as the reflexive. So it looks like we need to make (7) even more specific:

(11)   An anaphor must have an antecedent in the same minimal IP.

I want to take this opportunity to stress how important it is that we be as careful and explicit as possible when we're formulating our principles. There are ways of saying things which might look the same, but which have very different implications. For example, (12) sounds very much like the principle in (11):

(12)   The minimal IP which contains the antecedent must also contain the anaphor.

Before Continuing: Use (9) to show that (11) and (12) make different predictions and are therefore different statements.

A moment's thought will reveal that (12) is not the right principle. Consider again the tree representing (8), which we saw just above in (9). We want to make sure that our rule correctly predicts that (8) is ungrammatical, but (12) predicts the opposite. The minimal IP containing the antecedent is the IP *Mary thinks that Bill likes herself*. Is the anaphor within that IP? It sure is. So (12) incorrectly predicts that (8) should be grammatical. (11), on the other hand, makes the correct prediction. What's gone wrong is that we need to make sure that our algorithm looks for the *anaphor's* minimal IP. not the antecedent's. Otherwise, we might get something which looks right. but has things backwards.

5.1.2 The C-Command Requirement

Even though (11) and not (12) is the right principle to account for things so far, we're going to have to modify (11) still further. Consider (13):

(13) *[John$_i$'s mother]$_j$ likes himself$_i$.

Before Continuing: Explain why (13) presents a problem for (11).

Nothing that we've said so far explains why (13) is ungrammatical. There's no embedding of clauses here. The minimal IP which dominates the anaphor is the matrix IP *John's mother likes himself*. The intended antecedent *John* is within that IP, and therefore (11) predicts that (13) should be grammatical.

(13) isn't really all that different from the grammatical (1b) above. However, there's a sharp difference in grammaticality. The crucial difference would seem to be that the antecedent of the reflexive is not the subject, as it was in the grammatical (1b), but is instead buried inside the subject. We can confirm that we're focusing in on the right difference if we change the gender of the reflexive and make *John's mother* the antecedent:

(14)   [John$_i$'s mother]$_j$ likes herself$_j$.

The antecedent of the reflexive *herself* is now the whole subject *John's mother*, and not a subpart of the subject. As expected (14) is perfect.

How can we account for the contrast between (14) and (13)? We could simply say that anaphors must always have a subject as their antecedent. However, this would clearly be the wrong move to make, as (15) shows:

(15)   John$_i$ gave Mary$_j$ a picture of herself$_j$.

If it was the case that anaphors just always had to refer back to the subject, we'd expect that (15) should be ungrammatical. However, since the anaphor *herself* appears capable of referring to *Mary*, an indirect object, that doesn't seem like the right move to make.

As always, when we're in a situation like this, the first thing we should try to do is draw the tree. Perhaps there's a structural difference that we can look to for a solution.

(16)

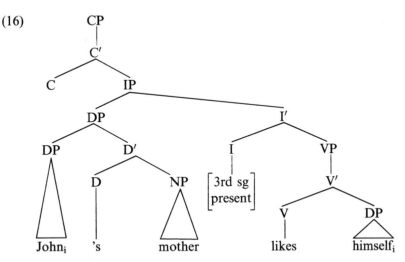

To put the problem in a nutshell, the relationship between *John's mother* and the anaphor in direct object position must be OK, but the relationship between *John* and a direct object anaphor seems not to be. What could be the difference?

Well, it looks like c-command might be relevant here. Recall the definition from Chapter 2:

(17)   One node A c-commands another node B if and only if the first branching node which dominates A dominates B.

If we apply this definition to (13) and (14) above, it looks like c-command captures the difference between the two. In the ungrammatical (13), the antecedent *John* fails to c-command the anaphor *himself*. The first branching node which dominates *John* is DP, and that DP node does not dominate *himself*. On the other hand, in the grammatical (14), the antecedent is the whole subject DP *John's mother*. The first branching node which dominates *that* DP is the IP node. And *that* IP node does dominate the anaphor *herself*.

(18)

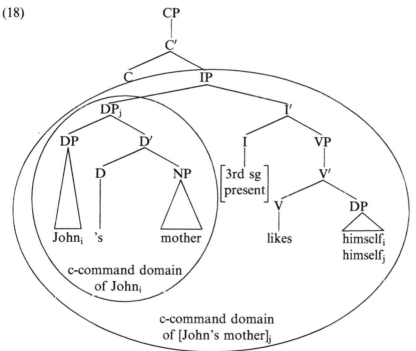

So c-command looks like it's definitely relevant, but we still need to hang on to our 'minimal IP' requirement. Otherwise, we'd be back to incorrectly predicting that *Mary thinks that John likes herself* is grammatical. Just like *John's mother*, the DP *Mary* will c-command the anaphor *herself*. The first branching node dominating *Mary* is the matrix IP, and the matrix IP dominates *herself*. So it looks like what we need to say is (19):

(19)   An anaphor must be c-commanded by an antecedent in the same minimal IP.

Another – and, in fact, the usual – way of saying that an element β is c-commanded by another element α which is its antecedent is to say that α *binds* β. (That'll also make it clearer why this topic is called Binding Theory!) We can then replace (19) with (20), which just says exactly the same thing using the new terminology, including a definition for binding in (21):

(20)   *Principle A (preliminary)*
       An anaphor must be bound in the minimal IP which contains it.

(21)   α binds β if α c-commands and is coindexed with β.

5.1.3   The Problem of ECM Contexts

Exceptional Case Marking configurations pose a problem for the anaphor rule in (20) as we've developed it so far. Consider the contrast in (22):

(22)a.   *Mary$_i$ believes that herself$_i$ is smart.
    b.   Mary$_i$ believes herself$_i$ to be smart.

(22a) behaves as predicted. Although *Mary* c-commands *herself*, the minimal IP containing the anaphor is the embedded IP *herself is smart*. Since the antecedent *Mary* is not within this IP, the sentence is correctly predicted to be ungrammatical. However, in (22b), the minimal IP containing the anaphor is *herself to be smart*. The antecedent *Mary* is not within this IP, and (22b) is also predicted to be ungrammatical. But in this case that's the wrong prediction.

So what's different about ECM complements, and how can we use that difference to explain the contrast in (22)? The only structural difference between (22a) and (22b) is that in the ungrammatical (22a), *believe* takes a CP complement (even if the complementizer is not expressed, don't forget) whereas the complement is an IP in the grammatical (22b), so whatever's going on is surely related to that.

As we saw in Chapter 4, the fact that ECM infinitives are IPs and not CPs means that the verb *believe* is able to assign accusative Case to the subject of the infinitive, so you get contrasts like (23):

(23)a.   I believe her to be smart.
    b.   *I believe she to be smart.
    c.   *I believe that her is smart.
    d.   I believe that she is smart.

Let's suppose that it's the verb's ability to reach down into the subject position of the infinitive clause to assign Case to an element there that allows an anaphor in that position to look up to the higher clause to find its antecedent. It's as if the verb's Case assigning creates a bridge between the subject position and the higher clause.

We need to work this idea into our theory, but, as it turns out, it's not quite Case assignment *per se* that's relevant. It's a slightly more general notion called *government*, of which Case assignment is a special case. Government is defined as in (24):

(24) α governs β if and only if
     (a) α is a head, and
     (b) α m-commands β, and
     (c)   no barrier intervenes (where any maximal projection except infinitival IP is a barrier).

Does this look familiar? It's the definition of Case assignment from the previous chapter, with one minor change. In (a), instead of saying 'α is a Case assignor (i.e., V, I, or P)', it says 'α is a head'. So heads always govern everything that they m-command (provided no barrier intervenes), and if the head is one of the special heads that assigns Case, then the head can assign Case to one of their governees too.

So, in the ECM case, because the verb governs the subject of the infinitive, an anaphor in that position can look up to the matrix clause for an antecedent. Notice that in other cases, where we don't want the anaphor to be able to reach up to the matrix clause, government from above isn't possible:

(25)a.   *Mary$_i$ believes [$_{IP}$ John to [$_{VP}$ like herself$_i$]].
    b.   *Mary$_i$ thinks [$_{CP}$ that herself$_i$ is smart].

In (25a), the anaphor is in the direct object position of an ECM infinitive, and government by *believe* is blocked. The infinitival IP may be defective as a barrier to government, but we've still got the barrier constituted by VP. In (25b), government from outside the embedded CP is straightforwardly blocked by the CP, which acts as a barrier.

So it looks as though when the anaphor in question is governed from outside the IP that it's in, it's allowed to look up to that higher IP for an antecedent. Let's incorporate this into our rule:

(26)   *Principle A of the Binding Theory (version 2)*
     An anaphor must be bound in the minimal IP which contains:
     (a)   the anaphor, and
     (b)   a governor for the anaphor.

The domain in which an anaphor has to find its antecedent is usually called the 'governing category' of the anaphor, so we can rewrite (26) completely equivalently as (27), with the appropriate definitions (with 'bound' repeated from above):

(27)   *Principle A of the Binding Theory (final version)*
       An anaphor must be bound in its governing category.

(28) α *binds* β if α c-commands and is coindexed with β.

(29)   The *governing category* for an element α is the minimal IP containing:
       (a) the element α, and
       (b) a governor for α.

Although we now have the final statement of Principle A of the Binding Theory in (27), it's going to turn out that we need to modify the definition of governing category just a little bit more.

5.1.4 'Subjects', Accessible and Otherwise

The last notion that we'll need to incorporate in order to give a complete account of anaphors is that of 'subject'. To see why that's going to be necessary, compare the sentences in (30):

(30)a.   John$_i$ liked the drawing of himself$_i$.
    b.   *John$_i$ liked Mary's$_j$ drawing of himself$_i$.
    c.   John liked Mary's$_j$ drawing of herself$_j$.

Whatever's going on, the contrast is pretty clear. It looks like the anaphor in (30b) and (30c) wants to have *Mary* as its antecedent, not *John*, in contrast with (30a), which is happy with *John* as its antecedent. The only difference between the two is that the definite article *the* in (30a) is replaced by the DP *Mary's* in (30b) and (c). What could be the reason for the contrast we're seeing?

Well, notice that DPs which have a DP specifier have some similarities to sentences. For example, the DPs in (31) contain roughly the same information as the full sentences in (32), a point we made when we introduced DPs in Chapter 3:

(31)a.   Mary's drawing of him.
    b.   Bill's destruction of Carthage.

(32)a.   Mary drew him.
    b.   Bill destroyed Carthage.

In (32), *Mary* and *Bill* each receive an Agent θ-role and are interpreted as the subjects of their respective sentences. *Him* and *Carthage*, the complements of the verbs in question, receive θ-roles appropriate for their direct object status. If *Mary* receives the Agent θ-role in (32a), there seems to be no reason not to assign *Mary* that same role in (31a). After all, *Mary* is understood as being in exactly the same relation to *drawing* as she is to *drew* in (32a). So even though (31a) is not a sentence, but a DP, it seems reasonable to say that *Mary* is functioning like a subject in both cases.

Let's try to develop this idea. Maybe, all along, when we were saying that the antecedent has to look for its antecedent in the appropriate minimal IP, it wasn't really IP *per se* that was relevant. Maybe the anaphor needs to find its antecedent in the minimal XP that has a *subject*. Under normal circumstances, it's usually only IPs that have subjects, so most of the time we'll be looking for IP. However, in those cases where you have a DP which has a 'subject', the domain in which the anaphor must have its antecedent is that DP. This means we'll need to revise (29) a little bit:

(33)   The *governing category* for an element α is the minimal XP containing
    (a) the element α,
    (b) a governor for α, and
    (c) a subject.

We can now explain the pattern of grammaticality that we saw in (30). In (30b) and (c) the DP *Mary's drawings of himself/herself* has *Mary* as a subject, and the governing category for the anaphor is the DP. In (30a) on the other hand, the DP *the drawing of himself/herself* does not have a subject, and therefore the governing category for the anaphor will be IP.

So far, so good. All we need to do now is make one tiny change to the notion 'subject' to take care of the following situation, and we'll be all set. Consider (34):

(34)   John$_i$ thinks that a picture of himself$_i$ is on sale.

Before Continuing: show that (33) wrongly predicts that (34) is ungrammatical.

(34) contrasts sharply with other cases where the anaphor is in an embedded CP, like (35), which we've seen before, and (36):

(35)   *John$_i$ thinks that Mary bought a picture of himself$_i$.

(36)   *John$_i$ thinks that himself$_i$ should win the election.

However, (33) as it currently stands predicts that (34) to (36) should all be ungrammatical. (34) is the surprising one, so let's take a closer look at how

(33) wrongly predicts it to be ungrammatical. Once we clearly understand where we're going wrong, we can think about how to fix things.

We're looking for the minimal XP which contains the anaphor, the anaphor's governor, and a subject. The preposition *of* is the governor of the anaphor, so the PP *of himself* is the minimal XP which contains the anaphor and the anaphor's governor. However, the PP does not contain a subject. Continuing up the tree, we eventually get to the embedded IP *a picture of himself is on sale*. Does this IP have a subject? Yes indeed. The subject is the DP *a picture of himself*. Therefore, the minimal XP which contains the anaphor, the anaphor's governor, and a subject is the embedded IP. However, the antecedent for the anaphor, *John*, is not within the embedded IP. We therefore predict that (34) should be ungrammatical, and that's not the answer we want.

Clearly, we need to make some change to our rule in (33) in order to account for the difference between (34) on the one hand, and (35) and (36) on the other. First of all, let's think about where in (33) we have room to make changes. It's hard to see how we could make a change to (a) or (b) in order to account for (34) that wouldn't incorrectly predict that (35) should be grammatical too. (c) on the other hand might be more promising. At least the subject is different in (34) vs. (35). Perhaps that's the hook that we need to hang the distinction on.

Notice that in (34), the anaphor is inside the subject of the embedded clause *a picture of himself*, whereas in (35) the anaphor is inside the direct object. Perhaps the subject position is special in some way. They can't be too special, though, because as (36) shows, if the anaphor is itself a subject, then the sentence is ungrammatical just as we would expect. So the key thing must be that the anaphor in (34) is a subpart *inside* the subject. How can we implement something that will correctly predict that (34) is grammatical while ruling out (35) and (36)? Basically, what we need is something that will make the embedded IP the relevant domain in (35) and (36), but allow the anaphor to look up to the matrix clause in the grammatical (34).

Chomsky (1981) introduced the notion of the 'accessible' subject as a way of solving the problems posed by (34)–(36). In order for a subject to count as an 'accessible' subject for an anaphor, it has to meet the following condition:

(37)   α is an accessible subject for an anaphor β if and only if (hypothetical) coindexation between the anaphor and the subject violates no grammatical principle.

That sounds complicated, but it's actually straightforward once you see it in action. On a personal level, I'm not sure how persuasive I find Chomsky's solution. It seems very *ad hoc*. However, it does look as though *something* needs to be said, and since I don't have anything better to suggest, I can't complain too loudly.

Let's start with the grammatical (34). What we want to make sure happens is that the embedded IP is *not* the relevant domain for the anaphor. Instead, we want the matrix IP to be the governing category. Let's see how (37) helps us. The minimal XP containing the anaphor and the anaphor's governor is still the NP *picture of himself*, so now we're looking for an accessible subject. The embedded IP has a subject, namely *a picture of himself*, but we need to see whether that subject is accessible or not. In order to do that, we need to see whether hypothetical coindexing of the proposed subject and the anaphor violates any grammatical principle. We say 'hypothetical' here because we're not proposing that the two things are supposed to be actually coindexed. A picture of something is inanimate, but a person is animate, so it wouldn't make any sense to literally coindex the two. This is just a hypothetical test of a situation – if we were to do it, would there be a problem?

Let's see what happens when we do that. If we hypothetically coindexed the anaphor *himself* with the proposed subject *a picture of himself*, we get the following configuration:

(38)   John$_i$ thinks that [a picture of himself$_i$]$_i$ is on sale.

Does this violate any grammatical principle? Well, it does actually. The principle is called the i-within-i filter, and basically rules out any configuration in which a smaller subpart of something is coindexed with the larger whole thing, as illustrated by (39):

(39)   *I-Within-I Filter*
       *$[\ldots X_i \ldots]_i$

You need something like (39) to avoid referential circularity. Basically, as a general rule, if you're trying to figure out what some expression refers to, you need to know what all of the component parts refer to. So in (39), in order to figure out what the whole thing refers to, part of what you need to figure out is what X refers to. However, if X and the whole expression are coindexed, you can't figure out what X refers to until you know what the whole thing refers to. But to do that you need to know what X refers to, and so on. You go round in circles. (39) rules out these configurations.

To give a slightly less abstract illustration of the same point, consider the sentence in (40), which also contains an i-within-i violation:

(40)   *[The picture of it$_i$]$_i$ is on the table.

In order to determine what *the picture of it* refers to, we need to know what *it* refers to. But in order to know what *it* refers to, we need to know what *the picture of it* refers to, and we're back where we started. If you try to imagine what (40) could mean, you end up with an infinite regress of pictures going into the distance, as if you had two mirrors reflecting each other. If, on the other hand, we have an indexation which does not create an i-within-i configuration, there's no problem:

(41)   [The picture of it$_j$]$_i$ is on the table.

In (41), *it* has index 'j', and so refers to some previously mentioned entity, like your new computer or something. There's no referential circularity here, and thus no problem with interpretation.

So, let's return to (34), our binding theory problem:

(34)   John$_i$ thinks that a picture of himself$_i$ is on sale.

The key intuition behind the notion 'accessible' subject is that *a picture of himself* can't serve as a subject for the anaphor *himself*, because that would require coindexation between *himself* and *picture of himself*, which is an i-within-i violation. Therefore, although the minimal XP which contains the anaphor, its governor, and a subject is the embedded IP, the subject of that IP isn't accessible to the anaphor. Therefore, we are allowed (and required) to look higher in order to find an antecedent for *himself*.

Once we've gone past the embedded IP, the next category which has any kind of subject at all is the matrix IP *John thinks that a picture of himself is on sale*. The subject is of course *John*. Would hypothetical coindexation of *John* and *himself* violate any grammatical principle? In particular, would it create an i-within-i configuration? No. Neither *John* nor *himself* is contained within the other, so there's no problem. *John* is a subject which is accessible to *himself*. Therefore, the minimal XP which contains the anaphor *himself*, a governor of *himself*, and a subject which is accessible to *himself* is the matrix IP. Do we find an antecedent for *himself* within this category? Yes, it's *John*. Therefore, the sentence in (34) is predicted to be grammatical.

Now that we've found a way to make (34) grammatical, let's make sure that we haven't lost anything along the way by taking a look at (35) and (36) again, both of which were ungrammatical. We need to make sure that our changes don't result in our incorrectly predicting that those two sentences are grammatical.

(35)   *John$_i$ thinks that Mary bought a picture of himself$_i$.

(36)   *John$_i$ thinks that himself$_i$ should win the election.

Just as with (34), the minimal XP containing the anaphor and a governor for the anaphor is the NP *picture of himself*. Moving upward in search of a subject, the next category which we need to take a look at is the embedded IP *Mary bought a picture of himself*. Does hypothetical coindexing between

Mary and *himself* create an i-within-i violation? No. Neither *Mary* nor *himself* is a subpart of the other. Therefore, *Mary* is an accessible subject for *himself*. So that means that the minimal XP containing the anaphor *himself*, a governor for *himself*, and a subject which is accessible to *himself* is the embedded IP *Mary bought a picture of himself*. Since *himself* has no *actual* antecedent in the embedded IP, (35) is still correctly predicted to be ungrammatical.

Now let's turn to (36). Here the situation might be a little bit more confusing. The difference between (34) and (36) is that in (34) the anaphor is *inside* the subject DP, whereas in (36) it *is* the subject. The governor for himself is now the embedded I, since it's assigning *himself* nominative Case. So the minimal XP containing the anaphor and its governor is the embedded IP *himself should win the election*. Does this IP have a subject? Yes, it's *himself*.

Now we need to answer the following question: can *himself* serve as an accessible subject for itself? We know the answer that we want. We want the answer to be 'yes'. That way, the anaphor will need to find a c-commanding antecedent in the embedded clause. Since there isn't one, we would then correctly predict that (36) is ungrammatical. What would be the justification for saying that an anaphor can serve as an accessible subject for itself? Well, if we were to consider the issue of hypothetical coindexation, what we'd be doing would be just giving something the same index over again. It's hard to see why that would be a problem. I suppose it could be taken to be redundant or something, but it certainly wouldn't create an i-within-i configuration. You're not coindexing something with a *subpart* of it, which is what the i-within-i filter prohibits.

Therefore, the minimal IP which contains *himself*, a governor for *himself*, and a subject which is accessible to *himself* is the embedded IP. *Himself* does not have an antecedent within this IP, and (36) is correctly predicted to be ungrammatical.

So it looks like we're all set; adding the 'accessibility' requirement to the subject would seem to correctly allow the grammatical (34), while ruling out the ungrammatical (35) and (36). So let's incorporate that into our complete version of Principle A:

(42)   *Principle A of the Binding Theory (final version)*
       An anaphor must be bound in its governing category.

(43) α *binds* β if α c-commands and is coindexed with β.

(44)   The *governing category* for an element α is the minimal XP containing
       (a) the element α,
       (b) a governor for α, and
       (c) a subject which is accessible to α.

(45)   α is a subject which is accessible to β if and only if (hypothetical) coindexation between the anaphor and the subject violates no grammatical principle.

(46)   *I-Within-I Filter*
       *[... X_i ...]$_i$

5.2   PRONOUNS AND PRINCIPLE B

Fortunately, as promised, now that we have Principle A under our belts, Principles B and C are a piece of cake. Principle B of the Binding Theory concerns pronouns. Unlike anaphors, pronouns will be familiar to you from traditional grammar instruction. They're words like *we*, *her*, *them*, *I*, and so on.

5.2.1   The Complementarity of Pronouns and Anaphors

We mentioned, in passing, one difference between pronouns and anaphors at the beginning of the previous section, when we were talking about discourse antecedents. It turns out that anaphors don't allow discourse antecedents, but pronouns do. So we have contrasts like in (47):

(47)   I saw John$_i$ yesterday. He$_i$/*Himself$_i$ just quit his job.

If we look at more of the examples we discussed at the beginning of the anaphor section, we see more in the way of complementary distribution. That is, for any given syntactic position, if an anaphor can be there, then a pronoun can't be, and vice versa. (48a), for example, contrasts with (48b):

(48)a.   John$_i$ likes himself$_i$.
    b.   *John$_i$ likes him$_i$.

Although I've mentioned this issue before, it's worth repeating. (48b) illustrates the importance of considering the indexation when looking at example sentences in a Binding Theory context. (48b) is only ungrammatical on the interpretation where *John* and *him* are intended to refer to the same person. Put another way, (48b) can't mean the same thing as (48a). On the other hand, (49) is fine:

(49)   John$_i$ likes him$_j$.

The same complementarity seems to run through other examples as well:

(50)a.   *John$_i$ thinks that Mary$_j$ likes himself$_i$.
   b.   John$_i$ thinks that Mary$_j$ likes him$_i$.

(51)a.   *[John's$_i$ mother]$_j$ likes himself$_i$.
   b.   [John's$_i$ mother]$_j$ likes him$_i$.

(52)a.   Mary$_i$ believes herself$_i$ to be smart.
   b.   *Mary$_i$ believes her$_i$ to be smart.

(53)a.   *John$_i$ liked Mary's$_j$ picture of himself$_i$.
   b.   John$_i$ liked Mary's$_j$ picture of him$_i$.

(54)a.   John$_i$ thinks that a picture of himself$_i$ is on sale.
   b.   *John$_i$ thinks that a picture of him$_i$ is on sale.

So, if anaphors and pronouns are in complementary distribution, then it would seem that we only need to make a minor modification to Principle A in order to get Principle B, the principle that deals with pronouns. If an anaphor must be bound in its governing category, then a pronoun must be *not* bound (i.e., 'free') in its governing category:

(55)   *Principle B of the Binding Theory*
     A pronoun must be free in its governing category. (where 'free' = 'not bound').

Therefore, in precisely the same domain in which an anaphor *must* have an antecedent, a pronoun *cannot*, and we build in the complementary distribution which seems to hold between pronouns and anaphors.

The important thing to notice about (55) is that it doesn't *require* that a pronoun have an antecedent. It just says that, if it does, then the antecedent has to be outside the pronoun's governing category. So (56), for example, is ambiguous between two readings: one where *him* refers to John, and another where *him* refers to a third, unmentioned person:

(56)   John$_i$ thinks that Mary$_j$ likes him$_{i/k}$.

The governing category for the pronoun will be the IP *Mary likes him*. Therefore, if *him* has an antecedent, then it must be outside *him*'s governing category. This allows *him* to have index 'i', referring back to *John*, since *John* is not within the IP *Mary likes him*.

5.3   R-EXPRESSIONS AND PRINCIPLE C

Having looked at both anaphors and pronouns, it's time now to move on to the last of the three kinds of DPs constrained by Binding Theory. Proper names like *John* and *Mary* are the canonical examples of R-expressions. Not only do they not need an antecedent, they also pick out a specific person or thing in the universe of discourse. If we've been discussing our friends Bob, John, and Mary, and I say 'John left', you know exactly who I'm talking about. If, on the other hand, I use a pronoun, and start by saying 'He left', you don't know which of the two male friends I have in mind.

At first glance, R-expressions look like they're going to pattern with pronouns:

(57)a.   *John$_i$ likes him$_i$.
   b.   *John$_i$ likes John$_i$.

However, when we look a little further, it becomes clear that R-expressions are subject to a slightly stronger requirement. In particular, it doesn't look like moving the binding antecedent to a position outside of the governing category does any good:

(58)   *John$_i$ thinks that Mary$_j$ likes John$_i$.

Just as we saw with the previous examples involving pronouns, the governing category for the R-expression *John* in direct object position of the embedded clause would be the embedded IP *Mary likes John*. The antecedent for *John* is not within the embedded IP. It would therefore seem that R-expressions must be different from pronouns with respect to the Binding Theory. Notice as well that the effect is identical when the antecedent is a pronoun rather than another R-expression, so what's wrong with (58) has nothing to do with repeating a previously mentioned R-expression or something:

(59)a.   *He$_i$ likes John$_i$.
   b.   *He$_i$ thinks that Mary$_j$ likes John$_i$.

One possible approach might be to see whether R-expressions just have a wider governing category than anaphors or pronouns. However, it quickly becomes apparent that that solution won't work. It looks like you can have as many IPs in the sentence as you like, and the sentence remains ungrammatical:

(60)a.   *John$_i$ believes that Mary$_j$ said that Alice$_k$ likes John$_i$.
   b.   *John$_i$ believes that Mary$_j$ said that Alice$_k$ wondered whether Jill$_l$ liked John$_i$.

However, it does look as though c-command is still playing a role. If the R-expression isn't c-commanded by its antecedent, the sentence improves considerably:

(61) [John's$_i$ mother]$_j$ likes John$_i$.

So, it looks like binding is relevant, but not governing categories. Nothing hard there. All we have to say is (62):

(62) *Principle C of the Binding Theory*
      An R-expression must be free. (again, free = not bound)

This way, any configuration where an R-expression is c-commanded by a coindexed antecedent will be ruled out.

In addition to proper names, like *John*, there are other kinds of DPs which seem to function as R-expressions with respect to the Binding Theory. For example, DPs of the kind which in the philosophy literature would be called definite descriptions also function as R-expressions. An example of this would be a DP like *the man I saw yesterday*, where there is a specific person in mind:

(63) *He$_i$ told me that [the man I saw yesterday]$_i$ was a local politician.

Compare (63) with (64):

(64) [The man I saw yesterday]$_i$ said that he$_i$ was a local politician.

In (64) the R-expression is not c-commanded by the pronoun and so no Principle C violation arises.

However, my favorite R-expressions are a class of elements called *epithets*. These are DPs like *the fool, the bastard,* or *the president*, which can be used as a way of descriptively referring back to some previously mentioned person:

(65) I saw John$_i$ yesterday. The bastard$_i$ didn't have the 10 000 pesetas he owes me.

These elements might feel more like pronouns, in that they pick out a specific person only when they have an antecedent. However, (66) shows that epithets obey Principle C of the Binding Theory:

(66) *John$_i$ said that the bastard$_i$ was going to the store.

The epithet can't be interpreted as coreferential with *John*. In other words, (66) can't be interpreted as the grammatical (67):

(67) John$_i$ said that he$_i$ was going to the store.

Similarly, sentences like (68) are ill formed:

(68)   *He$_i$ said that the president$_j$ would be addressing the nation tonight.

Just as with (63) and (64), reversing the pronoun and the epithet R-expression solves the problem:

(69)   The president$_i$ said that he$_i$ would be addressing the nation tonight.

5.4 SUMMARY

In this chapter, we've argued that in order to properly account for what you know about your language, we need to assume that there are three different kinds of DP: anaphors, pronouns, and R-expressions. The distribution of these three different kinds of DP is governed by Binding Theory, one of the most written about topics in Chomskyian linguistics.

Anaphors include reflexives, such as *herself* and *ourselves*, and reciprocals, such as *each other*. These DPs cannot independently refer, instead requiring that there be an antecedent for them within the appropriate domain. This requirement is expressed in Principle A of the Binding Theory:

(42)   *Principle A of the Binding Theory*
       An anaphor must be bound in its governing category.

(43)   α *binds* β if α c-commands and is coindexed with β.

(44)   The *governing category* for an element α is the minimal XP containing
       (a) the element α,
       (b) a governor for α, and
       (c) a subject which is accessible to α.

(45)   α is a subject which is accessible to β if and only if (hypothetical) coindexation between the anaphor and the subject violates no grammatical principle.

Pronouns, such as *she* and *us*, seem to be in complementary distribution with anaphors. Wherever you can have an anaphor, you can't have a pronoun and vice versa. This complementarity with anaphors is built into Principle B of the Binding Theory:

(55)   *Principle B of the Binding Theory*
       A pronoun must be free in its governing category. (where 'free' = 'not bound')

R-expressions include proper names, definite descriptions, and anaphoric epithets. Unlike anaphors and pronouns, they do not have a governing category of any kind. R-expressions may not co-refer with a DP that c-commands them, no matter how far away it is. This requirements is expressed in Principle C:

(62) *Principle C of the Binding Theory*
      An R-expression must be free. (again, free = not bound)

OPEN ISSUE: NON-COMPLEMENTARITY OF PRONOUNS AND ANAPHORS

As we mentioned above in discussing Principles A and B of the Binding Theory, pronouns and anaphors look like they're in complementary distribution, and this complementarity is built directly into Binding Theory. Anaphors must be bound in their governing category, and pronouns must be free in their governing category. The situation couldn't be more black and white than that. The problem is that, even in English, anaphors and pronouns are ... not ... quite ... fully ... exactly ... 100 percent ... in complementary distribution. It's a painful thing to admit. Trust me.

Unfortunately, the relevant cases are not even very complicated either. Consider the contrast (or lack thereof) in (70):

(70)a. They$_i$ think that pictures of each other$_i$ are on sale.
   b.   They$_i$ think that pictures of them$_i$ are on sale.

It looks like here we've got exactly what we didn't want to see. *Each other* is an anaphor, subject to Principle A, and *them* is a pronoun, subject to Principle B. Whatever the structure of the sentences in (70) is, we don't predict that you can get a pronoun and an anaphor in the same position. One of them should be grammatical and the other ungrammatical. But that's not what we see.

EXERCISE 2

Which of (70a) or (b) is predicted to be ungrammatical by Binding Theory as we've currently formulated it? Why?

There have been a number of attempts to come to grips with the problem represented by (70) and related problems in other languages. Huang (1983) takes essentially a syntactic approach. He argues that we do need to relax the complementarity that Binding Theory enforces, but we don't need to modify Principles A and B *per se*. Rather, the solution is to assume that governing categories are defined differently for pronouns and anaphors.

Huang (1983) starts by noticing that, in addition to the empirical problem posed by (70), we also have a potential conceptual problem when it comes to the notion of 'governing category', and, in particular, the 'accessible subject' requirement that we saw in Section 5.1.4. He observes that 'being a subject which is accessible to α' just seems to be another way of saying 'is capable of serving as an antecedent for α'. It makes sense to include a requirement like this for the governing category of anaphors. As Huang puts it (1983: 556): 'Since anaphors need antecedents, what the Binding Theory says is that they must be bound in the minimal domain whose [subject] is a possible antecedent (i.e., accessible).' However, it's precisely what makes the accessible subject requirement look right for anaphors that makes it look weird for pronouns. Pronouns can be free, as we've seen above. They don't ever *require* an antecedent. So in determining the governing category for a pronoun, why should finding a possible antecedent matter? Why should it matter whether the subject is accessible or not?

Huang claims that if we eliminate this conceptual weirdness, we also explain why both sentences in (70) are grammatical. Specifically, Huang suggests changing the definition of governing category from (44) to (71). (I've put the change in italics.)

(71)   The governing category for an element α is the minimal XP containing
       (a) the element α,
       (b) a governor for α, and
       (c) a subject which, *if* α is *an anaphor*, is accessible to α.

To see how (71) solves the problem, let's take a closer look at the sentences in (70).

(72)

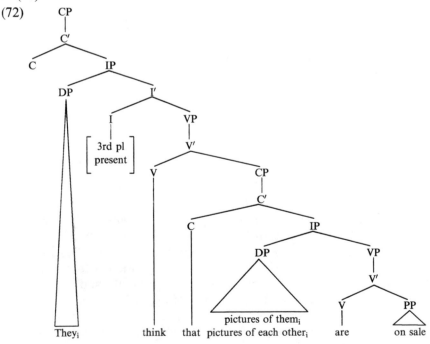

Let's start with the anaphor case in (70a). In this case, the situation is exactly the same as *John thinks that a picture of himself is on sale*, which we discussed in Section 5.1.4 above. The governor for the anaphor is the P *of*. However, neither PP nor NP nor DP has a subject. Therefore the minimal XP which contains the anaphor, the anaphor's governor, and a subject is the IP *pictures of each other are on sale*. However, since *each other* is an anaphor, we need to check whether this subject is an accessible one, and it turns out that it's not. If we were to hypothetically coindex the subject *pictures of each other* with the anaphor *each other*, we would create an i-within-i configuration. The next nearest category which has a subject is the matrix IP *They think that pictures of each other are on sale*. This subject, *they*, is accessible to the anaphor *each other*. Therefore, the governing category is the matrix IP, an antecedent for *each other* can be found within that domain, and the sentence is grammatical.

We proceed in exactly the same way with (70b)/(72b) to determine the governing category for the pronoun *them*. The first likely governing category is the embedded IP *pictures of each other are on sale*. This IP has a subject, but, since *them* is a pronoun, we don't need to check to see if the subject is accessible. Therefore, the governing category for the pronoun *them* is the embedded IP. Now, as Principle B requires, the pronoun *them* is free in its governing category, and (70b) is now correctly predicted to be grammatical.

BIBLIOGRAPHY

The general topic of anaphora (the conditions under which two DPs can co-refer) has long been a topic of investigation within Chomskyian generative grammar. The original discussion of Binding Theory using the terms that we've used in this chapter can be found in Chomsky (1981), but work in this area dates back many years prior to that. Chomsky (1981) can be *extremely* difficult to read, however, so I don't suggest that people start there. There are discussions of Binding Theory more or less as we have it here in most standard Chomskyian textbooks. I think the best discussions are in Lasnik and Uriagereka (1988) and Haegeman (1994). Webelhuth (1995a) also has a chapter on Binding Theory, but that discussion won't really be accessible until Chapter 9 has been completed. Also worth checking out is Lasnik (1989), which is a collection of articles on anaphora by Howard Lasnik, some written as early as 1973. It also contains an excellent historical overview of Binding Theory.

ANSWERS TO IN-TEXT EXERCISES

Exercise 1

Show that reciprocals do not allow discourse antecedents.

I saw [John and Mary]ᵢ yesterday. *I opened the door for [each other]ᵢ.

Exercise 2

Which of (70a) or (b) is predicted to be ungrammatical by Binding Theory as we've currently formulated it? Why?

(70)a.   They$_i$ think that pictures of each other$_i$ are on sale.
    b.   They$_i$ think that pictures of them$_i$ are on sale.

(70b), with a pronoun, is the one which is predicted to be ungrammatical. The governing category for the pronoun will be the entire IP *They think that pictures of them are on sale*. The minimal category containing the pronoun, the pronoun's governor, *of*, and a subject is the embedded subject *pictures of them*, but this is not an accessible subject for the pronoun. Hypothetical coindexation between the pronoun *them* and the subject *pictures of them* creates an i-within-i violation. The next higher category which contains a subject is the main clause. Coindexation between the main clause subject *they and* the pronoun *them* creates no i-within-i violation. Therefore, the minimal category containing the pronoun, a governor for the pronoun, and a subject which is accessible to the pronoun is the entire IP *they think that pictures of them are on sale*. Since the pronoun is bound in its governing category, Principle B is violated.

ADDITIONAL EXERCISES

Exercise 1

(a)   Draw the trees for the following sentences.
(b)   Identify all anaphors, pronouns, and R-expressions.
(c)   Show how Principles A, B, and C of the Binding Theory make the indicated predictions.

1.   John bought their$_i$ books about each other$_i$.
2.   Sue$_i$ likes her$_j$.
3.   *Bill Clinton$_i$ expected the discussion about the president$_i$ to be brief.
4.   *Bob hopes that Mary's$_j$ pictures of himself$_i$ will sell well.
5.   Mary$_i$ wondered whether she$_i$ would like the pictures of herself$_i$.
6.   *John$_i$ thought that Bill$_j$ said that Mary$_k$ liked John$_i$.
7.   The problems with John's$_i$ car surprised his$_i$ friends.
8.   For Mary$_i$ to support John$_j$ would help him$_j$.
9.   *For Mary$_i$ to support John$_j$ would help herself$_i$.
10.   [The employee of John's$_i$ firm]$_j$ deposited his$_{i/j}$ cheque.

Exercise 2

How does the sentence in (1) provide an argument for the existence of PRO, which we introduced in the last chapter?

(1)   To behave oneself in public is every citizen's duty.

Exercise 3

Jackendoff et al. (1993) make some interesting observations about the interpretation of the word 'home', as illustrated in (1):

(1)   John went home.

What are the interpretive possibilities for (2) and (3)? Put another way, whose 'home' is the destination?

(2)   John said that Mary went home.

(3)   John's friend went home.

What do these facts suggest to you about how to understand the interpretation of 'home' in the above examples? Be sure to discuss (2) and (3) in detail and draw the trees for them.
    Now consider (4):

(4)   John and Mary went home.

Is the interpretation of 'home' in this sentence problematic for your proposal? Why or why not? (If your judgment regarding the interpretation of 'home' in (4) is unclear, discuss the *possible* interpretations and which ones (if any) *would* be a problem for your proposal.)

6 Movement and Chains

Topics: Passive, Raising, Wh-movement, Topicalization, successive cyclicity, Subjacency.

Open Issue: parametric variation in bounding nodes (Italian).

6.0 INTRODUCTION

In the previous chapters, your attention has been deliberately directed toward certain kinds of examples. We argued in Chapter 4, for example, that a verb like *devour* must take a DP direct object. It can only be inserted in a phrase-structure tree under a V node which has a DP sister. By imposing this requirement, we explained contrasts like the one seen in (1):

(1)a.   John devoured his dinner.
   b.   *John devoured.

However, this requirement seems manifestly violated in cases like (2):

(2)   What did John devour?

In this case, it seems as though *devour* does not have the requisite DP sister, yet the sentence is grammatical. And if we try to add one, the sentence becomes ungrammatical:

(3)   *What did John devour the pizza?

We have a similar kind of mystery with respect to Binding Theory. In the previous chapter, we concluded, among other things, that an anaphor must be bound in its governing category by its antecedent, and in order to have binding we have to have c-command. This was intended to explain cases like (4) and (5):

(4)   *Himself$_i$ likes John$_i$.

(5)   *John's$_i$ mother likes himself$_i$.

However, in the course of our discussion we neglected to mention sentences like (6):

(6)   Which picture of himself$_i$ does John$_i$ like?

Assuming that *John* is in Spec IP as usual, it surely doesn't c-command the anaphor *himself*, wherever it is that the anaphor is actually sitting. Contrary to expectations though, (6) is grammatical.

The problems posed by the cases mentioned above aren't trivial. We seem to have evidence both that *devour* requires a DP sister and that it doesn't require one, and both that there *is* a c-command requirement on anaphors and there *isn't*. In this chapter, we will address sentences like (2) and (6), suggesting that, despite outward appearances, they, in fact, support the theory that we've been developing so far, with one important additional assumption.

6.1   TRANSFORMATIONS: AN INTRODUCTION

Consider for a moment the contrast between (1a) and (2):

(1)a.   John devoured his dinner.

(2)   What did John devour?

(2) presents a serious problem for the notion 'direct object' as we've formulated it so far. In this book, we're taking a configurational approach to terms from traditional grammar like 'subject' and 'direct object'. In other words, in the particular case at hand, we've said that something qualifies as a 'direct object' in virtue of being a sister to the verb. In (2), however, we have something different. *What* bears the same relationship to *devour* in (2) that *his dinner* does in (1a). They're both assigned the Patient θ-role. *What* is interpreted as a direct object, but it's not a sister to the verb.

One thing we could do is modify our configurational approach to direct objects. We could say that direct objects can either be generated as sisters to the verb (what we've seen until now) or in a sentence-initial position, which we'll assume for the moment is the specifier of CP.

However, it's not clear that this solution is going to buy us much in the long term. To begin with, it's not simply direct objects which can appear in Spec CP. Essentially, anything can – arguments, adjuncts, or even whole prepositional phrases. We would have to totally abandon configurational definitions of anything.

(7)a.   *What* did John buy at the store on Fridays?
   b.   *Why* did John put the book on the table?
   c.   *In which park* did Charles Mingus play for free last year?

Furthermore, allowing subjects, direct objects, adjuncts, and so on to be base-generated in Spec CP would undermine much of what we achieved in the previous chapters regarding the assignment of θ-roles and Case. Spec CP is certainly not a position which is governed by V. We would therefore be forced to give up the requirement that Case and θ-roles can only be assigned under government.

There is an alternative, however. Let's assume instead that the order that the words are actually pronounced in isn't the whole story. Suppose that our phrase-structure rules generate an underlying structure, which is then transformed by a rule into what we actually pronounce and perceive. Put another way, we have two kinds of operations: structure-*building* operations, as expressed by our phrase-structure rules, and structure-*changing* operations, which we'll call 'transformations'.

Intuitively, this approach has a certain appeal. For one thing, the idea that there are transformations allows us to account for the fact that, in (2), *what*, although in sentence-initial position, is interpreted as the direct object of *devour*. In an underlying representation, it *was* the direct object. Using the terminology that we'll adopt, (2) has as its *Deep Structure* the representation in (8):

(8)

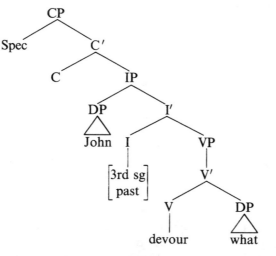

It is at this level of Deep Structure (usually abbreviated 'D-Structure') where θ-role assignment takes place. *What* is assigned the Patient θ-role under government from *devour*. The transformational rule of *Wh-Movement* takes *what* and moves it to Spec CP, leaving an unpronounced place-holder element, called a 'trace' (abbreviated 't'), to mark the original position. We thus have the Surface Structure (or 'S-Structure') representation in (9):[1]

(9)

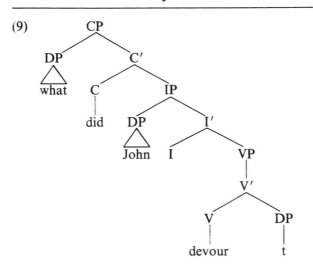

It should be clear from (9) why we want to say that Spec CP is the landing site for wh-words. The combination of word order and phrase structure almost forces that conclusion on us. Keeping our configurational definition of *subject*, (9) tells us that the subject must be in Spec IP. There are two words which must precede the subject, *what* and *did*. No other word orders are possible:

(10)a. *John what did buy?
    b. *What John did buy?
    c. *Did John what buy?
        etc.

The wh-word itself is a maximal projection (a DP, in fact, as it can surface in canonical DP positions like subject and direct object in echo questions (e.g., *John bought what?*)) and *do* is surely a head (presumably an I). As required, the CP projection provides exactly one host of each type (an XP position, Spec CP, and an X° position, C) in the right order (the XP position precedes the X° position). Therefore we seem justified in concluding that the landing site of Wh-movement is Spec CP. To introduce some terminology which will be useful in the chapters to come, positions where arguments of a predicate are generated at D-Structure (like the specifier of IP (subjects) or sister to the verb (direct objects)) are called argument positions or *A-positions*. Positions like the specifier of CP, where arguments of a predicate are not generated at D-Structure, are called *A'-positions* (read as 'A-bar', like X').

This idea, that there's a Deep Structure representation which is modified by transformations to give us what we see on the surface (S-Structure), would seem to explain the contrast between (1) and (2). The reason that *devour* does not take a DP sister in (2) is that it already had a DP sister which has been moved to Spec CP. However, being good scientists, we need to make sure that transformations are not just an *ad hoc* device for getting us out of this one problem. To that end, let's take a look at a couple of other problems that transformations seem to solve for us.

6.1.1　Further Evidence for Transformations

First, transformations do seem to get us out of that problem with respect to Binding Theory. We brought up sentences like (6) (repeated below), which we omitted in our discussion of Binding Theory in Chapter 5.

(6)　Which picture of himself$_i$ does John$_i$ like t?

If a sentence like (6) is base-generated (i.e., created by our structure-building phrase-structure rules rather than by a structure-changing transformation), then we need to throw out most of what we claimed about Principle A. It seems unlikely that *John* is somehow able to c-command *himself* in (6). The first branching node dominating the subject NP is IP, and Spec CP is not dominated by IP.

However, the assumption that (6) is derived by the same transformational rule of Wh-movement, and that Principle A applies to the D-Structure representation, not the S-Structure one, would seem to solve the problem. The S-Structure (6) would have (11) as its D-Structure representation:

(11)

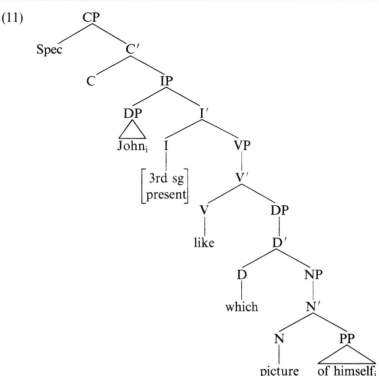

Here, the anaphor *himself* is bound in its governing category, just as Principle A requires.

Transformations also seem to be a good candidate for explaining certain subject-verb agreement facts. As we've seen in Chapter 3, the Infl node under Spec-Head agreement picks up the person and number features of the subject which are ultimately responsible for subject-verb agreement. With that in mind, consider the contrast in (12) and (13):

(12)a.   Which car did Bill say needs paint?
     b.   *Which car did Bill say need paint?

(13)a.   Which cars did Bill say need paint?
     b.   *Which cars did Bill say needs paint?

Assuming that the (a) sentences are directly generated by phrase structure rules (i.e., base-generated), the choice of *needs* versus *need* is hard to explain. Spec-Head agreement takes place between Spec IP and I, but in the (a) sentences there is no subject in the embedded Spec IP. One might expect that, since there's no subject to agree with, either (a) or (b) might be possible, or maybe that both would be ungrammatical. However, speakers of English have the unshakable intuition that the (a) sentences are grammatical and that the (b) sentences are not.

Transformations, on the other hand, allow us to say that, while there is no subject at *S-Structure*, there is one at *D-Structure*.

(14)

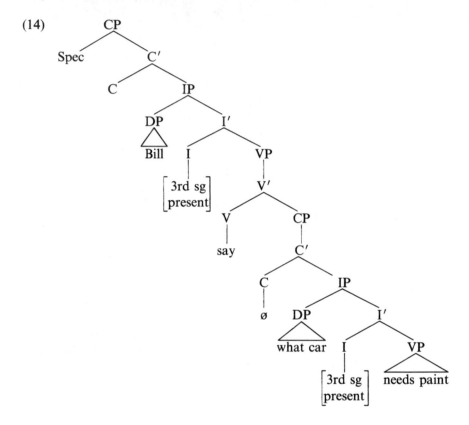

Subject-verb agreement takes place at D-Structure (as represented in (14)), and then Wh-movement moves the wh-phrase to Spec CP, creating the S-Structure representation in (15):

(15)

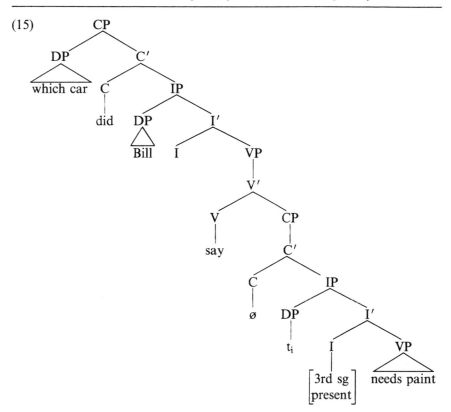

6.2   WH-MOVEMENT: SUBJACENCY AND SUCCESSIVE CYCLICITY

So far, we've seen examples of Wh-movement which involved either one clause (as in (16)) or two clauses (as in (17)):

(16)   [$_{CP}$ What $_i$ did [$_{IP}$ John devour t$_i$]]?

(17)   [$_{CP}$ Which car$_i$ did [$_{IP}$ Bill say [$_{CP}$ [$_{IP}$ t$_i$ needs paint]]]]?

In this section, we're going to take a look at Wh-movement more closely, examining in more detail how it works and what its limits are.

On the basis of (16) and (17) a natural question is whether Wh-movement can move a wh-word through any number of clauses, or whether there is some constraint on how far the wh-word can move.

Before Continuing: Provide examples of Wh-movement out of 3 clauses, 4 clauses, and 5 clauses respectively.

An examination of cases similar to (16) and (17) might suggest that Wh-movement can move a DP out of quite a few clauses:

(18) [CP Who$_i$ does [IP Alice think [CP that [IP Mary said [CP that [IP Bill liked t$_i$]]]]]]?

(19) [CP Who$_i$ did [IP Eunice say [CP that [IP John believed [CP that [IP Bill said [CP that [IP Peter liked t$_i$]]]]]]]]?

Examples like this can be continued *ad infinitum*.

There is, of course, a practical limit to the number of clauses out of which Wh-movement can take place, as a result of short-term memory limitations. If the sentence has 500 clauses, it's likely that you'll forget half of it before you get to the end. If you tried to move the wh-word to the beginning of a sentence with 500 trillion trillion clauses, you'd die before you finished saying it. However, we will assume that the fact that humans have a finite lifespan, or a fixed short-term memory, is a *performance*-related effect. As far as your linguistic *competence*, the underlying system of knowledge that you possess, is concerned, Wh-movement in a sentence with 500 trillion trillion clauses is in principle possible.

However, it turns out that this can't quite be the whole story. Consider the sentences in (20):

(20)a. John wondered where Bill saw *Midnight Cowboy*.
   b. John wondered why Bill saw *Midnight Cowboy*.
   c. John wondered who saw *Midnight Cowboy*.
   d. John wondered which film Bill saw.

The embedded clauses in (20) seem to have a lot in common with wh-questions:

(21)a. Where did Bill see *Midnight Cowboy*?
   b. Why did Bill see *Midnight Cowboy*?
   c. Who saw *Midnight Cowboy*?
   d. Which film did Bill see?

Although the sentences in (20) aren't questions, we still want to say that Wh-movement is taking place in the embedded clause, for all the same reasons that we would give for the sentences in (21).

EXERCISE 1

Using Binding Theory and the subject-verb agreement facts discussed in Section 6.1.1 above, provide arguments that Wh-movement takes place in sentences like (20).

Let's take a closer look now at (20a). If we were to question the object of *see*, asking what the thing was such that John was wondering about where Bill saw it, we get (22):

(22)   *What$_i$ did John wonder where$_j$ Bill saw t$_i$ t$_j$?

(22) is quite strongly ungrammatical, which comes perhaps as something of a surprise given what we saw with (18) and (19) above. (22) has fewer words than either one of those sentences, and seems as though it should be more or less on a par with (23):

(23)   What$_i$ did John say that he saw t$_i$?

It doesn't on the surface seem as though (23) is any more 'complicated' than (22), so there must be some other principle at work.

Before Continuing: Draw the tree for (23) and then (22).

As usual, the first step is to see if there is any structural difference between the two sentences which might provide an explanation. Comparing the trees for (22) and (23), we have (24) and (25):

(24)

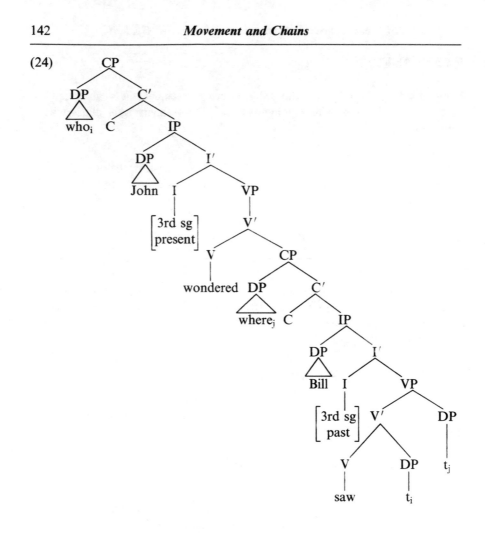

(25)

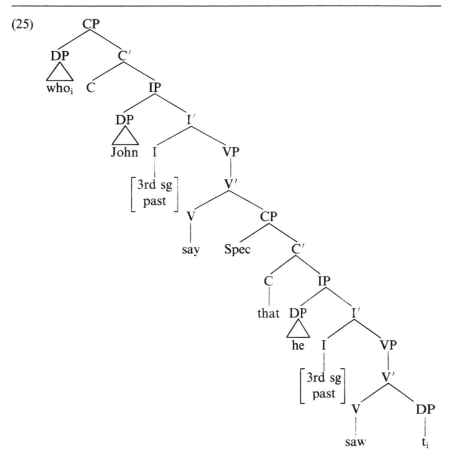

Although it is true that (22) and (23) have roughly the same number of words, notice that there is a crucial difference with respect to their structures. In the ungrammatical (22), there are *two* instances of Wh-movement, with the result that *where* is occupying the Spec CP position of the embedded clause. On the other hand, the grammatical (23) simply has complementizer *that* in the head position C.

This difference suggests a way to explain why (23) is grammatical but (22) is not: wh-words usually surface in Spec CP positions, whether it's the matrix (topmost) Spec CP as in (23) or an embedded one as in (20) above. Perhaps it's the case that wh-words don't just move in one fell swoop to the matrix Spec CP. Instead, perhaps there is some principle which forces them to move in a series of shorter steps *via intermediate Spec CP positions*. When one of these positions is already filled and the wh-word tries to 'skip' it, then this principle is violated, and the result is ungrammaticality. Let's refer to this principle as the *Successive Cyclic Hypothesis*: Wh-movement proceeds in a series of cycles, first moving to the Spec CP of the clause in which it is base-generated, and then from Spec CP to Spec CP until it reaches the matrix Spec CP. We could formulate such a principle informally as (26):

(26)   *Successive Cyclic Hypothesis*
       'Long-distance' Wh-movement must proceed via all intermediate Spec
       CP positions.

(26) will correctly account for the contrast between (22) and (23), and also correctly predict the grammaticality of the other 'long-distance' cases (18) and (19) which we saw above:

(18)   Who does Alice think that Mary said that Bill liked t?

(19)   Who did Eunice tell Mary that John believed that Bill liked t?

In both cases, the intermediate Spec CP positions are all open, and therefore *who* can use them to move successive cyclically to the matrix Spec CP.

EXERCISE 2

How many applications of Wh-movement do we need for (18) and (19) if we accept (26)? Draw the S-Structure tree for (18).

So it seems that we're beginning to get a handle on the question 'how far is too far' with respect to Wh-movement. Under the Successive Cyclic Hypothesis, it looks as though the farthest that an individual application of Wh-movement can go is from one Spec CP to the next highest Spec CP. This means that it's not the Wh-movement operation itself which is 'long distance'. Rather, the apparent distance is covered bit by bit as a series of shorter operations which are linked together.

Having formulated the Successive Cyclic Hypothesis, the next question is whether we've hit an irreducible axiom of the system, or whether the Successive Cyclic Hypothesis itself follows from some deeper principle. The traditional intuition in the literature is that there is indeed a deeper principle which underlies the Successive Cyclic Hypothesis. Specifically, the assumption is that certain nodes in the tree constitute *bounding nodes* for Wh-movement. Since Wh-movement can only proceed successive cyclically from clause to clause, it must be the case that some node in the clause constitutes a bounding node for Wh-movement. Under this assumption, we could then formulate a principle, which is referred to in the literature as *Subjacency*, along the following lines:

(27)   *The Subjacency Condition*
       A single instance of Wh-movement (whether from D-Structure
       position to Spec CP or from one Spec CP to another) can cross
       only *one* bounding node.

In order to be clear about what we mean by 'crossing' a node, let's give an explicit definition:

(28)   An instance of movement *crosses* a node X if X dominates the departure site but does not dominate the landing site.

Now we're in a position to see how a Subjacency Principle could force movement to be successive cyclic: when an intermediate Spec CP is filled, *two* bounding nodes must be crossed in order to get to the next Spec CP, and the result is ungrammaticality. Therefore, you have to move at most from one Spec CP to the next higher Spec CP.

If the Subjacency Principle is on the right track, the next task is to figure out which node or nodes might be the bounding nodes. Which node or nodes look like good possibilities? There aren't too many. Even in very simple clauses, the effect can still be seen. For example, consider (29), with some structure indicated:

(29)   *[$_{CP}$ What$_i$ did [$_{IP}$ John [$_{VP}$ wonder [$_{CP}$ why$_j$ [$_{IP}$ Bill [$_{VP}$ hit t$_i$t$_j$]]]]]]?

We're assuming now that we've crossed at least two bounding nodes in moving from direct object of *hit* to the matrix Spec CP, which is why the sentence is ungrammatical. Under this assumption, looking at the structure, the only real possibilities for bounding nodes are VP, IP, and CP. We can eliminate CP immediately. In moving from direct object position of *hit* to the matrix Spec CP, we cross only one CP, not two. (The matrix CP won't be crossed when you move to the matrix Spec CP because it dominates *both* the departure site *and* the landing site.) VP is a possibility, since there are at least two of them in (29). However, if we consider a sentence like (30), where the 'extra' auxiliaries are all Vs which take VP complements, Wh-movement still appears possible:

(30)   Who should [$_{IP}$ John [$_{VP}$ have [$_{VP}$ been [$_{VP}$ speaking to t]]]]?

Therefore, we seem left with IP as the only plausible candidate. Two IP nodes are crossed in (29). (They both dominate the departure site and both fail to dominate the landing site.) However, only one IP node is crossed in (30) above. Looking at the general case (moving successive cyclically from one Spec CP to the next), only one IP will be crossed.

Let's therefore introduce the definition of IP as a bounding node into the definition of Subjacency:

(31)   *The Subjacency Condition* (amended)
        A single instance of Wh-movement can cross only one bounding node, where IP is a bounding node.

Now you might be wondering why we've gone to all this trouble with respect to the Subjacency Condition when we already have the Successive

Cyclic Hypothesis. Given the cases we've seen so far, the Subjacency Condition just seems to be a different way of saying the same thing. However, we're about to see a case where the Successive Cyclic Hypothesis makes the wrong prediction, but the Subjacency Condition, with a slight addition, makes the right one.

Consider (32), with the tree in (33):

(32)   *Who did Bill reject the evidence that John hit t?

(33)

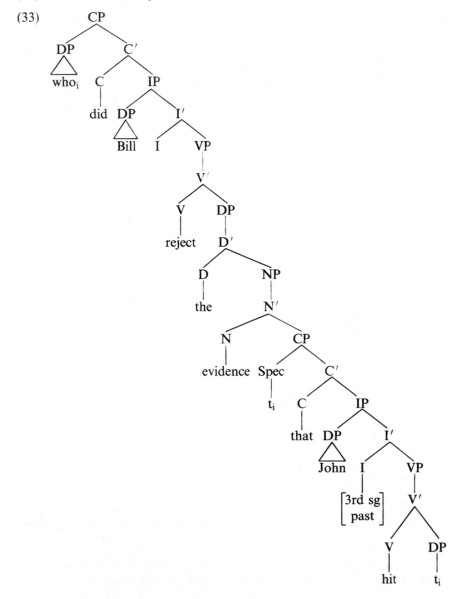

The Successive Cyclic Hypothesis, and the Subjacency Principle as we've formulated it so far, predict that (32) should be grammatical. The CP complement of the noun *evidence* has its specifier position open, and so the derivation should proceed in the following way: *who* first moves from its D-Structure position to the specifier of the CP complement, crossing one bounding node, the embedded IP, and then can move from there to the matrix Spec CP, crossing only one bounding node again, the matrix IP:

(34)

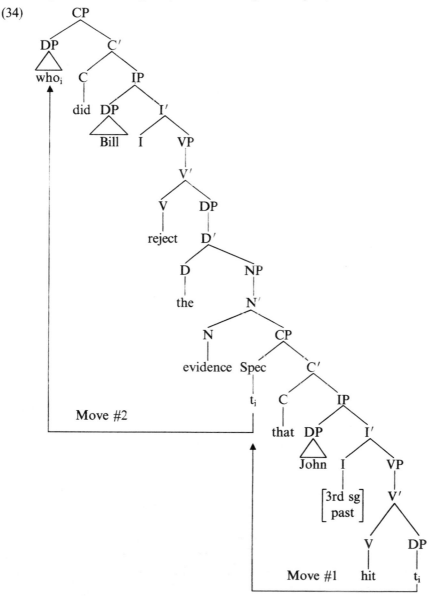

What the ungrammaticality of (32) would seem to indicate is that there's an extra bounding node that gets crossed somewhere along the line as part of one of those two moves. To try to figure out where that might be, let's take a closer look at the derivation of (32). The two moves of *who* are illustrated by the numbered arrows in (34).

It doesn't seem as though Move #1 is the one that's causing the problem. That move is just like the ordinary, garden-variety Wh-movement seen in (35):

(35)   Who did John hit t?

It doesn't seem as though there could be a mystery bounding node that's somewhere in (34) but not in (35). Therefore, the violation must be triggered during Move #2, when the wh-word moves from the embedded Spec CP to the matrix Spec CP.

Looking at Move #2, there is an obvious possible candidate for our mystery bounding node: the DP or the NP. We know that movement from a lower clause to a higher clause is in general possible. It must be the fact that what we have in (34) is a clause that's a complement of an N, rather than a V.

Under the assumption that either NP or DP is a bounding node in addition to IP, Move #2 in (34) from the embedded Spec CP to the matrix Spec CP will now cross two bounding nodes, NP/DP and the matrix IP, and the ungrammaticality of (32) will be explained. In order to figure out whether it's NP or DP that's the culprit, we need to look at the status of NPs that are not part of a larger DP. If we still see Subjacency effects, then NP is the crucial node. If, on the other hand, Subjacency effects disappear, then DP is causing the violation. As it turns out, NPs of this kind do seem to trigger Subjacency effects:

(36)a.   *Who did John reject suspicions that Bill hit?
    b.   *Who did John reject evidence that Bill hit?

This would seem to suggest that NP, rather than DP, is the relevant bounding node. So let's amend our definition of Subjacency to include NP among the class of bounding nodes:

(37)   *The Subjacency Condition* (final version)
       A single instance of Wh-movement can cross only one bounding node, where IP and NP are bounding nodes.

Hopefully, it's now clear why we needed to replace the Successive Cyclic Hypothesis. There's no obvious modification that we could make to the Successive Cyclic Hypothesis to ensure that Move #2 in (34) caused a violation. It's important to understand though that by replacing the Successive

Cyclic Hypothesis by the Subjacency Condition, we're not denying that Wh-movement takes place from Spec CP to Spec CP. It does, and we'll even continue to use the term 'successive cyclicity' to refer to the phenomenon. But it's understood that this is just a shorthand. Successive cyclicity is forced, not by the Successive Cyclic Hypothesis, but more indirectly by the Subjacency Condition.

6.3 MORE EVIDENCE FOR SUCCESSIVE CYCLICITY

In the previous section, we argued that 'long-distance' Wh-movement did not proceed in one fell swoop. Instead, we argued that Wh-movement proceeds in a successively cyclic fashion, via intermediate Spec CPs. However, the evidence that we saw for successive cyclicity was only indirect: it is only by moving from Spec CP to Spec CP that a Wh-element can satisfy the Subjacency Principle. English doesn't provide any direct, visible evidence for successive cyclicity.

However, once we move away from English, we see that other languages provide more direct support for the hypothesis that Wh-movement proceeds successive cyclically. Subject inversion in Spanish, and the choice of complementizer in languages such as Modern Irish seem to confirm that Wh-movement takes place in a clause-by-clause (CP by CP) fashion. In this way, we can confirm that Subjacency is a universal principle, which constrains Wh-movement not just in English, but in all languages.

6.3.1 Subject Inversion in Spanish

Torrego (1984) notes that Spanish, like many 'null subject' languages, allows 'free subject inversion', as illustrated in (38). (38a) represents the canonical Subject-Verb-Object word order of Spanish. In this respect, Spanish is exactly like English. However, under certain discourse conditions, the subject can appear in a rightward position, as in (38b):

(38)a. Juan contestó la pregunta.
      Juan answered the question.
   b. Contestó la pregunta Juan.

Interestingly, this subject inversion is in fact obligatory when certain wh-phrases appear in Spec CP, as illustrated in (39):

(39)a. Qué querían esos dos?
      What   wanted those two?
   b. *Qué   esos dos   querían?
      'What did those two want?'

(40)a.   Con quién vendrá   Juan hoy?
         With whom will come Juan today?
    b.   *Con quién Juan vendrá hoy?
         'Who will Juan come with today?'

Obligatory subject inversion in Spanish takes place both in main and embedded clauses, as illustrated in (41) and (42):

(41)a.   No sabía   qué querían   esos dos.
         Not knew-1sg what wanted-3Pl those two
    b.   *No sabía qué esos dos querían.
         'I didn't know what those two wanted.'

(42)a.   Es impredecible con quién vendrá   Juan hoy.
         Is not predictable with whom will come-3sg Juan today
    b.   *Es impredicible con quién Juan vendrá hoy.
         'It's impossible to predict who Juan will come with today.'

So, generalizing from the data in (39) to (42), it seems as though subject inversion is obligatory in any clause when Spec CP contains a wh-word of the appropriate type.

Now, let's look at cases involving 'long distance' Wh-movement. Consider the following declarative sentence (with the subjects italicized):

(43)   *Juan* pensaba que *Pedro* le había dicho que *la revista* había publicado
       Juan thought that Pedro him had said that the journal had published
       ya   el artículo.
       already the article
       'Juan thought that Pedro had told him that the journal had published
       the article already.'

When forming a wh-question about *el artículo*, *all* subjects obligatorily undergo subject inversion, not just the matrix one:

(44)a.   Qué pensaba *Juan* que le había dicho *Pedro* que había publicado
         What thought Juan that him had said Pedro that had published
         t *la revista*?
         the journal
         'What did Juan think that Pedro had told him that the journal had
         published?'
    b.   *Qué pensaba *Juan* que *Pedro* le había dicho que *la revista* había
         publicado?

If, on the other hand, the wh-word originates in a higher clause, inversion in the subordinate clause is not required:

(45) A quién   prometió *Juan* que Pedro se encargaría
      To whom promised Juan that Pedro self would-take-upon
      de que la gente   sacara   las entradas a tiempo?
      that   the people got   the tickets on time
      'To whom did Juan promise that Pedro would make sure that the
      people got the tickets on time?'

Under the assumption that a wh-word in Spec CP is what triggers subject
inversion, the contrast seen in (44) and the one between (44b) and (45) is
explained if Wh-movement proceeds successive cyclically. When it passes
through each intermediate Spec CP, it triggers subject inversion *with each
subject along the way*. In (45), since the wh-word originated in the matrix
clause and never passed through any of the embedded Spec CPs, the subjects
of the embedded clauses do not undergo inversion.

6.3.2 Complementizers in Irish

Additional support for the Successive Cyclicity Hypothesis can be found in
languages such as Modern Irish. In these languages, when a wh-word has
'stopped off' in an intermediate Spec CP position, the form of the
complementizer changes.
    Chung and McCloskey (1987) note that the normal subordinating particle
in Modern Irish is *go*, as illustrated by (46):[2]

(46) Dúirt sé go   dtiocfadh sé.
      Said he Comp would come he
      'He said that he would come.'

However, when Wh-movement has taken place, the complementizer *go* is
replaced by *aL*, as illustrated by (47):[3]

(47) an bhean$_i$ aL   chuir t$_i$ isteach air
      the woman Comp put   in   on it
      'the woman who applied for it'

Crucially for our purposes, when Subjacency would predict that successive
cyclic movement must have taken place, it turns out that every complementizer along the way changes to *aL*:

(48) an rud$_i$ aL   shíl   mé aL   dúirt tú aL   dhéanfá t$_i$
      the thing Comp thought I   Comp said you Comp would do
      'the thing that I thought you said that you would do'

This would seem to be further evidence that Wh-movement (in this case,
inside a relative clause) is proceeding in a successively cyclic manner.

6.4 MORE TRANSFORMATIONS: PASSIVE AND RAISING

So far in this chapter, we've concentrated exclusively on Wh-movement when discussing transformations. Movement of this kind is called *A'-movement*, because it involves movement to an A'-position, Spec CP. However, there are other sentences in natural language which involve movement to the specifier of IP, an A-position. This kind of movement is called *A-movement*, and we'll see that those phenomena, too, are best explained by transformations.

6.4.1 Passive

One familiar case of A-movement from traditional grammar instruction is that of passivization. Corresponding with an active sentence like (49), there is a Passive counterpart (50):

(49)   Big Business killed music.

(50)   Music was killed by Big Business.

(49) and (50) are essentially synonymous. The active verb *kill* is replaced by its passive counterpart *be killed*, the direct object of the active verb appears as the subject of the Passive, and the former subject of the active version appears in a prepositional phrase. The question is: what is the relation between an Active sentence and its Passive counterpart? Just as in the cases of Wh-movement, there are in principle two options. It could be that Passive sentences are directly base-generated by our phrase-structure rules. The alternative is that sentences like (50) are derived by transformation from an underlying Deep Structure.

In order to decide between these two options, let's take a closer look at some of the less obvious properties of Passive sentences. Recall from Chapter 4 that we discussed so-called *expletive* elements, elements which must not be assigned a θ-role. English has two expletives, *it* and *there*, depending on whether the associate of the expletive is a CP or a DP. Either one can appear in Spec IP when the verb has been passivized.

(51)a.   There was a man killed.
     b.   It is believed that John is a fugitive from justice.

From the grammaticality of (51a) and (b), we conclude that Spec IP is not a θ-position in Passives. That is, the subject of a Passive verb is not a position to which a θ-role is assigned.

But if that's the case, that would seem to be an argument against the base-generation hypothesis for Passives. The θ-Criterion tells us that all DPs need to be assigned a θ-role, but if *music* is base-generated in the subject position in (50), it won't receive one, and we'd expect (50) to be ungrammatical, on a par with (52):

(52)   *John seems that Bill is here

If, on the other hand, we assume that Passive sentences are transformationally derived, we don't have this problem. A sentence like (50) can be derived from a D-Structure like (53):

(53)

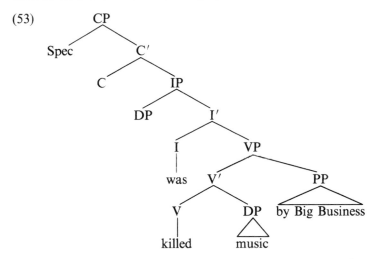

Since *music* is base-generated as the direct object of the verb, that's the θ-role that it receives.[4] The Passive transformation then moves the direct object to the empty subject position, generating the order that we see on the surface:

(54)

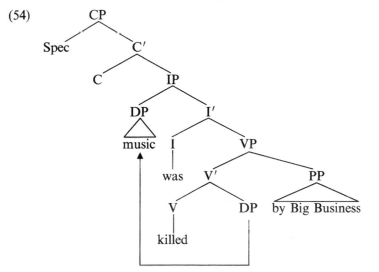

However, there's one more thing we need to say about Passives. On the basis of the discussion so far, we don't have an explanation for (55):

(55)   *There was killed music by Big Business

It seems as though the base-generated object can't just stay in its D-Structure position. It must move to subject position:[5]

(56)   Music was killed by Big Business.

A seemingly natural way to explain this is to say that, in addition to not assigning a θ-role to their subjects, Passive verbs also don't assign Accusative Case to their objects. (In fact, in what's come to be known as 'Burzio's Generalization', Luigi Burzio (1986) suggested these two properties are intrinsically connected.)

In this way, the following picture of Passives emerges: the direct object, base-generated in a position that receives a θ-role, but not Case, needs to move to a position to which Case is assigned. By the θ-Criterion, this Case position can't be a θ-position, since the object's already got its one θ-role. Fortunately, the subject position in Passives provides just such a position (Case, but no θ-role), and so the direct object moves there.

6.4.2   Raising

In addition to Passive verbs, there's another class of verbs (and adjectives, actually) which also have properties which seem to be best explained by a transformational analysis. These predicates are called *Raising* predicates. A canonical Raising predicate is the verb *seem*. In Chapter 4, we saw *seem* in its ordinary 'I take a CP complement' guise, as illustrated by (57):

(57)   It seems [CP that six executives like Guided by Voices].

However, *seem* has another guise, in which it takes an IP infinitival complement, as exemplified by sentences like (58):

(58)   Six executives seem [IP to like Guided by Voices].

Just as it does when it takes a CP complement, the subject position of *seem* is a non-θ-position when it takes an IP complement:

(59)   There seem [IP to be six executives here].

We therefore conclude that the DP *six executives* cannot have been base-generated in subject positions in sentences like (58). Instead, the DP is base-generated as the subject of the infinitive, where it receives its θ-role as the subject of *like*, and is subsequently 'raised' to the subject position of *seem*.

(60)   Six executives$_i$ seem [$_{IP}$ t$_i$ to like Guided by Voices].

An example of a Raising adjective is *likely*. Just as with Raising verbs, Raising adjectives can take a finite CP complement:

(61)   It is likely that six executives enjoy Guided by Voices.

(61) can alternate with an infinitival IP complement, as in (62):

(62)   Six executives are likely [$_{IP}$ to enjoy Guided by Voices].

The subject is still a non-θ-position:

(63)   There are likely to be six executives here.

We therefore conclude that the subject *six executives* in (62) was raised from the subject position of the infinitive, as illustrated by (64):

(64)   Six executives$_i$ are likely [$_{IP}$ t$_i$ to enjoy Guided by Voices].

EXERCISE 3

Consider the following four sentences:

(a)   John promised to go
(b)   John appeared to go
(c)   John is certain to go
(d)   John intends to go.

In each case, *John* is interpreted both as the promisor, appearer, and so on, and as the goer. Using the θ-Criterion and expletives as a test, discuss which of the four are Raising predicates and which are not.

6.5   LEVELS OF APPLICATION OF PRINCIPLES

We've been exploring the idea that phrase-structure rules generate D-Structures which are then operated on by transformations to give S-Structure. Given this revision of our model, there's a question we need to ask: now that we have two levels, D-Structure and S-Structure, which level or levels do Case marking, Binding Theory, θ-marking, and so on apply to? This question didn't arise before, since in previous chapters we were dealing only with one level, S-Structure.

We've mentioned a couple of cases in passing already. It was examples involving Binding Theory that we used to motivate the existence of transformations in the first place. Remember (6)?

(6)   Which picture of himself$_i$ does John$_i$ like t?

At S-Structure, *John*, the antecedent of the reflexive *himself*, fails to c-command it. (The first branching node dominating *John* is the matrix IP, which does not dominate Spec CP.) It is only at D-Structure that the relevant c-command relationship exists between *John* and *himself*. It must therefore be the case that Principle A of the Binding Theory applies at D-Structure.

θ-marking is another process which must take place at D-Structure rather than S-Structure. As we saw in Section 6.4, Passive and Raising move elements into positions which are not assigned a θ-role, as evidenced by the fact that these positions allow expletive *it* and *there*:

(65)   There were three men killed.

(66)   It is likely that John is here.

If θ-marking took place at S-Structure, we would expect sentences like (67) and (68) to violate the θ-Criterion:

(67)   Three men were killed t.

(68)   John is likely t to be here.

At S-Structure, *three men* and *John* are not in positions which are assigned a θ-role, and would be predicted to be ungrammatical. We therefore conclude that θ-marking must take place at D-Structure.

What about subject-verb agreement? This presents an interesting case, and one which will lead us directly into the next section, where we'll clarify the relationship between moved elements and their traces. We argued in Section 6.1 that certain facts about subject-verb agreement provided an argument for transformations. Recall the contrast in (13):

(13)a.   Which car did Bill say needs paint?
    b.   *Which car did Bill say need paint?

It is only at D-Structure that the requisite Specifier-Head relationship exists between the wh-phrase which is in the lower Spec IP position and I. We therefore concluded that, in order to account for choice of *needs* over *need*, subject-verb agreement had to take place at D-Structure.

However, if we take a close look at the cases of Passive and Raising that we saw in Section 6.4, they seem to argue for the opposite conclusion. The D-Structure representations for (67) and (68) are of course (69) and (70):

(69)   were killed three men

(70)   is likely John to be here

Unlike the contrast seen in (13), in (69) and (70) the requisite Specifier-Head relationship doesn't exist at D-Structure. It only exists at S-Structure.

So we seem to have a paradox: some instances of subject-verb agreement must take place at D-Structure, while others must take place at S-Structure. However, this paradox can be resolved by taking a closer look at the relationship between a moved object and its trace.

6.6   CHAINS

In this section we're going to introduce the idea of a *chain*, a technical concept concerning the relation between a moved element and its trace which plays a central role in the theory of movement. For purposes of discussion, consider the raising structure in (71):

(71)   John$_i$ seems t$_i$ to be here.

John is a DP. The trace too must be a DP, given its distribution (i.e., it appears only in DP positions: Spec IP, sister to V, sister to P, etc.). However, the relation between an antecedent and its trace is not just an ordinary relationship between two coindexed DPs, like the one in (72):

(72)   John$_i$ said that he$_i$ was late.

Syntactic requirements which hold of DPs treat the moved element and its trace as though they were a single DP. For this reason, we say that the moved element and its trace form *a chain*. In (71) the chain is created transformationally by raising of *John*. The chain has two members, *John* and the trace. In the case of a single DP which simply remains in its base-generated position, we say that that DP forms a *one-membered chain*.

Notice that this will require that the θ-Criterion and the Case Filter be redefined in terms of chains, but this is easily done. Chomsky (1986: 97) provides the following chain-based definition of the θ-Criterion:

(73)   *The θ-Criterion*
       Each argument A appears in a chain containing a unique ... θ-position P, and each θ-position P is ... a chain containing a unique argument A.

And the Case Filter can be revised as follows:

(74)   *The Case Filter*
       Each chain must be assigned Case.

The concept of the chain, and the reformulation of the θ-Criterion to
apply to chains, explains a multitude of otherwise odd facts. It first explains
why, as we saw above, *John* can (and indeed must) move to a position that
doesn't assign a θ-role. *John* itself doesn't need an independent θ-role in (71)
because it's linked up with a trace which already has one. Additionally, we
also explain the contrast in (75):

(75)a.   John$_i$ seems t$_i$ to be here.
   b.   *John$_i$ believes t$_i$ to be here.

If *John* already has a θ-role by virtue of its association with the trace, (75b)
is straightforwardly ruled out as a θ-Criterion violation, defined in terms of
chains, as the chain (*John*, t) receives *two* θ-roles.

We also resolve the paradox that we mentioned at the end of Section 6.5
regarding subject-verb agreement. In (13) (repeated below), which involved
Wh-movement, it seemed as though subject-verb agreement took place at
D-Structure:

(13)a.   Which car does Bill say needs paint?
   b.   *Which car does Bill say need paint?

In the case of Passive and Raising, it seemed as though subject-verb
agreement must take place *after* Passive or Raising, that is, at S-Structure:

(76)a.   John$_i$ is likely t$_i$ to be here.
   b.   *John$_i$ are likely t$_i$ to be here.
   c.   *[John and Mary]$_i$ is likely t$_i$ to be here.
   d.   [John and Mary]$_i$ are likely t$_i$ to be here.

However, the notion of the chain allows us to have elements be in two
places at once, in effect, at S-Structure. We can then say that subject-verb
agreement takes place at S-Structure, and that agreement can take place
either with the head of the chain (the moved element) or the tail of the chain
(the trace). In the case of Wh-movement, it's the tail of the chain that is in
the embedded Spec IP, but the embedded INFL agrees by virtue of the trace
being in a chain with *which car*. In (76), by contrast, the matrix INFL is
agreeing with the head of the chain (John, t), which is *John*.

6.7 SUMMARY

This chapter has motivated one of the most significant additions so far to our model of what speakers of a language know. One thing that speakers seem to know about their language is that certain sentences are not simply base-generated. Rather, they are derived from an underlying D-Structure representation. Transformations apply to this D-Structure representation, generating the S-Structure representation, which is what actually undergoes pronunciation. Schematically, we have the following model:

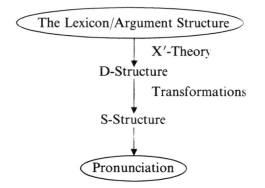

Notice that the facts we've discussed – facts which are intuitively obvious to any speaker of a language – again constitute clear examples of Plato's Problem. It appears to be the case that in order to account for what we know when we know a language, we need to say that speakers don't pay attention to just what there is on the surface. Rather, speakers know that sentences have multiple representations. There's a D-Structure representation, which in certain constructions (like Raising) never appear on the surface. Then there are also transformations which map these 'invisible' D-Structures into the S-Structures that are pronounced.

In particular, we looked at several different transformations, including Wh-movement, Passive, and Raising. We saw that Wh-movement in particular is subject to the Subjacency Principle:

(37)   *The Subjacency Condition*
       A single instance of Wh-movement can cross only one bounding node, where IP and NP are bounding nodes.

This principle forces Wh-movement to proceed successive cyclically, moving in stages from Spec CP to Spec CP. Although English doesn't provide any direct evidence for successive cyclicity, other languages, like Spanish and Irish do.

It also turned out that the relationship between an element moved by transformation and the trace it leaves behind was unlike anything we've seen before. It seemed as though the θ-Criterion and the Case Filter treat the moved DP and its trace as a single DP. As a result we introduced the notion of *a chain* and were led to modify our definitions of the θ-Criterion and the Case Filter from Chapter 4:

(73)   *The θ-Criterion*
Each argument A appears in a chain containing a unique ... θ-position P, and each θ-position P is ... a chain containing a unique argument A.

(74)   *The Case Filter*
Each chain must be assigned Case.

OPEN ISSUE: PARAMETRIC VARIATION AND BOUNDING NODES IN ITALIAN

In Section 6.2 we motivated the Subjacency Condition:

(37)   *The Subjacency Condition* (final version)
A single instance of Wh-movement can cross only one bounding node, where IP and NP are bounding nodes.

However, Rizzi (1982) noticed that certain Romance languages, such as Italian seem to present a problem for the Subjacency condition as we've formulated it.
   Consider the following sentence:

(77)   Tuo fratello, [$_{CP}$ a cui$_i$ [$_{IP}$ mi domando [$_{CP}$ che storie [$_{IP}$ abbiano
Your brother, to whom myself I-ask   which stories have-3pl
racontato t$_i$]]]], era molto preoccupato.
told   was very worried
'Your brother, to whom I wonder which stories they have told, was very worried.'

In particular, look at the subject DP, *your brother, to whom I wonder which stories they have told*. The English translation violates Subjacency – just like example (78), which we saw earlier:

(78)   *What $_i$ did [$_{IP}$ John wonder [$_{CP}$ why [$_{IP}$ Bill hit t$_i$]]]?

The movement crosses two bounding nodes (in this case, two IPs), but, unexpectedly, the result is grammatical in Italian.

There are a couple of different options we could pursue at this point. We could simply abandon the idea that Subjacency is a universal principle, and content ourselves with the work that it does for us in English and other languages. However, a brief look at some other data in Italian shows that this would be the wrong decision. Although the kind of Subjacency violations we saw in (78) don't seem to exist, violations involving 'complex' DPs like (32) above do:

(79) *Tuo fratello, [$_{CP}$ a cui$_i$ [$_{IP}$ temo [$_{DP}$ la [$_{NP}$ possibilità
Your brother, to whom fear-1sg the possibility
[$_{CP}$ che [$_{IP}$ abbiano raccontato tutto t$_i$, ...]]]]]
that have-3pl told everything, ...
'Your brother, to whom I fear the possibility that they have told everything, ...'

In (79) the wh-phrase *a cui* has crossed both an IP node and an NP node, and, as Subjacency would predict, the result is ungrammatical. So it seems clear that Subjacency needs to be modified rather than completely abandoned.

One obvious way to modify Subjacency would be to say that IP isn't a bounding node in Italian. What really matters in Italian is crossing an NP, and crossing only **one** bounding node will result in ungrammaticality:

(83) *Italian Subjacency (proposed)*
Movement cannot cross even one bounding node (where the bounding nodes are NP only).

(83) makes the correct predictions about (77) vs. (79). Movement crosses no NP nodes in (77), and so is correctly predicted to be grammatical. Movement crosses one NP node in (79), and so is correctly predicted to be ungrammatical.

However, (83) also predicts that movement can cross as many IPs as you like, provided that no NP is crossed. That prediction isn't correct. Consider the following subject noun phrase:

(84) *Franceso, [$_{CPx}$ che$_i$[$_{IPx}$ non immagino [$_{CPx}$ quanta gente [$_{IPx}$ sappia
Francesco, who not imagine-1sg how-many people know
[$_{CPz}$ dove [$_{IPz}$ hanno mandato t$_i$, ...]]]]]
where have-3Pl sent
'Francesco, who I can't imagine how many people know where they have sent, ...'

In (84), *who* has had to move in one fell swoop from its position as the direct object of *send* to Spec CP$_x$, because the intermediate Specs CP$_y$ and CP$_z$ are filled by *where* and *how many people* respectively. There's no NP node crossed here, only IPs, so (83) predicts that (84) should be grammatical. And that's not the right result.

So we're left with something of a mystery: what is it that distinguishes (77) from (79) and (84)? A closer look at the structure indicated in (77) suggests the answer. Notice that, while two IP nodes were crossed by *a cui*, only one CP node was crossed. (Remember the highest CP node isn't *crossed*, since it dominates both the departure site (sister to V') and the landing site (Spec CP)). In the ungrammatical (84), *two* CP nodes are crossed (CP_y and CP_z).

With this insight, Rizzi observed that Subjacency in Italian can be accounted for with a minimum amount of fuss. The only difference between English and Italian has to do with which nodes are bounding nodes. Thus, we have (85):

(85)   *Italian Subjacency (final)*
       Movement cannot cross more than one bounding node (where the
       bounding nodes are NP and CP).

So Subjacency seems to be subject to parametric variation. For a language like English, the bounding nodes are set to NP and IP, but for other Romance languages like Italian, the bounding nodes are NP and CP. This suggests that, while Subjacency is indeed a universal principle, the precise details are subject to parametric variation.

BIBLIOGRAPHY

The idea that there are structure-changing operations like transformations is one of the oldest ideas in Chomskyian generative linguistics, going back to Chomsky (1957) (although similar ideas can be found in other traditions hundreds of years earlier). The first observations about what we've been calling 'Subjacency' effects go back to John Robert Ross's (1967) dissertation, where he identified what he called 'islands'. As with some of the other topics we've discussed, any textbook on Chomskyian linguistics will have discussion of these ideas, including Lasnik and Uriagereka (1988) and Haegeman (1994).

ANSWERS TO IN-TEXT EXERCISES

Exercise 1

Using Binding Theory and the subject-verb agreement facts discussed in Section 6.1.1 above, provide arguments that Wh-movement takes place in sentences like (20).

We can construct sentences which are entirely parallel with those in Section 6.1.1 to show that the sentences in (20) cannot be base-generated, but instead must be derived by transformation. Consider (i):

(i)   John wondered [which picture of herself]ᵢ Mary liked tᵢ.

Although (i) is grammatical, the required c-command relationship would not exist between *Mary* and the anaphor *herself* if the sentences were base-generated. On the other hand, if (i) is transformationally derived from the D-Structure in (ii), then Binding Theory can be satisfied. At D-Structure, *Mary* does c-command *herself*:

(ii)   John wondered [CP Mary liked which picture of herself].

A similar situation exists for subject-verb agreement:

(iii)   John wondered which car Bill thinks needs paint.
(iv)   *John wondered which car Bill thinks need paint.

Unless sentences like (20) are transformationally derived and not base-generated, it's not clear why there should be a difference between (iii) and (iv).

Exercise 2

How many applications of Wh-movement do we need for (18) and (19) if we accept (26)? Draw the S-Structure tree for (18).

Clearly, if we accept (26), we're going to need one application of Wh-movement for each CP. (26) says that Wh-movement first moves an element to the nearest Spec CP, and then from Spec CP to Spec CP. Therefore, in (18) we need 3 applications of Wh-movement and in (19) we need 4.

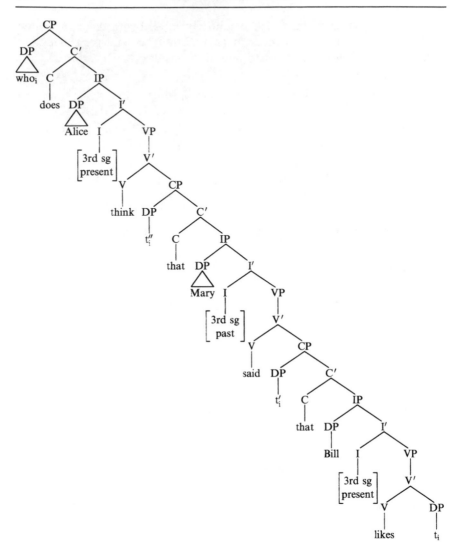

Exercise 3

Consider the following four sentences:

(a) John promised to go.
(b) John appeared to go.
(c) John is certain to go.
(d) John intends to go.

In each case, *John* is interpreted both as the promisor, appearer, etc. and as the goer. Using the θ-Criterion and expletives as a test, discuss which of the four are Raising predicates and which are not.

If the subject position of the verb allows an expletive, then it does not assign a θ-role. Therefore, by the θ-Criterion, the predicate must be a Raising predicate, with the subject getting its θ-role as the subject of the lower verb. Therefore, we have:

(ia)   *It promises that John will leave.
(ib)   *There promises to be a man here.

Conclusion: *promise* is not a raising predicate.

(iia)   It appears that John will leave.
(iib)   There appears to be a man here.

Conclusion: *appear* is a raising predicate.

(iiia)   It is certain that John will leave.
(iiib)   There is certain to be a man here.

Conclusion: *certain* is a raising predicate.

(iva)   *It intends that John will leave.
(ivb)   *There intends to be a man here.

Conclusion: *intend* is not a raising predicate.

ADDITIONAL EXERCISES

Exercise 1

Draw the D-Structure and S-Structure trees for the following sentences:

1.   Which book about linguistics did Mary write?
2.   Why did John think that Bill left the room?
3.   What did John believe Bill said that Mary had written?
4.   On which postcard has John drawn a picture of himself?
5.   For John to appear to be lying would be a political disaster.
6.   Toby intended to be seen at the party.

Exercise 2

Put traces in the appropriate places and identify the chains in the following sentences. How does each DP in the sentence satisfy the revised θ-Criterion and Case Filter?

1. John seems to have left the building.
2. The duck salesmen were attacked in the streets yesterday.
3. What did John say that he put on the shelf?
4. I believe Bob to have destroyed Carthage.
5. Who was killed?
6. Who does John seem to like?

Exercise 3

There's a kind of construction which we haven't look at here called Topicalization, which is exemplified by sentences like (1) and (2):

1. This book, John bought yesterday.
2. Beatles records, Bill likes.

Do you think that these sentences are directly generated by our phrase-structure rules, or derived by a transformation?

Exercise 4

One useful thing that Subjacency can do is provide a diagnostic test for phrase structure. Consider the following extraction from a sentential subject:

(1)   *What$_i$ did that Brian recorded t$_i$ yesterday bother Mike?

Examine the derivation. Does any application of Wh-movement lead to a Subjacency violation? How could we modify our analysis of the phrase structure of sentential subjects in order to make the correct prediction with respect to (1)?

Exercise 5

We argued in this chapter that Binding Theory is checked at D-Structure on the basis of sentences like (1):

(1)   Which picture of himself does John like?

However, consider the interpretive possibilities for *himself* in a sentence like (2):

(2)   Which picture of himself did John say that Bill liked?

Can *himself* refer to *John, Bill*, or either one? What problems, if any, do the co-reference possibilities present? Consider the derivation and whether *himself* would be bound in its Governing Category by its antecedent at D-Structure.

Exercise 6

The examples which show that Binding Theory applies at D-Structure have so far all come from Wh-movement. However, consider the following data from raising verbs:

(1) John$_i$ seems to me to like himself$_i$.

(2) They$_i$ seem to each other$_i$ to be good players.

What impact do (1) and (2) have on the claim that Binding Theory is checked at D-Structure? How can the concept of the chain help us here?

Exercise 7

Consider the following instances of 'long-distance' Passive and Raising:

(1) John was believed to have been attacked.

(2) Bill seems to be likely to lose the race.

Do Passive and Raising proceed successive cyclically? Are they subject to Subjacency too? Try to construct sentences in which 'one fell swoop' passivization and raising are forced because a potential intermediate 'stopping off' point is filled and see what the result is.

7   Logical Form

Topics: LF Wh-movement, Quantifier Raising, Expletive replacement as LF raising.

Open Issue: 'Superiority' and Discourse-linking.

7.0   INTRODUCTION

In the previous chapter we introduced the idea of transformations, and discovered that part of what you know about your language includes the fact that sentences have two kinds of representations: S-Structures, in which the words appear in the order in which they're pronounced, and D-Structures, which interface with the lexicon and encode information about the argument structure of the predicates. S-Structures and D-Structures are linked by transformations.

This might have seemed like a pretty radical step. What we claimed is that part of what you know about your language includes information about D-Structure representations – representations which *never* appear on the surface in many cases. And even S-Structure representations, in which the word order corresponds to the 'surface' word order, often have traces in them – elements which are present but which are *never* pronounced.

In this chapter, we're going to take this idea one step further. Not only are there *representations* which you never 'see', but there are also *transformations* whose effects you never 'see'. That is, there are transformations which are not concerned with deriving the surface order that is pronounced. In introducing this idea, we're going to modify our assumptions about the architecture of the grammar once again. (Don't worry! This is the last time.) So far, we have (1):

(1)

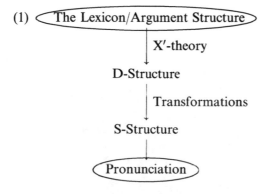

168

The structure-building operation, X′-Theory, together with the lexicon and argument structure of the words involved, creates D-Structure. D-Structure is then modified by transformations (if appropriate) to create S-Structure. S-Structure is then used as the input to phonology and pronunciation.

What we're going to claim in this chapter is that, after S-Structure, the computation 'splits', rather than going directly to pronunciation. As before, the phonological information is stripped out of the S-Structure representation and sent to the phonological component for processing. In the phonological component, intonational contours are assigned and other phonological operations happen, ultimately yielding a representation of pronunciation. What's new in this chapter is the idea that the *syntactic* computation (minus phonological features) actually continues, and specifically that there are other transformations which continue to manipulate the structure. When those transformations have been completed, we arrive at a level known as *Logical Form*, which is then passed on to the semantic component for semantic interpretation. *Logical Form* (LF) therefore serves as the 'interface' between the syntax and the semantics, just as S-Structure serves as the interface between the syntax and the phonology.

Therefore, instead of (1), what we really have is (2):

(2)   The Lexicon/Argument Structure

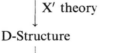

X′ theory

D-Structure

Transformations

S-Structure

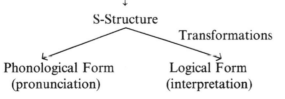

Transformations

Phonological Form   Logical Form
(pronunciation)   (interpretation)

This is known as the 'Y' model of grammar, because the shape of it looks something like an upside-down Y.

In Section 7.1, we'll take a look at Chinese and Japanese, particularly as they compare with English. Chinese and Japanese are languages in which wh-words *appear* not to undergo movement to Spec CP. That is, unlike in English, there are no Wh-movement effects visible in pronunciation. There is no *overt* movement. However, we'll argue that in those languages wh-words *do* undergo Wh-movement, but they do so *covertly*, after S-Structure in the LF component. We'll then go back to English, and argue that English has cases of LF Wh-movement too. In Section 7.2, once the idea of LF movement is more familiar, we'll talk a little more generally about Logical Form as a level of representation, in the context of another LF transformation, Quantifier Raising.

   Both LF Wh-movement and Quantifier Raising will turn out to be instances of covert A′-movement, so in Section 7.3 we'll turn our attention to LF A-movement, arguing that there's an LF-counterpart to Raising in English. We'll claim that in structures of the form *there ... DP*, the DP raises to the position of *there* in the LF component.

7.1   WH-MOVEMENT IN THE LF COMPONENT

In this section, we're going to take a look at two cases of LF Wh-movement; that is, Wh-movement which takes place but which you don't 'see'. In languages like Chinese and Japanese, following a line of analysis started by Huang (1982), it turns out that *all* Wh-movement happens in the LF component.

7.1.1   LF Wh-Movement in Chinese and Japanese

Chinese and Japanese represent two languages in which, on the surface, wh-elements like *what* and *why* do not undergo Wh-movement. Consider the following sentence from Japanese:

(3)   John-wa   nani-o   kaimashita ka?
       John-Top what-Acc bought   Q
       'What did John buy?'

As you'll recall from Chapter 3, Japanese is a head-final language. Therefore, *nani-o* 'what' is in a standard direct object position as a sister to V, as illustrated by (4):

(4)

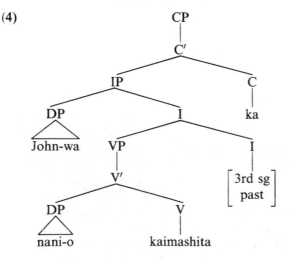

However, notice that *nani* (a wh-word in Japanese) has not undergone any Wh-movement in (3), despite (3) being the normal way to ask a wh-question in Japanese. The wh-word remains *in situ*, that is in its D-Structure position. We can see this when we replace *nani* with a non-wh word, as in (5):

(5) John-wa hon-o   kaimashita.
     John-Top book-Acc bought
     'John bought a book.'

In this section, we'll argue that, despite this apparent lack of *overt* Wh-movement, Chinese and Japanese have *covert* Wh-movement to Spec CP. Put another way, Chinese and Japanese are essentially identical to English with regard to their wh-questions. The difference between them is simply a matter of whether Wh-movement takes place between D-Structure and S-Structure (overtly) or between S-Structure and LF (covertly).

There are two kinds of arguments that we'll look at to support the idea of LF Wh-movement. The first will be a more conceptual, cross-linguistic kind. In looking at other languages, we'll see that they have overt movements which correspond to the covert ones that we're postulating (as in English, for instance). In Section 7.1.1.1, we'll try to make some of the same arguments for LF Wh-movement in Chinese and Japanese as we made for *overt* Wh-movement in English in the last chapter. However, in Sections 1.1.2 and 1.1.3, we'll try to go one better. We'll see that, even though the elements in question don't seem to move anywhere, the elements are behaving as if they did move, and are subject to some familiar constraints on movement.

7.1.1.1 An Argument from Selection
By way of introduction, let's take a quick look at an English sentence of a type we discussed in the previous chapter:

(6) John wondered what$_i$ Bill bought t$_i$.

Remember that we want to say that Wh-movement is taking place in (6) even though (6) as a whole does not have the semantics of a question. It's just a lexical fact about *wonder* that it requires a wh-word in the specifier position of the CP that is its sister. That's just part of the meaning of that verb. Other verbs which can take a +wh CP all fall into roughly the same semantic area, involving states of knowledge.

(7)a. I asked what$_i$ John bought t$_i$.
   b. I know what$_i$ John bought t$_i$.

Let's now contrast this situation in English with the situation in a language like Chinese. The Chinese translation of (6) is (8) (with the proper names changed to appropriate ones for the language, as is commonly done):

(8)   Zhangsan xiang-zhidao [CP [IP Lisi mai-le shenme]].
       Zhangsan wonder   Lisi bought what
       'Zhangsan wonders what Lisi bought.'

The obvious difference between (6) and (8) is that Wh-movement does not appear to have taken place in (8), just like the Japanese case that we saw in (4) above. In the S-Structure in (8), *shenme* is in the same position it's in at D-Structure. It has not moved to Spec CP.

How do we account for this difference between Chinese and English? We could say that the verb *xiang-zhidao* in Chinese is different from *wonder* in English. *Wonder* simply has a semantic requirement that *xiang-zhidao* lacks. *Wonder* requires a wh-word in its Spec CP, but *xiang-zhidao* does not.

The problem with that solution is twofold: first, it seems a little odd to say that *wonder* and *xiang-zhidao* differ to such a radical extent. Whatever precise semantic property it is which requires *wonder* to select a +wh CP is surely some part of its core meaning, which is not something that we'd expect to differ across languages. However, more concretely, the hypothesis that verbs like *xiang-zhidao* in Chinese don't select a +wh CP seems wrong when you consider how (8) contrasts with (9) and (10). (8) is a statement, (9) is a question, and (10) is ambiguous between a statement and a question:

(9)   Zhangsan yiwei Lisi mai-le shenme?
       Zhangsan think Lisi bought what
       'What does Zhangsan think that Lisi bought?'

(10)   Zhangsan jide   Lisi mai-le shenme?
       Zhangsan remember Lisi bought what
       'Zhangsan remembers what Lisi bought.' (statement meaning)
   or 'What does Zhangsan remember that Lisi bought?' (question meaning)

How can we explain the different interpretive possibilities in (8), (9), and (10)? In every case, *shenme* is in the same place. Why is (8) a statement, (9) a question and (10) ambiguous between the two?

Well, as we saw in the last chapter, we need to go beyond what we see on the surface. Notice that with respect to the three verbs in English, *wonder* requires that its CP sister is +wh, *think* requires that its CP sister is −wh, and *remember* can take either a +wh CP sister or a −wh one:

(11)a.   I wonder [what John bought].   +wh
     b.   *I wonder [that John bought a car].   −wh

(12)a. *I think [what John bought].   +wh
    b. I think [that John bought a car].   −wh

(13)a. I remember [what John bought].   +wh
    b. I remember [that John bought a car]. −wh

This looks like the key to understanding (8), (9) and (10). Let's say that *xiang-zhidao, yiwei,* and *jide* all have exactly the same semantics as English *wonder, think,* and *remember.* They *must, cannot,* and *may* select a +wh CP respectively.

Let's postulate that there's another level of representation, Logical Form, which is the input to semantic interpretation. Let's also suppose that LF is related to S-Structure via transformations, and that wh-words in Chinese move to the relevant Spec CP between S-Structure and LF, rather than between D-Structure and S-Structure. On these assumptions, it looks like we've got everything explained.

In (8), *xiang-zhidao* 'wonder' requires that a wh-word be in its sister's specifier at LF since it selects a +wh CP, so *shenme* can only move to the embedded Spec CP, resulting in the 'statement' interpretation. In (9), by contrast, *shenme* cannot move to the embedded Spec CP, as *yiwei* 'think' does not allow its sister CP to be +wh. Therefore, at LF *shenme* moves at LF to the main clause Spec CP, resulting in a wh-question interpretation for the sentence. Finally, in (10) *jide* 'remember' optionally may or may not take a +wh CP. If it does, then *shenme* must move to the embedded CP at LF, resulting in the statement interpretation. If it does not, then *shenme* moves to the matrix Spec CP, and a wh-question interpretation results. Since there is no morphological marking as to whether a given Spec CP is +wh or not, and there is no *overt* Wh-movement to Spec CP, (10) is ambiguous.

EXERCISE 1

Given the preceding discussion, would you expect the following Chinese sentence to be a statement, a question, or ambiguous?:

Zhangsan zhidao Lisi mai-le shenme
Zhangsan knows Lisi bought what

7.1.1.2 An argument from Subjacency
In addition to the argument from selection which we've just seen, there is also another kind of argument supporting the idea that Chinese wh-phrases

undergo covert movement. In the previous chapter we saw that *overt* movement was constrained by the Subjacency Condition:

(14)   *The Subjacency Condition*
       A single instance of Wh-movement can cross only one bounding node, where IP and NP are bounding nodes.

If we could show that Subjacency effects seem to obtain even when it looked like no overt movement was taking place, we'd have a strong argument that there were transformational operations going on between S-Structure and our new hypothesized level of Logical Form.
    To begin with, consider the following string of words:

(15)   Why did John say Mary had left?

(15) is actually ambiguous between two different interpretations. On one interpretation (with falling intonation), (15) is a question about why John said something. A possible answer would be 'because he thought he saw her car drive away'. On the other interpretation (with rising intonation), (15) is a question about why Mary left. A possible answer would be 'because she needed to get back home by 7 pm'.
    This ambiguity arises because the S-Structure in (15) can have either the D-Structure in (16a) or the D-Structure in (16b) as its source:

(16)a.   John said [Mary had left] why
    b.   John said [Mary had left why]

(16a) is the D-Structure associated with the 'why John said something' interpretation, since in this D-Structure *why* is a sister to, and therefore modifies, the V' *said Mary had left*. (16b) is the D-Structure associated with the 'why Mary left' interpretation, because *why* is a sister to the V' *left*.
    With this discussion in mind, consider now (17):

(17)   Why do you like the man that bought the books?

Unlike the example in (15), (17) is not ambiguous. (17) cannot be a question about why the man bought the books. It can only be a question about why you like the man. A possible answer to (17) would be 'because he seems like a nice person' (an answer to why you like the man). 'Because he needed them for work' (an answer to why the man bought the books) is not a possible response to the question posed by (17).
    The reason why the S-Structure in (17) is not ambiguous is because, unlike (15), there are not two possible D-Structure sources. This is because

the D-Structure in which *why* is a sister to the V' *bought the books* requires a Subjacency violation to move *why* to Spec CP:

(18)   *Why$_i$ do [$_{IP}$ you like [$_{DP}$ the man [$_{CP}$ t'$_i$ that bought the books t$_i$]]]?

The Wh-movement proceeds successive cyclically, but the movement from the embedded Spec CP to the matrix Spec CP crosses an NP and an IP bounding node. Since this D-Structure is not available as a source for (17), (17) cannot be a question about why the man bought the books.

On the other hand, if *why* is a sister to the V' *like [the man who bought the books]*, then no Subjacency violation occurs in moving to the matrix Spec CP:

(19)   Why$_i$ do you like [$_{DP}$ the man [$_{CP}$ who bought the books]] t$_i$?

Only a single bounding node (the matrix IP) is crossed by the movement in (19).

In this way, the string of words in (17) actually provides evidence for the Subjacency Condition, because the only interpretation possible is the one in which there is no Subjacency violation. A different interpretation for the D-Structure position of *why*, (18), which would involve a violation of Subjacency, isn't available.

With this in mind, consider the following Chinese sentences cited in Huang (1995):

(20)   *ni zui xihuan [$_{DP}$ weishenme mai shu   de   ren]?
       you most like   why   buy book Comp person
       'Why$_i$ do you like the man who bought the books t$_i$?'

Since Chinese is a language in which Wh-movement occurs at LF, rather than at S-Structure, there is not the same potential for ambiguity that we saw in (17) above. At S-Structure, the wh-word *weishenme* is in its D-Structure position, and is therefore clearly seen to be modifying the VP *bought the books*. If we assume that wh-words must move at LF to Spec CP of the matrix clause, mirroring the overt Wh-movement that we see in English, and we assume that Subjacency applies equally to LF movement as to S-Structure movement, then we can account naturally for the ungrammaticality of (20). As we expect, if we move *weishenme* to a position in which it modifies *like*, (21) becomes perfectly grammatical, with the interpretation that it's a question about why you like the man:

(21)   ni weishenme zui xihuan [$_{DP}$ mai shu   de   ren]?
       you why   most like   buy book Comp person
       'Why$_i$ do you like [the man who bought the books] t$_i$?'

7.1.1.3 C-Command in Japanese

Turning now from Chinese to Japanese, we can see another case in which overt movement (in English) and LF movement (in Japanese) seem to be subject to the same requirements.

In addition to Subjacency, there also a constraint against 'downward' movement. A moved element must always c-command its trace. To see an example, consider the S-Structure in (22):

(22)   *t_i wonder [$_{CP}$ who $_i$ [$_{IP}$ John likes Bill]]

Wonder has its usual requirement that it selects a +wh CP, but in this case we've tried to satisfy that requirement by lowering *who* from the matrix subject position to the embedded Spec CP.

Given our theory so far, it's not at all clear what's wrong with (22). Subjacency is not violated, neither is the θ-Criterion or the Case Filter. The chain {t_i, who$_i$} has both Case and a θ-role from the matrix subject position. However, under the assumption that antecedents must always c-command their traces, we can rule out the ungrammatical (22). This requirement is often referred to as the Proper Binding Condition.

For the moment, however, all we need to observe is that the Proper Binding Condition seems also to hold in cases where no overt movement takes place. This suggests that there *is* movement taking place, but that the movement isn't 'visible'. Consider the contrast in (23) (from Harada (1972), cited in Saito (1989)). *ka* is a 'scope marker', which indicates which Comp the wh-phrase is to be interpreted in:

(23)a.   John-ga [$_{CP}$ [$_{IP}$ dare-ga   sono hon-o   katta] ka]
        John-Nom   who-Nom that book-Acc bought Q
        siritagatteiru koto
        want-to-know fact
        'the fact that wants to know Q who bought that book'

   b.   *dare-ga [$_{CP}$ [$_{IP}$ John-ga   sono hon-o   katta] ka]
        who-Nom   John-Nom that book-Acc bought Q
        siritagatteiru koto
        want-to-know fact
        'the fact that who wants to know Q John bought that book'

If we assume that the wh-element *dare* undergoes movement between S-Structure and LF, the Proper Binding Condition immediately gives us an account of the contrast, as can be seen from the partial structures in (24):

(24)a.

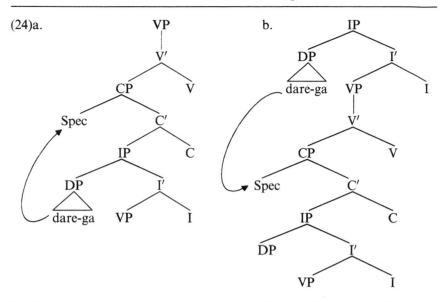

In (23a), the scope marker *ka* indicates that *dare* 'who' moves at LF *up* to a *higher* position from which it can c-command its trace. By contrast, in (23b) the scope marker indicates that *dare* is to move 'downward' at LF, to a non c-commanding position. The Proper Binding Condition would seem to explain the contrast between the two, and we therefore have more evidence for the 'reality' of covert LF movement. To the extent that proposed LF movements seem to be subject to the same constraints that apply to overt movements, we have a strong argument for their existence.

7.1.2   LF Wh-Movement in English

Having discussed LF Wh-movement in a couple of different languages, we're now in a better position to come back to English. Contrary to what we've been implying so far, English actually does have instances of LF Wh-movement. It's just that it only happens when you have *two* wh-words. In that case, only one of the wh-words moves to Spec CP, the other stays *in situ*. Consider the question in (25), focusing in on the wh-word *what*:

(25)   Who told Mary about what?

With rising intonation, (25) is interpreted as an 'echo' question, where *what* essentially means 'I didn't hear whatever words came after *about*'. (This can also be used to indicate surprise or disbelief, if *what* is heavily stressed.) However, with falling intonation, (25) is a double wh-question, where both *who* and *what* are being questioned. An expected answer would be a set consisting of pairs of people and what they told Mary about (e.g., *John told Mary about linguistics, Alice told Mary about history*, etc.).

EXERCISE 2

Assuming the 'double question' interpretation, give two answers each to the following questions:

(a) Who gave the book to John when?
(b) What did Bill put where?

It's the double wh-question interpretation which we're interested in here in (25). In order to account for the fact that it's *both* people *and* things which are being questioned, we want to say that *who* and *what* have *both* moved to Spec CP. Since we don't see any movement at S-Structure, however, it must be the case that *what* is moving at LF. (In order not to completely undermine Subjacency, though, we'll have to say that these multiply filled Spec CPs are allowable only at LF, not at S-Structure, otherwise there would be no Subjacency violations ever.)

We can see even more clearly how moving to the main clause Spec CP means that a wh-word is part of the question if we take a look at a famous example, first discussed by Baker (1970). Consider (26):

(26) Who$_i$ t$_i$ is wondering where$_j$ we bought what t$_j$?

Notice that (26) is ambiguous. Under one interpretation, it is a single question asking who the person is who is wondering something, namely where we bought what. An answer would be: 'Mary is. Mary's wondering where we bought what.' However, (26) can also be interpreted as a double question, asking for a list of people paired with objects. An answer to *that* question would be: 'Mary is wondering where we bought the car. John is wondering where we bought the violin', and so on.

If we assume that *what* is undergoing Wh-movement at LF, we get a nice explanation for this ambiguity. There are two possible Spec CPs that *what* could be moving to, and those correspond to the two possible interpretations. First, *what* could be moving at LF to the embedded Spec CP:

(27) [$_{CP}$ Who$_i$ [$_{IP}$ t$_i$ is wondering [$_{CP}$ what$_k$ where$_j$ [$_{IP}$ we bought t$_k$ t$_j$]]]?

If *what* moves at LF to the embedded CP, then the only wh-word in the matrix Spec CP is *who*. We therefore get a single question interpretation. We want to know who the person is who is wondering something. An answer is 'Mary is wondering where we bought what'.

The other possibility is that *what* is moving at LF to the matrix Spec CP:

(28) [$_{CP}$ what$_k$ who$_i$ [$_{IP}$ t$_i$ is wondering [$_{CP}$ where$_j$ [$_{IP}$ we bought t$_k$ t$_j$]]]].

If *what* moves at LF to the matrix Spec CP, then it's a question involving *who* and *what*, and we get the multiple-wh interpretation. The question we're asking has *two* elements to the answer. We want to know about pairs of (1) people and (2) things that they're wondering. Thus an expected answer is 'Mary is wondering where we bought the car. John is wondering where we bought the violin', and so on. (We'll address the potential Subjacency violation in the next section.)

In a language like Polish, we can actually see multiple Wh-movement at S-Structure. So, in Polish, all Wh-movement takes place overtly between D-Structure and S-Structure.[1] Consider the following example from Lasnik and Saito (1984):

(29)a. Zastanawiam sie *kto co*   przyniesie.
         Wonder-1sg   who what will bring
         'I wonder who will bring what.'
    b. *Zastanawiam sie *kto* przyniesie *co*.
         Wonder-1sg   who will bring what

In (29) both wh-phrases must move to Spec CP at S-Structure. This is unlike the English multiple questions which we've seen, where one wh-word moves at S-Structure and the others wait until LF.

This Polish data seems to further confirm the general theory. What we see is that all multiple wh-questions have the same structure at Logical Form, but there are variations as to the timing of Wh-movement. All Wh-movement happens overtly in Polish. In English, one wh-word moves overtly and any others move covertly, and in Chinese all wh-words move covertly.

7.1.2.1 English LF Wh-Movement and Subjacency

So far, we've seen some arguments that English does in fact have LF Wh-movement in the case of multiple wh-questions. Not only does it seem to account for the multiple-question interpretation that multiple wh-sentences can have, but also we've seen a language (Polish) where it appears as though what happens at LF in English happens at S-Structure in this language. What we now want to do, paralleling our discussion of Wh-movement in Chinese and Japanese, is to look at parallels between overt movement and LF movement. To the extent that our postulated LF movements pattern with similar overt movements, then we'll have some good evidence that movement that we don't see really is taking place.

In particular, we saw in Section 1.1.2 that we could use Subjacency as a diagnostic for LF Wh-movement in Chinese, and it turns out that we can use it again in English. As usual, the logic of the argument is that wherever we're postulating covert LF movement, we should check to see if this 'movement' obeys constraints that we know hold of overt movement.

In that context, consider (30), from Huang (1995):

(30)   *Who likes the man [who fixed the car how]?

We might expect that (30) should be a perfectly well-formed double question, asking for pairs of people and ways in which the men that they liked fixed the car. However, (30) is ungrammatical. We can explain this in the same way as we did in Section 1.1.2. We're assuming that *how* must undergo movement at LF to the matrix Spec CP, but we have again a classic 'complex DP' Subjacency configuration. *How* can't move to the matrix Spec CP without crossing an IP and a NP node, and the ungrammaticality of (30) now follows.

However, this argument must remain slightly tentative. As the eagle-eyed among you may have noticed, the claim that Subjacency constrains LF movement as well as overt movement causes problems for (26), which we looked at in the previous section:

(26)   Who is wondering where we bought what?

We said a moment ago that (26) can be interpreted as a multiple question, asking for pairs of people and things that they're wondering where we bought. Therefore *what* must be able to move to the matrix Spec CP. But, given what we've just said, that should create a Subjacency violation just like (30), since again Spec CP is blocked in precisely the same way. Movement from the position of the direct object of *buy* to Spec CP should cross two IP nodes.

Unfortunately, we'll have to leave this as an outstanding problem for the time being. In Chapter 9, when we look at constraints on movement in more detail, we'll have a way of dealing with this contrast. It'll turn out that adjuncts are subject to slightly different principles than arguments when extracted from certain kinds of Subjacency configurations. It is also possible that the ideas that we'll discuss in the 'Open Issue' section at the end of this chapter could be relevant.

7.2   QUANTIFIER RAISING: ANOTHER LF TRANSFORMATION

Now that you're getting used to the idea of covert LF movement, I want to step back for a minute and talk a little more about Logical Form as a level of representation. As we mentioned briefly in the introduction, it is assumed that the language faculty interfaces with two other systems: the articulatory–perceptual system (phonetics/phonology), and the conceptual–intensional system (semantics). This is intended to encode the traditional intuition that what's at the heart of language are sound/meaning pairs. Logical Form is the level which provides the interface between the syntax and the conceptual–intensional system. What's represented at LF are those aspects of semantic interpretation which are determined by the syntax. In this section, we're going to look at 'quantificational' DPs, and argue that they too undergo LF movement in English.

7.2.1   Introduction to Quantifiers

Quantifiers are words in a language like *every, some, all,* and *many*. The effect that they have is to create DPs which do not pick out a specific entity in the world. Rather, what these quantificational DPs do is delimit a range of possible entities and then focus in on some (quantified) part of that range.[2] This contrast can be easily seen if you compare a good, old-fashioned R-expression to a quantificational expression:

(31)a.   *John* likes The Beatles.
    b.   *Every sane person* likes The Beatles.

In (31a), a particular person in the universe of discourse is picked out, namely *John*, and it is claimed that it is true of him that he likes The Beatles. On the other hand, when I assert (31b), I'm not referring to a specific person and making a claim about him or her. Rather I'm picking out a group or range of people whoever they might be (in this case the class of people who are sane) and saying that it is true that every person who falls into that group likes The Beatles. As first argued for by the philosopher Bertrand Russell (1905), if we were to express the claim made in (31b) using logical notation, we would express it using the following formula:

(32)   ($\forall$x: x is a sane person) (x likes The Beatles)

(32) is read 'for every x, x a sane person, x likes The Beatles'.
    Notice that quantifiers seem to have a lot in common with wh-words and phrases. wh-words/phrases are also DPs which don't pick out specific entities, but rather draw our attention to groups or ranges of entities. And they have the same logical structure in (32). Consider the S-Structure in (33):

(33)   [Which eighties pop group]$_i$ does John admire t$_i$?

Just as with quantifiers, there's no specific eighties pop group which is being referred to by the wh-phrase. Rather, what the wh-word does is identify a range of things (eighties pop groups) and asks which one within that range is the one such that John admires it:

(34) (which x: x is an eighties pop group) (John admires x)

In fact, it's commonly assumed that wh-words consist of an interrogative feature together with a quantifier like *some*.

We'll use the term *operator-variable structures* to refer to structures like (32) and (34). The *operator* portion expresses the range and what subpart of it we're dealing with (whether it's every member of the range, most members of the range, some member(s) of the range, etc.). The *variable* portion tells us where in the corresponding sentence we would plug in the individual member of the range to see if the sentence is true or false. So, for example, assuming that the range of sane people is {Maria, Erich, John}, when I assert something like *every sane person likes the Beatles*, I'm saying that if you plug Maria, Erich, and John in place of the x, the sentences *Maria likes the Beatles*, *Erich likes the Beatles*, and *John likes the Beatles* will all be true. In (32) and (34), the operators are the quantifier and the wh-phrase respectively. The variable in both cases is the trace.

However, quantifiers and wh-words differ in that, in the case of wh-words, their operator-variable structure is represented in the syntax, at least in English. The wh-word/phrase, which corresponds to the operator part, moves to Spec CP. This operation leaves behind a trace, which corresponds to the variable part. As we saw in Section 7.1, languages which don't have overt Wh-movement like Chinese and Japanese still have covert Wh-movement at LF . Therefore, at the level of Logical Form, the operator-variable structure of wh-questions is always represented.

This is not too surprising, though, when you think about it. The level of Logical Form is the interface with the conceptual-intensional systems, which contain things like semantics and real-world knowledge. Presumably the operator-variable nature of questions is the same in all languages.

But if quantifiers also have operator-variable structure, then we might expect that this would also be represented at LF. Unlike wh-questions, though, we don't have any overt movement of the quantifier in English. It remains in its D-Structure position (or S-Structure position if it's undergone Raising or Passive). However, the operator-variable structure could still be represented at LF if quantifiers, in fact, undergo a process of Quantifier Raising (QR). This gives us a type of conceptual argument for saying that there should be a transformation in the LF component which targets quantifiers.

7.2.2 The Landing Site of QR and 'Scope'

If quantifiers undergo movement at Logical Form, we need to know what the landing site for the movement is. What is generally assumed is that QR 'adjoins' the quantifier to IP, so that the S-Structure in (35) has the LF in (36):

(35) [CP [IP John likes everyone]].

(36)

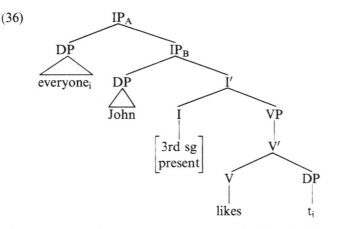

The process of adjunction targets the maximal projection and 'splits' it into two *segments*. IP_A and IP_B in (36) are *not* two maximal projections. They together count as only one. We therefore have no violation of X'-Theory, as there is still one head and one maximal projection. (The process of *Topicalization*, which we mentioned back in Chapter 2, is a transformation in the overt syntax which also adjoins an element to IP.)

A traditional idea, which will be particularly important in the next section, is that quantifiers have *scope*. In other words, they have a domain in which they have effects. Within our system, the scope of a quantifier is its c-command domain at LF. Therefore, the scope of the quantifier *everyone* in (35) is everything dominated by IP_B. If quantifier A c-commands quantifier B at LF, quantifier A is said to have *wide* scope relative to quantifier B. Quantifier B on the other hand is said to have *narrow scope* relative to quantifier A.

EXERCISE 3

Draw the tree for the LF representation of

(a) **Everyone saw Bill,**
(b) **John gave the book to every student.**

7.2.3 Scope Ambiguities and QR

We've seen in the previous section that quantificational DPs seem to undergo a process of Quantifier Raising which adjoins them to IP. This process happens in the LF component in many languages, including English, but can be seen overtly in languages like Polish and Hungarian.

However, we've only seen cases involving one quantifier so far. When there are two (or more) quantifiers in a clause, they can interact in interesting ways to create what's known as *scope ambiguity*. By way of illustration, consider (37):

(37)   Every politician avoided some journalist.

(For some speakers, (37) is more natural with *some* replaced by the indefinite article *a*, which can also function as a quantifier.) Notice that there are two quite different situations under which (37) could be true. First, it could be the case that for every politician, there was some journalist or other that he/ she avoided (a different journalist for every politician). However, (37) is also true if there's one specific journalist and every politician avoided him/her. To make this a bit clearer, look at the following diagrams which each illustrate one of the readings:

(38a)   Politician #1 → Journalist #1   (38b)   Politician #1
        Politician #2 → Journalist #2   Politician #2
        Politician #3 → Journalist #3   Politician #3 → Journalist #1
        Politician #4 → Journalist #4   Politician #4
        Politician #5 → Journalist #5   Politician #5
        and so on   and so on

Interpretation (38a) is referred to as the reading in which *every* has wide scope relative to *some* (for every politician x, there is some journalist y such that x avoided y). Interpretation (38b) is referred to as the reading in which *some* has wide scope relative to *every* (there is some journalist y, such that for every politician x, x avoided y).

Taking the scope of a quantifier to be its c-command domain at LF, and assuming that we can apply QR to the quantified expressions in either order, we can explain the interpretational ambiguity of sentences like (37).

Let's start by looking at the S-Structure for (37):

(39)   [$_{CP}$ [$_{IP}$ every politician$_i$ [$_{VP}$ avoided some journalist$_j$]]]

We know that both quantified phrases *every politician* and *some journalist* must undergo QR at LF because one of the main functions of LFs is to represent quantifier scope. If we apply QR to *some journalist* first, we get (40):

(40)   [$_{CP}$ [$_{IPA}$ some journalist$_j$ [$_{IPB}$ every politician$_i$ [$_{VP}$ avoided t$_j$]]]]

We then QR *every politician*, giving us (41) (which I've done as a tree to make it easier to see):

(41)

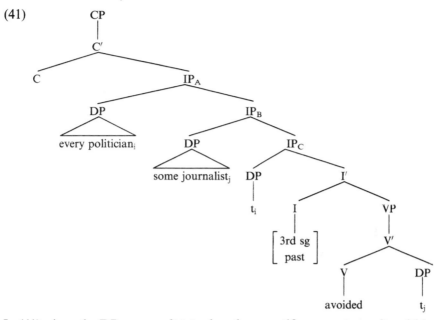

In (41), since the DP *every politician* has the quantifier *some journalist* within its scope at LF, we can encode the fact that *every politician* is interpreted as having wider scope than *some journalist*, resulting in interpretation (38a).

(42)

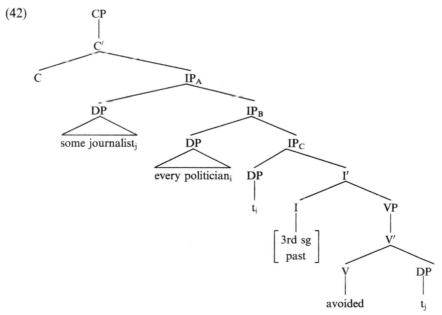

If, on the other hand, QR applies to *every politician* first and then to *some journalist*, the LF representation in (42) will result (see page 185). This corresponds to the interpretation in which there is some journalist such that every politician avoided him/her.

EXERCISE 4

Discuss the scope ambiguities present in the following sentences:

(a)   Some student leaves home every day,
(b)   John showed three books to every customer.

7.2.4   Quantifier Raising and Constraints on Movement

Now that we've talked a little bit about quantifiers and how Quantifier Raising works, and given some conceptual arguments for the LF movement of quantifiers, it's time to turn to the arguments based on constraints on movement. As with LF Wh-movement in Section 7.1, if we can show that QR obeys the same constraints that overt A′-movement shows, we'll have a strong argument that covert A′-movement is in fact taking place.

7.2.4.1   Quantifier Raising and Subjacency

As with LF Wh-movement in the previous section, our first instinct should be to check Subjacency. If QR looks like it's subject to Subjacency, we'll have a good argument that movement is really taking place, even if we don't 'see' it. Unfortunately, the facts about Subjacency and QR are ultimately inconclusive for independent reasons. I want to discuss the issue, though, as an example of how you can get a seemingly 'negative' result which *isn't* a problem.

The core of the problem is that Subjacency constrains 'long-distance' movement, but QR can't move quantifiers in a 'long-distance' fashion. QR can adjoin them to the closest IP which dominates them, but can go no higher. Consider (43):

(43)   [$_{IPA}$ some student thinks that [$_{IPB}$ John saw every band]]

If *some student* adjoins to IP$_A$ and *every band* adjoins to IP$_B$, we have the LF in (44):

(44)   [$_{IPA}$ some student$_i$ [$_{IPA}$ t$_i$ thinks that [$_{IPB}$ every band$_j$ [$_{IPB}$ John saw t$_j$]]]]

Some student c-commands *every band*. Therefore *some student* has wide scope relative to *every band* and the interpretation is that there is a single student who thinks that John saw every band. If, on the other hand, *every band* could adjoin to the higher IP, IP$_A$, we should be able to generate the LF in (45):

(45)   [$_{IPA}$ every band$_j$ [$_{IPA}$ some student$_i$ [$_{IPA}$ t$_i$ thinks that [$_{IPB}$ John saw t$_j$]]]]

But this LF, in which *every band* has wide scope relative to *some student*, is interpreted as meaning that there is a multiplicity of students and bands. For every band, there is some student who thinks that John saw them: Mary thinks John saw Guided by Voices, Bill thinks that John saw Baby Ray, and so on.

But (43) is not ambiguous between these two readings. *Some* can have wide scope relative to *every*, but not vice versa. There can only be a single student who has some thought, namely that John saw every band. There can't be a multiplicity of students, who each think that John saw a different band.

Notice that we can't use the impossibility of the reading represented by (45) as an argument for QR. There's no Subjacency problem there. IP_B is crossed but not IP_A since all the 'segments' of IP_A don't dominate the landing site. It just seems to be the case that, for whatever reason, quantifiers must adjoin to the closest IP and go no further. Therefore, we can't use Subjacency to argue for LF movement of quantifiers. It simply turns out not to be relevant.

7.2.4.2   Inverse Linking and C-Command

Although we have problems with Subjacency, we can now turn to a phenomenon called 'inverse linking', originally discussed by May (1977) and one of the most persuasive arguments I know for QR, and for the idea of LF (covert) transformations as a whole. It's essentially the Proper Binding Condition from Section 7.1.1.3. The traces that would be left behind if you assumed covert QR was taking place look like they need to be c-commanded by the QRed element, just like the traces of overt movement. This suggests that movement really is taking place.

In Section 7.2.3, we saw how two quantifiers can create ambiguity, depending on which one undergoes QR first (and thus has narrow scope). With that discussion in mind, consider the following sentence, which also has two quantifiers:

(46)   Every man in some Italian city likes opera.

Before Continuing: What scope relations are possible in (46)? Is (46) ambiguous?

Taking the discussion in the previous section, we might expect that (46) should have two possible readings, just like the other cases we saw with two quantifiers, since QR can apply to either one of the quantifiers first. (There's only one IP, and so we don't have the problems that we saw with example (43) in the previous section.) If *every* has wide scope with respect to *some*, then (46) should mean that for every man who loves opera, there is some Italian city in which he resides. Alternatively, if *some* has wider scope, then (46) should mean that there is some single Italian city such that every man in that city likes opera. These two readings are represented graphically in (47) and (48).

(47)   Man #1 → City #1
       Man #2 → City #2
       Man #3 → City #3
       Man #4 → City #4
       Man #5 → City #5
       and so on

       every > some

(48)   Man #1
       Man #2
       Man #3 → City #1
       Man #4
       Man #5
       and so on

       some > every

Interpreting sentences with multiple quantifiers is a notoriously difficult thing to do, but if you're having particular difficulty getting the reading in (47), in which *every* has wider scope than *some*, there's a reason. Unlike the cases in (37) that we saw in the previous section, (46) has two quantifiers but is **not** ambiguous! The only reading possible for (46) is the one in which *some* has wider scope than *every*. (46) can only mean that there is some specific Italian city and every man in that city likes opera. This is really quite surprising. What could it be that allows two quantifiers to interact to create ambiguity in (37) but not in (46), when one quantified expression is contained within another?

May suggested that an answer could be found by looking at what the two readings would look like if we assumed that Quantifier Raising was taking place in the LF component. Let's first take a look at the reading in which *some* has wide scope – the permitted reading. Since the last quantifier to undergo QR is the one which has the widest scope, we want to begin by targeting the DP which is headed by *every*. That DP is the DP *every man in some Italian city*. Applying QR to that DP gives us the representation in (49):

(49)

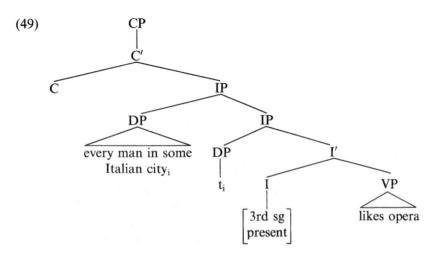

We then QR the DP *some Italian city* resulting in the LF representation in (50):

(50)

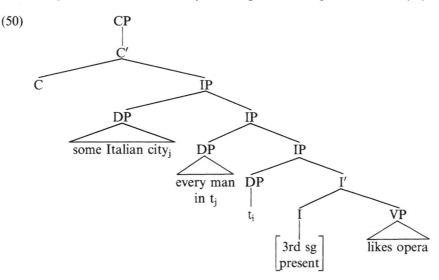

However, let's take a look at what happens if we try to derive the impossible reading – the one in which *every* has wider scope than *some*. First we QR *some Italian city* from within the subject DP and then the DP *every man in t*, resulting in the representation in (51):

(51)

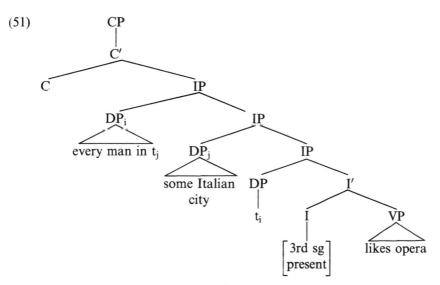

Notice now what's happened in the course of the derivation. When we QRed *every man in t*, it took the trace of *some Italian city* with it. This has the result that the DP *some Italian city* now no longer c-commands its trace.

But we saw in Section 7.1.1.3 that covert LF movement is constrained by the Proper Binding Condition; that is, traces of LF movement, just like traces of overt movement, must be c-commanded by their antecedents. That was one of the arguments we gave for saying that a LF Wh-movement was taking place in Japanese. And we can use it again here. Even though there are two quantifiers in (46), there aren't two possibilities for applying QR. If we QR *every man in some Italian city* followed by *some Italian city*, nothing goes wrong. Therefore, as predicted, the wide scope reading of *every* is available in (46). On the other hand, to QR *some Italian city* followed by *every man in t* would violate a general principle which we know to hold of transformations – The Proper Binding Condition. We therefore can't apply QR in that order, and we correctly predict that (46) cannot be interpreted with *some* having wider scope than *every*.

7.2.4.3 QR and Weak Crossover

A final area that we'll look at is the behavior of quantifiers in what are called 'weak crossover' configurations. It has long been noted that pronouns cannot have a 'bound-variable' interpretation after certain kinds of Wh-movement have taken place. The interesting thing for our purposes turns out to be that quantifiers also can prohibit pronouns from taking on this bound-variable interpretation, even though no movement *appears* to be taking place. However, if there really is movement, in the form of Quantifier Raising at LF, then everything is explained.

But first, what exactly does it mean for a pronoun to have a 'bound-variable' interpretation? How is this different from a pronoun's normal interpretation? The easiest thing to do is take a sentence where this bound-variable interpretation is possible, but not necessary, and compare the two interpretations. Consider a sentence like (52):

(52)   Who$_i$ t$_i$ thinks that he$_{i/j}$ is smart?

The most natural interpretation for the pronoun in (52) is one in which it has index 'i', referring to the same person as the wh-word. This interpretation, where the pronoun refers back to a wh-phrase, is called the *bound-variable* interpretation. The pronoun is in effect acting as a second variable in addition to the wh-trace, both of them being bound by the operator *who*. Under the bound variable interpretation, (52) means something like 'who is the person that thinks that he or she is smart?' or, slightly awkwardly, 'who thinks himself smart?'. A possible answer would be 'John thinks that he is smart', meaning 'John thinks that John is smart'. The pronoun, unlike normal, does not refer to a specific person, but instead varies over the same individuals that the wh-phrase does.

In fact, the use of 'inclusive' or 'non-sexist' language can sometimes aid in bringing out the bound-variable interpretation. Masculine pronouns such as *he* or *his* are sometimes replaced by both masculine and feminine pronouns *he/she* or *his/her* when the actual gender of the person is not known or irrelevant. For example (53):

(53)   As for the new employee, his/her duties will include ...

In the context of a wh-word, this use of 'non-sexist' language can force the bound variable interpretation. In rewriting (52) as (54), it makes it clearer that the bound-variable interpretation is intended[3]:

(54)   Who$_i$ t$_i$ thinks that he/she$_i$ is smart?

By contrast, if the pronoun has index 'j', and is therefore not coindexed with the wh-word, then the pronoun is not acting as a bound variable. It instead refers to some unspecified other person. For example, say we've been talking about our friend John, I could produce (55):

(55)   Who$_i$ t$_i$ thinks that he$_j$ is smart?

In this case, the pronoun *he* is not acting as a bound variable and simply refers to *John*. A possible answer to the question in (55) might be '*Bob* thinks that he (i.e., John) is smart'.

Having explained what 'bound variables' are, we now need to explain what 'weak crossover' is. So-called 'weak crossover' configurations are illustrated by sentences like (56):

(56)   *Who$_i$ does [his$_i$ mother] like t$_i$?

The configuration is a 'crossover' configuration because the wh-word has 'crossed over' the pronoun in moving from its D-Structure position to the matrix Spec CP. It's a 'weak' crossover configuration because the pronoun does not c-command the wh-trace at S-Structure. (There are also 'strong crossover' configurations, in which the pronoun *does* c-command the wh-trace.)

The thing to notice about weak crossover configurations (and strong ones too, actually) is that the pronoun in (56) *cannot* act as a bound variable, coindexed with the wh-word *who*. If it did, it would mean 'who is the person x, such that x's mother likes x?'. In other words, it would be the same question as (57):

(57)   [Whose mother]$_i$ t$_i$ likes him$_i$?

But (56) can't mean what (57) means. In (56) *his* must have a different index from *who*, meaning we've been talking about our friend John, and I'm asking 'who does his [i.e., John's] mother like?'.

Compare the question in (56) with the following question:

(58)   Who$_i$ t$_i$ likes his$_i$ mother?

Here, the bound-variable interpretation for the pronoun *is* possible. (58) can be put as 'who likes his own mother?'. This is because in (58), the wh-word does not 'cross over' the pronoun in moving to Spec CP, and so the bound-variable interpretation for the pronoun is perfectly possible.

If we use our 'inclusive language' test, we can see the difference between (56) and (58):

(59)a.   ??Who does his/her mother like?
   b.   Who likes his/her mother?

The contrast between (59a) and (60) is clear. The strangeness of (59a) comes from the fact that (59a) represents a 'weak crossover' configuration, in which the bound-variable interpretation is prohibited. However, by using *his/her* we're trying to *force* a bound-variable interpretation. In (59b), on the other hand, does not represent a potential crossover configuration. There is therefore no such strangeness when you try to force a bound-variable interpretation.

Now let's take what we've seen about crossover configurations with respect to Wh-movement and see what happens when we replace the wh-word with a quantifier. Consider first (60):

(60)   Everyone$_i$ loves his$_i$ mother.

Here there's no problem with a bound-variable interpretation for the pronoun. (60) can perfectly well mean 'for every x, x loves x's mother', and, in fact, that's the most natural interpretation of the sentence (although, of course, as always a non-bound-variable interpretation is possible as well).

Compare (60) with (61), though, and you see something interesting:

(61)   *His$_i$ mother loves everyone$_i$.

In (61), the pronoun seems unable to act as a bound variable. (61) can't mean something like 'for every x, x's mother loves x', making (61) synonymous with (60). Why should this be? It can't be that there's a general prohibition on pronouns acting as bound variables with things to their left, as (62) shows (from Reinhart (1983: 129)):

(62)a.   Near his$_i$ child's crib nobody$_i$ would keep matches.
   b.   For his$_i$ birthday, each of the employees$_i$ got a Mercedes.

However, if we assume that *everyone* undergoes Quantifier Raising, then in (61) we'll have a weak crossover configuration at LF:

(63)   [$_{IP}$ everyone$_i$ [$_{IP}$ his$_i$ mother loves t$_i$]]

Therefore, under the assumption that *everyone* undergoes QR, we can explain why the bound-variable interpretation is impossible in (61). Again, the 'inclusive language' test also gets the same results as it did with Wh-movement:

(64)a.   Everyone loves his/her mother.
   b.   ??His/her mother loves everyone.

Although we haven't really specified what it is about weak crossover configurations that interferes with a bound-variable interpretation (unlike strong crossover, which we'll see in the next chapter is due to Principle C of the Binding Theory), what we do see is quantifiers patterning with wh-words. It seems not only that quantifiers semantically function as operators, but also that the operator-variable structure of quantifiers is ultimately syntactically represented at LF.

7.3   LF A-MOVEMENT: EXPLETIVE REPLACEMENT

So far, we've seen various examples of LF A'-movement. The landing sites of the movements have all been places like Spec CP or adjoined to IP. These are A'-positions – not positions to which a grammatical function like subject or object is assigned. However, there's nothing in principle that says that LF movement is restricted to A'-movement, and in this section we'll examine expletive replacement, which is an instance of LF movement to an A-position – specifically, subject position.

One of the distinctive features of expletive *there* constructions in English is that the verb shows subject-verb agreement with the 'associate' of the expletive (as it's called) rather than the expletive itself:

(65)a.   *There is two people in the garden.
   b.   There are two people in the garden.

This is a fairly straightforward challenge to what we've seen so far about agreement.[4] *There* is occupying the Spec IP position, and if agreement always takes place in a specifier-head relationship at S-Structure, it's unclear how to handle this situation. Clearly *two people* is not in the requisite specifier-head relationship with the verb. How can we handle this situation?

Well, the title of this section probably gives the answer away. It looks as though we can kill two birds with one stone if we assume that *two people* moves to subject position and replaces the expletive. Since this movement is obviously something that you don't 'see', then it must be happening between S-Structure and LF. We can then say that although subject-verb agreement is present at S-Structure, it actually represents the LF configuration. It is whatever's in the specifier of IP *at LF* that the verb is actually agreeing with. If we examine the LF representation of (65b) under this expletive replacement assumption, we have:

(66)   Two people$_i$ are [$_{PP}$ t$_i$ in the garden].

All we've got to worry about is the chain {two people, t}, and it will have Case (from the subject position) and a θ-role (from its D-Structure position). Again, if subject-verb agreement is determined by the LF representation, there will be no problems there either.

7.3.1   Expletive Replacement and Constraints on Movement

As always, the next question is whether or not we can dig up any independent evidence for the expletive replacement hypothesis just presented, apart from the fact that it seems to provide a nice solution to several potentially thorny problems. Well, just as we saw with the other instances of LF movement that we've discussed, expletive replacement also seems to share a lot of properties with overt movement. To begin with, notice that sentences in which you have expletive/associate relationships alternate with configurations in which overt A-movement takes place:

(67)a.   There have been six records broken. [Passive]
    b.   Six records$_i$ have been broken t$_i$.

(68)a.   There seems to be a man in the garden. [Raising]
    b.   A man$_i$ seems t$_i$ to be in the garden.

However, we can make an even stronger argument by checking configurations in which overt A-movement *isn't* possible, and seeing whether an expletive associate relationship is possible. For example, as (68b) illustrates, Raising is possible when the embedded clause is infinitival. However, Raising is not possible when the embedded clause is tensed:

(69)   *A man$_i$ seems that t$_i$ is in the garden.

We'll see exactly what's wrong with (69) in the next chapter. However, the thing to notice about the configuration in (69) is that an expletive-associate relationship is also impossible.

(70)   *There seems that a man is in the garden.

Chomsky (1995:156–7) points out a number of other configurations in which both overt movement and expletive-associate relationships are disallowed.

(71)a. *A man$_i$ seems that John saw t$_i$.
   b. *There seems that John saw a man.

(72)a. *A man$_i$ was thought that pictures of t$_i$ were on sale.
   b. *There were thought that pictures of a man were on sale.

We'll see in more detail in the next chapter exactly why these configurations should be ungrammatical. For the moment, it is enough to notice that these examples suggest that whatever principles are constraining overt movement are also constraining expletive-associate relationships. That's a good indication that there really is movement happening in (70) even though it's covert rather than overt.

7.4 SUMMARY

In this chapter, we've taken the ideas from the previous chapter and gone one step further. Not only are there levels of representation that you don't 'see', like D-Structure, but there are also transformations that you don't 'see' – those that happen between S-Structure and Logical Form. As a result, the computational system of the language faculty now looks like this:

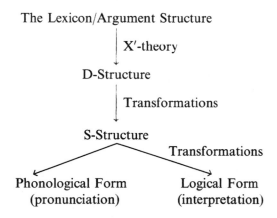

Figure 7.1 The computational system of the language faculty.

Every example and argument in this chapter has served to motivate and defend this claim about the existence of covert, post S-Structure movement. In Section 7.1, we looked at the question of Wh-movement, and suggested that both in Japanese and in English, there were wh-words which appeared *in situ*, that is in their D-Structure position, but which moved to Spec CP at LF. In Section 7.2, we made the same claim about quantificational DPs in English. In Section 7.3, we looked at structures of the *there ... DP* form and argued that the DP raised at LF and replaced to the expletive.

What I hope to have convinced you of is that just because these transformations happen covertly doesn't mean that we can't find evidence for them. On the one hand, we saw a couple of instances where it looked as though transformations we were postulating at LF actually take place overtly in some languages. If semantically identical sentences in different languages are *structurally* identical at LF, then seeing a transformation which happens overtly *could* be evidence that it's happening at LF in another language where you don't 'see' anything. However, we also looked at evidence which to my mind is a little stronger. If the 'Y' model of grammar is right, and transformations are the same whether they happen between D-Structure and S-Structure or between S-Structure and LF, then they should be subject to the same constraints, like Subjacency, or the Proper Binding Condition. To the extent that we find proposed LF movements patterning identically with their overt counterparts, we have strong evidence that the same thing is at work.

OPEN ISSUE: 'SUPERIORITY' AND DISCOURSE-LINKING

Chomsky (1973) observed something which he called 'superiority' effects, which occur in multiple wh-constructions in English. A typical example is seen in the contrast in (73):[5]

(73)a.　　Who$_i$ t$_i$ bought what?
　　b.　　*What$_i$ did who buy t$_i$?

Descriptively, when you have two wh-phrases either of which could move to Spec CP, it is the higher-up or 'superior' one which must move. Various people at more or less the same time (including Jaeggli (1982), Aoun, Hornstein and Sportiche (1981), and Chomsky (1981)) claimed that superiority effects provided another argument that there was LF Wh-movement taking place in English multiple wh-constructions, which was the conclusion we were arguing for in Section 1 above. We'll consider their arguments in detail in Chapter 9.

However, Pesetsky (1987), citing observations by Chomsky and by Richard Kayne, notes that we don't see the superiority effects we'd expect when we turn from wh-words like *who* and *what* to lexical wh-phrases like *which book*. There are also some unexpected instances in Japanese where we don't see the Subjacency effects that we should.

To start off, Pesetsky considers the following contrast:

(74)a. Which man$_i$ did you persuade t$_i$ to read which book?
  b. Which book$_i$ did you persuade which man to read t$_i$?

Descriptively, (74b) seems to resemble the superiority configuration that we saw in (73b) above. However, while we had a contrast in (73), there's no contrast in (74). Why is that?

The problem is compounded by (75):

(75) Which man knows where which woman will live?

This looks like a real problem. (75) displays exactly the same ambiguity that we saw in (26) in Section 7.1.2 above. (75) can be interpreted either as a single question or as a double question. In the first case, there is only the one man whose identity is in question and the sentence is essentially synonymous with (76):

(76) Which man knows where each woman will live?

In the second interpretation of (75), there is a set of man–woman pairs that we need to find out about, with each man knowing where a different woman will live.

Just as we did when we talked about (26), that would seem to indicate that movement is really taking place, with the ambiguity residing in whether the movement is to the embedded Spec CP (single question) or the matrix Spec CP (double question). However, notice that *which woman* is not in a position from which overt movement is possible.

(77) *Who$_i$ does John know where t$_i$ will live?

We seem to have a contradiction. We want, on the one hand, to say that *which woman* does undergo LF movement because of the ambiguity (and because that's the general position that we've been arguing for in this chapter). On the other hand, (77) makes it look like we want to say that *which woman* doesn't undergo movement, since the leading idea is that movement is movement, whether it happens at S-Structure or at LF, and the same constraints should apply. Therefore (77) and (75) should be the same.

We could just stipulate things, and say that there's something different about wh-phrases. However, there's also a problem first noted by Lasnik and Saito (1984) concerning an absence of Subjacency effects in Japanese. Consider (78a) and its English translation in (78b):

(78)a. Mary-wa [$_{DP}$ [$_{CP}$ John-ni nani-o   ageta] hito-ni] atta-no?
    Mary-Top   John-Dat what-Acc gave   man-Dat met-Q
  b. *What$_i$ did Mary meet [$_{DP}$ the man [$_{CP}$ who gave t$_i$ to John]]?

The movement crosses two bounding nodes, NP and the embedded IP, and the result should be ungrammaticality. Unfortunately, we only see the ungrammaticality in English, not in Japanese.

There are various possible approaches to this problem. The standard one is that of Lasnik and Saito (1984, 1992), who say that Subjacency simply doesn't hold of LF movement, only of S-Structure movement. Notice that this would be a real problem for us, though. Many of our arguments for LF movement have assumed that Subjacency *does* constrain LF movement. Empirically, there's good evidence that it does. And conceptually, being able to say that all movement is the same, no matter where it happens, is also something we'd like to hang on to if we can.

Fortunately, Pesetsky (1987) has an approach which doesn't require saying that LF movement is any different from S-Structure movement. Instead, Pesetsky suggests that the difference is between two kinds of wh-words/phrases which appear *in situ*, and that this will address both the problem presented by (74)/(75) and (78). Pesetsky claims that some *in situ* wh-phrases are 'discourse-linked' (or 'D-linked') and others are not. *Which*-phrases are normally D-linked. That is to say, by using a *which*-question, the speaker is implying that there is some set of possible answers/objects which the speaker and the hearer (implicitly) share or have in mind. Thus, a question like *which band does John like?* is very odd without any context or background. One would expect that if that question were asked that there would have been a previous discourse about music or bands. On the other hand, 'pure' wh-words such as *who* or *what* are normally not D-linked. A question such as *what does John like?* does not contain any presupposition of sets or previous discussion, and would be a perfectly appropriate way to open a new topic of conversation, for example.

The core of Pesetsky's suggestion is that non-D-linked wh-phrases have their scope decided by moving to a particular Spec CP at LF, which is what we've been assuming so far for all wh-phrases. On the other hand, those which are D-linked have their scope assigned by simple coindexation. Essentially what happens is that the +wh feature that's present in either the matrix or embedded CP has an index, like the ones we used for Binding Theory. All wh-words also have an index, and they're interpreted as being in whichever CP corresponds to the index they have. The crucial difference is that there's no actual movement of the wh-word under this indexation route.

This would explain all of the facts that we've seen so far. The reason why *which woman* in (75) is able to appear in a position from which movement isn't normally possible is that, being D-linked, it doesn't actually move at all. If the wh-word *nani* in the Japanese example (78) can also be shown to be D-linked, then we predict that it should not move and the lack of a Subjacency violation is expected. This is a potentially very interesting hypothesis, allowing us to retain the claim that all movement no matter where it happens is constrained by the same principles.

As Pesetsky observes, one way we could argue for this approach would be to take a normally D-linked wh-phrase and find a way to 'un-D-link' it somehow. If we could do this, we'd expect that it should then undergo movement and be subject to the constraints on movement that we've seen. Pesetsky suggests that phrases such as 'what the hell' or 'what on Earth' are ways to create an explicitly non-D-linked wh-element. In a question like *what the hell/what on Earth did you read that in?*, the point is to emphasize the surprise and imply a lack of connection to the previous discourse. *What the hell* can be also used colloquially as in (79), creating a wh-phrase which is, in Pesetsky's terms, 'aggressively non-D-linked':[6]

(79)   What the hell book did you read that in?!?!

Interestingly, Japanese appears to have something which corresponds to *the hell* in English:

(80)   Mary-wa John-ni ittai   nani-o   ageta-no?
       Mary-Top John-Dat the hell what-Acc gave-Q
       'What the hell did Mary give to John?'

Now if we were to go back and look at (78a) again, and this time use *ittai* to force a non-D-linked interpretation, we would predict that Subjacency effects would re-emerge, since the aggressively non-D-linked wh-phrase should undergo movement at LF. This seems to be the case:

(81)   *Mary-wa [DP [CP John-ni ittai   nani-o   ageta]
        Mary-Top   John-Dat the hell what-Acc gave
        hito-ni] atta-no?
        man-Dat met-Q
        'What the hell did Mary meet the man who gave to John?'

It's not that you can't use *ittai* in embedded clauses or something. (82), which isn't a Subjacency configuration, is perfect:

(82)   Mary-wa [CP John-ga ittai   nani-o   yonda to] itta-no?
       Mary-Top   John-Nom the hell what-Acc read that   said-Q
       'What the hell did Mary say that John read?'

So it looks like there might be way in which we can maintain our assumption that S-Structure and LF movement both obey Subjacency, but still account for the lack of superiority effects in English that we saw in (74) and the lack of Subjacency effects in Japanese. It's not that there's any difference between S-Structure and LF movement. It's just that D-linked wh-phrases don't undergo movement.

BIBLIOGRAPHY

Although the idea of Logical Form had been around in linguistics previously, the first systematic discussion of some of the ideas we've seen in this chapter is Robert May's (1977) dissertation, which was finally made more widely available in 1990. (It had originally been distributed only by the Indiana University Linguistics Club.) May was the first, for example, to propose and investigate Quantifier Raising as a transformation on a par with other overt movement. The idea that Wh-movement is taking place between S-Structure and LF has been most thoroughly explored by James Huang since his dissertation in 1982. He has a good overview/summary in the Logical Form chapter of Webelhuth (1995a). Also, most Chomskyian syntax textbooks have discussion of Logical Form and the ideas that we've been talking about. I particularly recommend Lasnik and Uriagereka (1988), but there's also good material in Haegeman (1994). There are also two books called simply *Logical Form* – one by May (1985) and one by Hornstein (1995). They've both got some interesting arguments, but can be a little difficult. I wouldn't recommend looking at them directly until after Chapter 9.

ANSWERS TO IN-TEXT EXERCISES

Exercise 1

Given the preceding discussion, would you expect the following Chinese sentence to be a statement, a question, or ambiguous:

Zhangsan zhidao Lisi mai-le shenme
Zhangsan knows Lisi bought what

Since we're operating under the assumption that the semantics of *know* and 'zhidao' are identical, we should see whether *know* requires, does not permit, or allows its sister to be a +wh CP in English. Depending on which of these is true, we would expect the sentence to be a statement, a question, or ambiguous in Chinese, respectively.

(a)   John knows [what Bill bought]   +wh
(b)   John knows [that Bill bought a car]   −wh

Since *know* appears to allow either a +wh CP or a −wh CP as its sister, *shenme* will move to either the embedded CP or the matrix Spec CP as appropriate. *Know* is therefore similar to *remember*, and we predict that the sentence in Chinese should be ambiguous between a statement and a question.

Exercise 2

Assuming the 'double question' interpretation, give two answers each to the following questions:

(a) Who gave the book to John when?
(b) What did Bill put where?

Under the 'double question' interpretation, (a) is asking for pairs of people and the times when they gave John the book. Two appropriate answers would be 'Bill gave the book to John yesterday' and 'Mary gave the book to John three days ago'. Example (b) is asking for pairs of things and locations where Bill put them. Two appropriate answers would therefore be 'Bill put the money in the drawer' and 'Bill put the keys on the tray'.

Exercise 3

Draw the tree for the LF representation of

(a) Everyone saw Bill,
(b) John gave the book to every student.

(a)

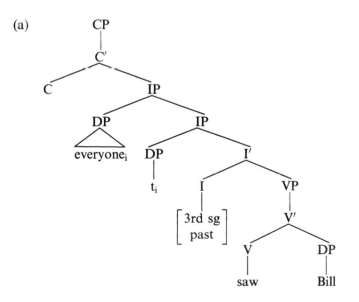

(b)

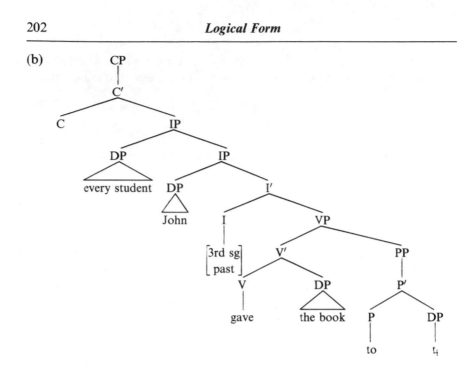

Exercise 4

Discuss the scope ambiguities present in the following sentences:

(a)   Some student leaves home every day,
(b)   John showed three books to every customer.

In the (a) sentence, either *some student* or *every day* may have wide scope relative to the other, creating a scope ambiguity. If *some student* has wide scope relative to *every day*, then the interpretation of the sentence is that there exists a single student who leaves home every day. If, on the other hand, *every day* has wide scope, then the sentence is interpreted as meaning that during every day there is some student or other who leaves home. In the (b) sentence, we see an ambiguity between the numeral quantifier phrase *three books* and the universal quantifier *every customer*. If *three books* has wide scope, then there are three specific books which John showed to every customer. If *every customer* has wide scope, then for every customer, John showed three books to them, and they need not be the same three each time.

ADDITIONAL EXERCISES

Exercise 1

Draw the LF representation for the following sentences:

1. Everyone left yesterday.
2. John said that Bill believed some politician.
3. Zhangsan xiangzin [shei mai-le shu]?   [Chinese]
    Zhangsan believe   who bought book
    'Who does Zhangsan believe bought books?' ˙

Exercise 2
As we mentioned in passing in this chapter, the indefinite article *a(n)* can also serve as an existential quantifier like *some*. Show that this is the case by constructing an argument using scope ambiguity like the one in Section 7.2.3.

Exercise 3
Consider the following sentences:

1. Some student whispered that Bill read every book.
2. Some student believed that Bill read every book.

What are the relative scope possibilities for *some* and *every* in (1) and (2)? Does either one create a problem for our theory?

Exercise 4
Under the assumption that a pronoun must be c-commanded by an operator in order to serve as a bound variable, the following sentences can be used to argue for the existence of QR. How?

1. A report card about every student$_i$ was sent to his$_i$ parents.
2. *The woman who loved every man$_i$ decided to leave him$_i$.

Exercise 5
We assumed in Section 4.3.2 that, at LF, expletive *there* was replaced at LF by its associate, so that a sentence like 1 has the LF in 2:

1. There is a man in the room.
2. A man$_i$ is t$_i$ in the room.

What problem for this idea is created by the following pair of sentences?

3. There weren't many books on the shelf.
4. Many books weren't on the shelf.

Exercise 6
In section 7.4.3, we saw that subject-verb agreement had to be checked at LF, rather than D-Structure, in order to account for sentences like 1:

1. There were six people in the office.

Does the level at which Binding Theory applies need to be similarly changed? What relevance do the following examples have?

2. John$_i$ bought every picture of himself$_i$.
3. *He$_i$ liked every picture that John$_i$ took.

Is your conclusion affected by the following example?

4. Which claim that John$_i$ made did he$_i$ deny?

8 The Binding Theory and Empty Categories

Topics: Binding Theory status of DP-trace, wh-trace, *pro* and PRO, the PRO Theorem, determination of empty categories.

Open Issue: does *pro* exist in English?

8.0 INTRODUCTION

In Chapter 5, we introduced Principles A, B, and C of the Binding Theory and showed how DPs fell into one of three types: anaphors (which include both reflexives and reciprocals), pronouns, and R-expressions. We saw that anaphors were subject to Principle A, pronouns to Principle B, and R-expressions to Principle C. In this chapter, we're going to re-examine this division based on what we saw about traces in Chapter 6 and come to some interesting new conclusions about the types of unpronounced elements in natural language.

To begin with, notice that we can pare our theory down a bit and eliminate a few stipulations. At the moment, we have three different 'labels' for DPs: anaphors, pronouns, and R-expressions. We could reduce those three labels to two, by saying that there aren't three different kinds of DPs, rather DPs possess two features or properties, 'a' and 'p'. These features would indicate whether an element was subject to Principle A (the 'a', or anaphoric, feature) or Principle B (the 'p', or pronominal feature). If a DP had the $+$a feature, it would be subject to Principle A. If it had the $-$a feature, it would not be subject to Principle A. The features $+$p and $-$p would work in the same way. Anaphors as we saw them in Chapter 5 would then correspond to $[+a, -p]$ – a DP that was subject to Principle A and not Principle B. Pronouns would be the reverse, and therefore $[-a, +p]$. What about $[-a, -p]$? This would correspond to a DP which is subject to neither Principle A nor Principle B. Have we seen such a DP? Yes. R-expressions, which are subject to Principle C. But what about the fourth possibility $[+a, +p]$? Well, this would have to be a DP which is subject to *both* Principle A and Principle B simultaneously. That would require a DP to be both bound and free in its governing category at the same time, which seems impossible. It therefore seems as though we don't need to worry about that case. It would seem to be excluded on logical grounds. So, summarizing, we have Table 8.1.

However, we are now going to look at a further kind of DP that doesn't seem to have a place in Table 8.1: traces. Remember we argued in Chapter 6 that traces of Passive, Raising, and Wh-movement were DPs in their

Table 8.1 DPs and Their Feature Combinations

Feature Combination	Type of DP
+a, −p	anaphor
−a, +p	pronoun
−a, −p	R-expression
+a, +p	cannot exist

own right. The question obviously arises: are they anaphors, pronominals, R-expressions, or none of the above?

You might be inclined just to place them outside the system by saying that Binding Theory applies only to overt DPs, that is, DPs which are pronounced. Since traces aren't pronounced, Binding Theory doesn't apply to them. However, Chomsky (1982) suggested a more interesting way of looking at things. He argued that there are different kinds of unpronounced, or 'empty' categories, which correspond to all four feature possibilities, including [+a, +p].

We've obviously got some work to do here. We've gone from just worrying about whether traces fit in to our a/p system to suddenly claiming that, using the terms of that system, there are four different kinds of empty categories! What we'll see in this chapter is that traces actually break down into two different kinds: traces of A-movement (Passive and Raising), which are anaphors [+a, −p], and traces of A'-movement (Wh-movement), which are R-expressions [−a, −p]. Null pronouns, which would have the features [−a, +p] are usually assumed not to exist in English, but if we take a look at other languages, like Italian and Spanish, we can see them pretty clearly. The last one [+a, +p] will turn out to be our old friend PRO, the unexpressed subject of infinitivals, and we'll finally be able to clear up some of the things we had to leave as loose ends back in Chapter 4.

Before we can begin, though, we need to introduce one additional stipulation regarding Binding Theory which we didn't discuss in Chapter 5. Since that Chapter came before we introduced movement, we only discussed DPs that were in A-positions like Spec IP or sister to V. (You need movement in order for DPs to get to A'-positions like Spec CP or 'adjoined to IP'.) It turns out that elements in A'-positions are 'invisible' for Binding Theory. When looking to see, for example, whether a given trace is bound in its governing category, only DPs in A-positions are considered.

8.1 THE BINDING THEORY STATUS OF DP-TRACE

In trying to decide the status of different DP-traces, let's take a look at a typical case of A-movement, with a view toward what kind of DP the trace might be:

(1) $Mary_i$ seems t_i to be the best candidate.

Before Continuing: Draw the tree for (1) and determine the governing category for the trace.

One possibility seems to be excluded immediately. It doesn't look as though the trace could be an R-expression. R-expressions, remember, are subject to Principle C, which means that they can't be bound by an element in an A-position. But that's exactly what we have here. *Mary* is in an A-position, subject of the matrix clause. It c-commands the trace, and it's coindexed with the trace. Therefore *Mary* binds the trace, and (1) would be predicted to be ungrammatical if the trace were an R-expression.

Let's see what the governing category of the trace is. That way, we can see whether *Mary* is outside it or inside it, and that will tell us whether we should home in on Principle A or Principle B. The first step as always is to draw the tree, and that gets us (2):

(2)

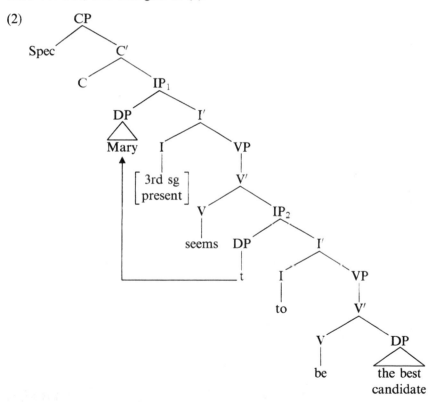

We need to find the minimal XP which contains: (a) the trace; (b) a governor for the trace; and (c) a subject which is accessible to the trace. IP₂ is the minimal maximal projection containing the trace, but it doesn't contain a governor for the trace (remember that infinitival *to* doesn't govern), so we'll have to look higher. V is a member of the class of governors, and no barrier intervenes between the V *seems* and the subject (remember that IP doesn't count as a barrier). So the governing category could be VP. We're two-thirds of the way there. The problem is that, of course, VP doesn't contain a subject, so we need to go higher still. The matrix IP_1 contains a subject, *Mary*, and that subject is accessible to the trace, since coindexation between them does not create an i-within-i configuration.

So it looks like the matrix IP is the governing category for the trace. We've already established that trace is bound by *Mary*, and *Mary* is within the matrix IP. *Mary* is also in an A-position. Therefore the trace is bound, rather than free, in its governing category and we have our answer. The trace has to be [+a, −p], subject to Principle A and not Principle B, which makes it an anaphor.

EXERCISE 1

Using the same logic, show that the traces of Passive must also be [+a, −p]. (e.g., John$_i$ was killed t$_i$)

The conclusion that traces of A-movement are anaphors is of more than just academic interest. It does some important work for us. Consider a sentence like (3) (these sentences are often referred to as 'superraising' violations):

(3)   *[$_{IP1}$ John$_i$ seems that [$_{IP2}$ it is believed t$_i$ by everyone]].

It's not immediately obvious why (3) isn't grammatical, meaning something like 'It seems that John is believed by everyone'. In particular, notice that Subjacency is *not* violated. The movement crosses only one IP: IP_2. IP_1 is not crossed, as it dominates both the departure site and the landing site. However, if traces of A-movement are anaphors, we have the explanation we're looking for. Since *John* is moving to an A-position (subject of the matrix sentence), t$_i$ must be an anaphor. But if that's the case, notice that t$_i$ won't be bound in its governing category. Its governing category is going to end up being the finite IP_2, and *John* is not within IP_2. Therefore the ungrammaticality of sentences involving 'superraising' violations follows from Binding Theory.

8.2   THE BINDING THEORY STATUS OF WH-TRACE

Having looked at traces of A-movement, let's now take a look at traces of A'-movement. In Chapter 6, we didn't differentiate between the two. However, a moment's reflection will make it clear that we now need to. As just discussed, traces of Passive and Raising are anaphors, but traces of

A′-movement clearly can't be. To see this, consider a simple case of Wh-movement, like (4):

(4)   [$_{CP}$ Who$_i$ [$_{IP}$ t$_i$ left]]?

If t$_i$, the trace of Wh-movement, is an anaphor, (4) ought to be a Principle A violation. The trace is bound by *who*, but of course *who* is in Spec CP, which is not an A-position. *Who* will therefore be 'invisible' to Binding Theory, and this means that there is no element that can serve as a binder for the trace. So if traces of Wh-movement were anaphors, (4) would be predicted to be ungrammatical.

The fact that (4) is perfectly fine means that traces of A′-movement can't be anaphors. They must be something else. What other possibilities are there? The fact that the trace has no binder in an A-position would seem to rule out the trace being any kind of anaphor, either [+a, +p] or [+a, −p]. That leaves us with only two remaining possibilities. The wh-trace could be [−a, +p], a null pronoun, or [−a, −p], a null R-expression.

Notice that the grammaticality of (4) is compatible with either possibility. Because the trace has no A-binder whatsoever, it would satisfy either Principle B or Principle C. So (4) by itself doesn't tell us whether the trace is a pronoun or an R-expression. What would distinguish the two possibilities is a sentence where the wh-trace is A-bound by a coindexed pronoun, but where the pronoun falls outside the trace's governing category. That's a case where Principle B would be satisfied, but Principle C would be *violated*. If the trace is a null pronoun, that configuration should be grammatical. If the trace is a null R-expression, the resulting sentence should be ungrammatical, since R-expressions must be A-free, full stop. Here's the relevant test sentence:

(5)   *Who$_i$ does he$_i$ think [$_{CP}$ t$_i'$ that Mary likes t$_i$]?

In (5), the pronoun is attempting to act as a bound variable, creating a 'crossover' configuration. In this case, it is an instance of *strong* crossover because the coindexed pronoun c-commands the wh-trace. If this indexation were possible, then (5) would be synonymous with (6):

(6)   Who$_i$ t$_i$ thinks that Mary likes him$_i$?

From a structural point of view, both (5) and (6) should have the interpretation 'which person x is such that x thinks that Mary likes x'. However, (5) cannot have that interpretation. It looks like the pronoun *he* can't have the same index as the wh-trace when the pronoun c-commands the wh-trace, as it does in (5). The pronoun must have a different index from the wh-trace, as in (7):[1]

(7)   Who$_i$ does he$_j$ think [$_{CP}$ t$_t'$ that Mary likes t$_i$]?

We can explain this by assuming that traces of Wh-movement are null R-expressions; that is, they have the features [−a, −p]. Under this assumption, the wh-trace must be A-free. There can be no element in an A-position which c-commands the trace and is coindexed with it. But that's precisely the situation which arises in the ungrammatical (5). The pronoun in the matrix subject position c-commands the trace, which is in direct object position of the embedded clause. So if the pronoun and the trace have the same index, as would happen if we were trying to force the bound-variable interpretation, you violate Principle C, and the result is ungrammaticality. If the pronoun has a different index than the wh-trace, as in (7), no A-binding of the pronoun takes place (remember *who* is in an A'-position), and there's no violation of Principle C.

Notice that this is now an argument that traces of A'-movement can't be pronouns. The offending pronoun *he* is outside the governing category of the wh-trace. If traces were [−a, +p], we'd predict that both (5) and (7) should be grammatical. Only the assumption that traces of A'-movement are null R-expressions correctly predicts that (5) is ungrammatical, but (7) is fine.

EXERCISE 2

Show that the wh-trace in (5) is not bound in its governing category.

8.3   THE SEARCH FOR NULL PRONOUNS

We now seem to have discovered analogues to two of the three kinds of overt NPs. We've got traces of A-movement, which are anaphors (+a, −p), and traces of A'-movement, which are R-expressions (−a, −p). Let's now see if we can find a null counterpart to overt pronouns. We're looking for some kind of empty category which is subject to Principle B of the Binding Theory.

Unfortunately, English isn't helpful here. We've exhausted the empty categories of English. The one outstanding empty category we haven't talked about is PRO, but we'll have reason to see in Section 8.4 that PRO is [+a, +p].

However, let's look at 'null subject' languages like Spanish and Italian, where the subject of a finite verb is normally unpronounced. So for example, the neutral way of saying *I am going to Madrid* in Spanish is:

(8)   Voy   a Madrid.
      go-1sg to Madrid
      'I am going to Madrid.'

In general, unless you were emphazising that *you* were going to Madrid, as opposed to someone else, you would leave out the first person singular subject pronoun *yo*. Null subject languages contrast (unsurprisingly) with 'non-null subject' languages like English and French, where the subject pronoun must always be expressed.[2]

(9)   *am going to Madrid

(10)   *vais   à Madrid   (French)
       go-1sg to Madrid
       'I am going to Madrid.'

How do we approach sentences like (8) and the contrast between null subject and non-null subject languages? We could just say that a sentence like (8) has no subject, that is, that there's no DP in Spec IP, but it's pretty clear why we wouldn't want to do that: the argument structure of the verb *to go* is the same in Spanish and in English. The semantics are certainly the same. It's not that the Spanish sentence (8) has no concept of 'goer' in it. And if that's the case, then there will be an Agent θ-role which the verb will have to assign at D-Structure. An obvious way out of this problem is to say that (8) *does* have a subject, merely an unpronounced one.

So if Spanish and the other languages have a null subject where English would have a subject pronoun, could this null subject be the null pronoun that we're looking for? Let's take a look at a slightly more complicated sentence:

(11)   Juan$_i$ dijo que ___ va a Madrid
       Juan said that ø goes to Madrid
       'Juan$_i$ said that he$_i$ is going to Madrid.'

For the same reasons as in (8), it must be the case that the embedded clause has a subject in Spec IP even though nothing is pronounced. (We've put 'ø' in (8) as a indication that there's some kind of empty category present.) Therefore, it must be the case that there is an empty category of some kind serving as the subject. Furthermore, that empty category is coindexed with the subject *Juan*, as can be seen from the interpretation.

Could this empty category which we've indicated as ø be either of the two that we've seen before? It seems unlikely. It can't be a trace of A-movement [+a, −p]. Those are anaphors. ø$_i$ does have a binder: *Juan*. But *Juan* is outside ø$_i$'s governing category, so Principle A won't be satisfied. That rules out ø$_i$ being [+a, +p] as well. But the fact that *Juan* is binding ø$_i$ from an A-position (albeit an A-position outside ø$_i$'s governing category) means that ø$_i$ can't be a trace of A′-movement. Those are R-expressions and need to be A-free.

So what we've got is an empty category that can be A-bound, but outside its governing category. Sound familiar? It should! ø$_i$ has to be a null pronoun, [−a, +p]. By a process of elimination, that's the only possibility we're left with. Fortunately, this seems right. The subject position of the embedded clause in (11) is the place where pronouns can appear. It's a θ-position and is Case marked by finite I. Also, most tellingly, an overt pronoun can appear in that position when the embedded clause subject is not coreferential with the matrix clause subject.

(12)   Juan dijo que vosotros vais   a Madrid.
       Juan said that you−pl go-2pl to Madrid
       'Juan said that you(pl) are going to Madrid.'

Furthermore, this null element seems to have all of the interpretive possibilities that overt pronouns have. That is to say, in addition to being bound outside its governing category, this null element can also be free, just like an overt pronoun. So, for example, if we're having a conversation about our friend Juan, I can say:

(13)   ø$_i$ Dijiste que ø$_j$ va   a Madrid
       ø said-2s that ø go-3s to Madrid
       'You said that he is going to Madrid.'

Here we've got empty categories both in the subject position of the matrix clause and the subject position of the embedded clause, and both are free. This makes it even more likely that we're dealing with null pronouns here.

We'll refer to this null pronominal element as '*pro*', which is usually read/ said as 'little *pro*'. The lowercase letters are important, because we need to keep it separate from PRO, the unexpressed subject of an infinitive, which we saw in Chapter 4 (which is called 'big *pro*'). English does of course have PRO, as we've seen, but it doesn't have *pro*, since subjects of finite verbs can't be null in English.[3]

8.3.1 Null Objects in Italian

So far, we've only seen *pro* as a subject. If *pro* really is just an empty pro-noun, it should be able to turn up in other positions as well. After all, overt pronouns aren't just restricted to subject position. They can be objects of verbs, prepositions – in fact, anywhere an overt DP can turn up.

Rizzi (1986) argues that *pro* can also appear as the object of certain verbs in Italian, like *condurre* 'to lead'. Rizzi points to contrasts like the following:

(14)a.   Questo conduce la gente$_i$ a [PRO$_i$ concludere quanto segue].
         This   leads   people inf.   to conclude what follows
         'This leads people to conclude what follows.'

b. Questo conduce pro a [PRO$_i$ concludere quanto segue].
   This   leads   inf.   to conclude what follows
   'This leads one to conclude what follows.'

In one respect, the argumentation follows exactly the same line as we saw in Section 8.3. From the appearance of the DP *la gente* in (14a), it seems as though *condurre* has a θ-role to assign to its object. Since no DP is present phonetically in (14b) to receive that θ-role, the θ-Criterion requires that there be a phonetically unrealized DP there. You might be inclined to object to this line of reasoning with the observation that perhaps *condurre* in Italian is like *eat* in English, in which the object θ-role is only optionally realized.

(15)a.   John ate dinner.
   b.   John ate.

However, this possibility doesn't look too strong when we take a look at the English equivalent of *condurre*. As the translation indicates, *lead* seems to obligatorily assign a θ-role to its object.

(16)a.   Societal problems should lead people to question the political system.
   b.   *Societal problems should lead – to question the political system.

If *lead* were like *eat* in having an internal θ-role which is optional, then we'd expect that (16a) and (16b) should both be grammatical, on a par with (15a) and (b). The fact that they aren't suggests that the internal θ-role possessed by *lead* is obligatory. Since optionality/obligatoriness of θ-role assignment with respect to a given predicate is not something that we expect to vary cross-linguistically, given the close ties between θ-role assignment and semantics, the fact that *lead* in English has an obligatory internal θ-role strongly suggests that *condurre* does in Italian as well.

In fact, it seems that *pro* provides exactly the solution that we're looking for. *Lead* and *condurre* each have an internal θ-role which must be assigned. In Italian, that internal θ-role can be assigned to *pro*, which is phonetically null, so (14b) is grammatical. English, on the other hand, doesn't have *pro*, as we've seen, so (16b) constitutes a θ-Criterion violation.[4]

8.4   [+a, +p] REVEALED!

We've managed to track down three of the four logical feature possibilities in the domain of empty categories: Traces of A-movement are null anaphors [+a, −p], traces of A′-movement are null R-expressions [−a, −p], and *pro* is our null pronoun [−a, +p]. That leaves [+a, +p].

Now you might think that [+a, +p] is going to be a lost cause. When we talked about the typology of *overt* elements at the beginning of the chapter, we just wrote off the possibility of [+a, +p] with the simple, if plausible, assertion that such a thing couldn't exist because it would have to be both bound and free in its governing category; which is, of course, impossible. However, I hope that by now you've learned not to jump to conclusions, however apparently plausible (my recommended approach to things in general, by the way, not just syntax). As it turns out, things are a little bit more complicated. What I'm going to argue is that PRO ('big pro'), the phonologically null subject of infinitivals and gerunds, has the features [+a, +p].

We saw in Chapter 4 that PRO seems to split into two types with regard to its interpretation. On the one hand, we have *controlled* PRO, as in (17):

(17)   John$_i$ promised PRO$_i$ to go home early.

Unlike ordinary pronouns, which can take an antecedent but don't have to, controlled PRO does requires an antecedent. There's no possible situation under which (17) could mean 'John promised that somebody or other would go home early'. It can only mean 'John promised that he (John) would go home early'.

On the other hand, we also have *arbitrary* PRO, as in (18):

(18)   PRO to go home early would be a terrible mistake.

Here PRO's interpretation has a much more pronominal feel to it. In fact, it's essentially synonymous with something like 'for one to go home early would be a mistake'.

8.4.1   The PRO Theorem

Now it's one thing to say that PRO has both anaphoric and pronominal interpretive tendencies and quite another to say that it literally has the Binding Theory features [+a] and [+p]. We still haven't addressed the fundamental question of how something could simultaneously satisfy both Principle A and Principle B of the Binding Theory.

Let's begin by taking a closer look at Principles A and B, and see if we've got any hitherto unsuspected room to maneuver.

(19)a.   *Principle A*
         An element with the feature [+a] must be bound in its governing category.
   b.   *Principle B*
         An element with the feature [+p] must be free in its governing category.

On the surface, they do look contradictory, but let's dig a little deeper. The contradiction is coming about because of the way *bound* and *free* are defined. Since *free* means 'not bound', it's hard to imagine how something could be both bound and not bound.

However, don't lose sight of that last little prepositional phrase 'in its governing category'. The Binding Theory doesn't say that an anaphor must be bound, full stop, or that a pronoun must be free, full stop. What it says is that they need to be bound or free *in their governing categories*. How does that help us? Well, if you had an element which *didn't have* a governing category for some reason, maybe that would fall outside the system somehow because Principles A and B presuppose that the element *does* have a governing category.

Let's pursue that thought. The first thing we need to think about is how you could ever have an element which didn't have a governing category. From Chapter 5 you'll remember that the governing category for a given element is the minimal maximal projection which contains: (i) the element itself; (ii) a governor for the element; and (iii) a subject which is accessible to the element. If for whatever reason an element didn't have one of these three things, then it could be reasonably said that it didn't have a governing category.

Starting with (i), it looks like there's no help there. There will always be some category which contains the element. (iii) doesn't look too promising either. As we saw back in Chapter 5 the subject of the clause that the element is in will always be an accessible subject, unless the element is inside a subject, in which case the subject of the next higher clause will serve.

(ii) looks more promising. If an element had no governor, then it makes sense to say that the element has no governing category. And it looks like PRO fits the bill. First, let's take a look at a partial structure for (17), the case of controlled PRO:

(20)

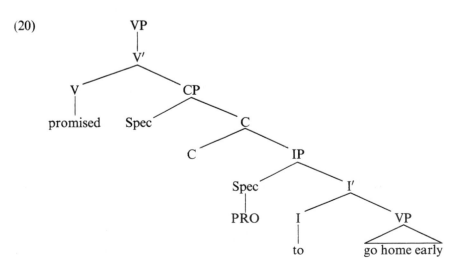

Here PRO doesn't have a governor. Government from outside the CP, by *promise* for example, is blocked by the barrier CP. And there's no government from I, the other possible source. Remember that non-finite I is defective: unlike finite I, it doesn't govern its specifier position, Spec IP.

The same situation obtains in the case of arbitrary PRO. If we take a look at a partial structure for (18), we've got (21):

(21)

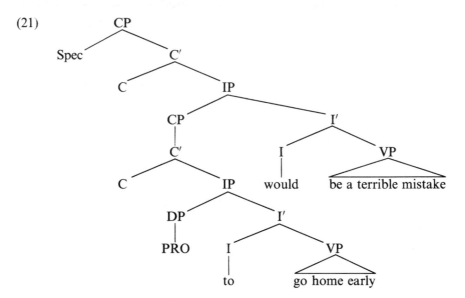

Again, government from the matrix finite I is blocked by the barrier CP and there's no government from non-finite I because it's defective.

So it looks like PRO, both controlled and arbitrary, has no governor. It therefore seems plausible to say that PRO has no governing category. So what effect does this have with respect to Principles A and B? Are Principles A and B satisfied or violated by an element which has no governing category?

The traditional claim is that elements which have no governing category *satisfy* Principles A and B automatically. This intuition might seem slightly odd. (19a) is 'satisfied' by an anaphor that has no governing category? But I think the intuition becomes clearer if we reverse things, and ask ourselves whether Principle A or B is *violated* by an element which has no governing category. If you can't figure out whether something is bound or free in its governing category because it simply has no governing category, it's hard to say that Principle A or B is violated. And it seems reasonable to define 'satisfies' as equivalent to 'doesn't violate'. This is what we will do.

This is not just a bit of terminological juggling. If we can find it in our hearts to say that Principles A and B are satisfied when an element has no governing category, it turns out that some interesting (and correct) predictions about the distribution of PRO seem to follow automatically from the assumption that it is both [+a] and [+p]

If not having a governing category is the only way to satisfy both Principles A and B at the same time, then it follows automatically that PRO can *never* appear in a governed position. That is, it follows that it can never be the subject of a finite INFL, object of a verb, subject of an ECM infinitive or object of a preposition. These predictions all seem right:

(22)a.   *PRO goes to the market every Sunday
   b.   *I hit PRO
   c.   *I believe PRO to be here
   d.   *I gave the book to PRO

If we hadn't made the assumption that PRO was [+a, +p], and therefore couldn't appear in a governed position, it's hard to see what other principle rules out (22a) to (d). Interpretively, PRO can either be controlled or arbitrary, so, on a par with (18), (22a) could mean that some unspecified person or people in general go to the market every Sunday. And (22b) could mean something like *I hit myself*. But the fact is that they don't. They're just ungrammatical. But fortunately, instead of having a mystery, we have an explanation.

Putting all of these ideas and argumentation together, we have what's known as the PRO Theorem:

(23)   *The PRO Theorem*
       PRO must be ungoverned.

This is nice in that it's a genuine *theorem*, as opposed to a description, or rule-of-thumb or something. That is to say, this fact about PRO follows completely from other principles. Once we say that PRO has the both the feature [+a] and the feature [+p], it follows that PRO cannot have a governor.

Notice that at last we've got a genuine explanation for why there's no overt counterpart to PRO; that is, an overt element which has the features [+a] and [+p]. As we've seen, the only way that such an element could satisfy both Principles A and B of the Binding Theory would be to have no governing category, and for that it would have to have no governor. But if an element doesn't have a governor, then it can't be assigned Case. (Remember from Chapter 4 that you have to govern an element in order to Case mark it.) And an overt element which doesn't get assigned Case is always going to violate the Case Filter. Therefore, you could never have an overt element which was [+a, +p] as it would always result in a Case Filter violation. *Voila!*

8.5   INTERLUDE: A NOTE ON PLATO'S PROBLEM

Let's pull back and reflect on what we've just discovered. When you think about it, all these things that we've just been talking about are vivid examples of Plato's Problem. Remember from the Introduction that Chomsky argued that you seem to know a lot more than just what you could have figured out from the data/acoustic disturbances that you were exposed to in childhood. There must be some guiding hand, in the form of a Language Acquisition Device, which makes possible the acquisition of such a body of knowledge, which is not only very intricate, but also quite independent of anything you can actually see or hear.

First of all, there's the concept of empty categories in general. We've found what I think is pretty solid evidence that part of knowing your language consists of knowing that there are elements in the grammar *which are never pronounced*. That in itself is really surprising. In acquiring English, you could have had no direct evidence that they were there, so how did you figure out what was going on? It would be like trying to learn the rules of chess by watching games played, but where crucial pieces were invisible.

Furthermore, it's not just that you know that there are invisible pieces. You know that there are, and you distinguish between, different *kinds* of invisible pieces – *three* if you're an English or French speaker and *four* if you're an Spanish or Turkish speaker. And they all have different properties! In English, you've got traces of A- and A'-movement, which are anaphors and R-expressions respectively and you've also got PRO which is *both* an anaphor *and* a pronominal – something which couldn't exist if it were an overt category. And if you're a speaker of a null subject language, you've got all these plus *pro* to deal with.

It's hard to see how analogy, inductive generalization or any other kind of generalized learning mechanism could explain how you know facts like these. Nonetheless, the intuitions are sharp and something that every speaker knows. It's these kinds of issues that lie at the heart of Chomsky's 'Logical Problem of Language Acquisition'. Not only did you manage to figure out all this information from the data you were exposed to, but *everybody* did regardless of intelligence. How did everyone converge on exactly the same thing given the varying primary linguistic data they were exposed to? The only answer seems to be that an innate, inborn guiding force, Universal Grammar, is at work in the acquisition process.

8.6   THE FUNCTIONAL DETERMINATION OF EMPTY CATEGORIES

In this section, we're going to investigate an implicit assumption that we've been making about how empty categories are created. So far, we've been assuming that empty categories are *intrinsically* determined. A-movement leaves an empty category that's an anaphor because that's how we define A-movement. Similarly for A'-movement: the trace of A'-movement is an R-expression because we say that's the way A'-movement works, and so on with PRO and *pro*. These are independent elements which are just defined in the lexicon as having certain properties.

Now we didn't just define things this way for no reason. Sections 8.1–8.4 were all about giving arguments that A-traces, A'-traces, PRO, and *pro* had specific anaphoric and pronominal features. However, that doesn't alter the fact that, at its core, what we've got are four separate stipulations.

However, Chomsky (1982) suggested that there is a more interesting way of looking at things. Expanding on a proposal originally made by Koopman and Sportiche (1982), he proposed what's known as the *functional* determination of empty categories. In this system, there is in effect only one kind of empty category, which intrinsically has no [a] or [p] features. These features get assigned at Logical Form by a general algorithm, which assigns the empty category [±a] and [±p] features depending on the context that the empty category is in.

Here's the algorithm as given by Lasnik and Uriagereka (1988:67) (with some slight modifications for clarity (see Lasnik and Uriagereka (1988:67ff.)). Don't worry about trying to assimilate it all at once. It'll become much clearer when we've gone through a few examples.

(24) *Functional Determination Algorithm*
   a. An empty category is [−a, −p] if it is in an A-position and its nearest binder is an operator in an A'-position.
   b. An empty category in an A-position that is not [−a, −p] has the feature [+a].
   c. An empty category in an A-position that is not [−a, −p] has the feature [+p] if it is free or its nearest binder is in an A-position and has an independent θ-role. Otherwise, it has [−p].

It would be really interesting if this algorithm worked. We could eliminate some stipulations from the theory, reducing ourselves to a single, contextually defined empty category. First of all, though, we need to make sure that this algorithm gets the basic facts right. (It will be helpful to have (24) in front of you in what follows.)

8.6.1 The Functional Determination of Anaphors

Consider a simple Raising case of the sort that we saw in Section 8.1 above. (Since we don't know what kind of empty category we're dealing with until we run through the Functional Determination Algorithm, we'll leave the empty category marked as 'e' in the examples we're looking at.)

(25)   Mary seems e to be the best candidate.

The answer we want from the Functional Determination Algorithm is that 'e' here is an anaphor [+a, −p] and that it's coindexed with *Mary*.

You'll notice that the algorithm doesn't assign indices. It just assigns [a] and [p] features. So we have to specify beforehand what the indices are. Let's begin by assuming that *Mary* and *e* do have the same index:

(26)   Mary$_i$ seems e$_i$ to be the best candidate.

e_i is in an A-position (subject of the infinitive) and its nearest binder is *Mary*. (That is, *Mary* c-commands e_i and is coindexed with it.) So, beginning with part (a) of the algorithm, e_i isn't [−a, −p]. e_i is in an A-position, but *Mary*, its nearest binder, is neither an operator nor in an A′-position. Therefore, by part (b), e_i must be [+a].

Turning now to part (c), we've got to check two things. An empty category gets assigned the feature [+p] *either* (1) if it's free *or* (2) its nearest binder is in an A-position and has an independent θ-role. Clearly e_i's not free. It's bound by *Mary*, so (1) isn't relevant. *Mary* is in an A-position, though, so we need to see whether *Mary* has an independent θ-role. However, it doesn't. The subject position of *seem* is not a θ-position, but the trace position is. Therefore *Mary* must be dependent on the trace for a θ-role, otherwise we'd have a θ-Criterion violation. Therefore (2) doesn't apply either, and we conclude that e_i is [+a, −p], exactly the result we wanted.

Now let's see what happens if we give *Mary* and *e* different indices:

(27)   Mary$_i$ seems e$_j$ to be the best candidate.

Now e_j has no binder at all, so it will not be [−a, −p], and must therefore be [+a] by parts (a) and (b). By part (c), though, e_j will be assigned the feature [+p]. Therefore, the Functional Determination Algorithm tells us that e_j is PRO. But PRO can't appear in the position e_j is in! *Seem* takes an IP complement, and infinitival IP isn't a barrier to government. If PRO is there, it will be governed by *seem*, in violation of the PRO Theorem. So it looks like the Functional Determination Algorithm does some nice extra work for us predicting the ungrammaticality of (27). In addition to telling us that *e* is [+a, −p] when it's coindexed with *Mary*, it also indirectly tells us that *e must* be coindexed with *Mary*. Otherwise you get an impossible result.[5]

8.6.2   The Functional Determination of Variables

Now let's look at a simple case of A′-movement. In this case, the answer we want is that the empty category left by the movement of the wh-expression is [−a, −p]. Starting with a simple example, we have (28):

(28)   Who does Bill like e?

Who and *e* will be coindexed, and have a different index from *Bill*:

(29)   Who$_i$ does Bill$_j$ like e$_i$?

This one's easy. The nearest binder for *e* is *who*. *Bill* is nearer, but not coindexed, so there's no binding. *Who* is an operator, and it's also in an A'-position (Spec CP), so, by part (a), *e* is automatically [−a, −p], which is the result we want.

Notice that, again under the Functional Determination Algorithm, the indexation we want turns out to be the only one possible. If we try to create a 'strong crossover' configuration, by having *Bill* coindexed with *e*, we have this:

(30)   Who$_i$ does Bill$_i$ like e$_i$?

Now, the nearest binder to *e* is *Bill* rather than *who*. Therefore, part (a) of the algorithm won't be invoked. *Bill* is not an operator, nor is it in an A'-position. Therefore, *e* will be assigned [+a]. With respect to part (c), we again have to check two things. Clearly *e*'s not free, so it won't get [+p] that way. However, its nearest binder, *Bill*, does have an independent θ-role. *e* is assigned the Theme θ-role, as the object of *like*, and *Bill*, being the subject, is assigned Experiencer. Therefore, the Functional Determination Algorithm, under the indexation in (30), determines *e* as [+a, +p] or PRO. But sister-to-V isn't a possible position for PRO, since the position is governed by V. Therefore, under Functional Determination, we need say nothing extra about strong crossover.

However, we should say something in the context of Wh-movement about the status of intermediate traces of successive cyclic movement. They seem to be 'invisible' for the purposes of the Functional Determination Algorithm. Consider a standard case like (31):

(31)   What$_i$ did John say [$_{CP}$ t$'_i$ that [$_{IP}$ Bill liked t$_i$]]?

If intermediate traces were considered by the Functional Determination Algorithm, we'd end up with *two* variables in (31):

(32)   [for what x [John said [x that [Bill liked x]]]]

But this is not the interpretation that (31) has. It's interpreted as though it has only *one* variable, in the position of direct object of *like*.

Before we finish with variables, just for the sake of completeness, let's take a quick look at variables created by Quantifier Raising at Logical Form, which we introduced in the last chapter. The Functional Determination

Algorithm works just as well for these too. Consider a sentence like (33), and its representation at Logical Form (34):

(33) I like everyone.

(34) [$_{CP}$ [$_{IP}$ everyone$_i$ [$_{IP}$ I$_j$ like e$_i$]]]

Since 'adjoined to IP' is not a position where a θ-role is assigned, it must be an A′-position. That makes *everyone* the nearest binder for e$_i$. *Everyone* is also an operator, as we saw in the last chapter, and that means that the algorithm will determine e$_i$ as a variable, just as desired.

8.6.3   The Functional Determination of PRO

Now let's try PRO. As ever, there are two cases we need to take a look at, controlled PRO and arbitrary PRO.

(35) John$_i$ promised e$_i$ to go home early.

Under the indexation where *John* and *e* are coreferent, cranking through the Functional Determination Algorithm will get us the right result. *John* is the nearest binder so by parts (a) and (b) *e* is [+a]. And since *John* is in an A-position and has a θ-role which is independent from *e* (agent of *promise* vs. agent of *go*), part (c) will assign *e* [+p], and we have the result we want: [+a, +p], which is PRO.

Taking the arbitrary version of PRO, we have:

(36) e$_i$ to go home early would be a terrible mistake

The big difference here is that *e* has no binder at all in (36). So again by parts (a) and (b) it will be [+a], and by part (c) it will be [+p]. Again, the result we want.

However, notice that the case of PRO is different from the others that we've seen so far in that the Functional Determination Algorithm by itself doesn't uniquely tell us what the indexation must be. Consider (35) again, but where *e* has a different index from *John*.

(37) John$_i$ promised e$_j$ to go home early.

Because part (c) will assign an empty category [+p] if either it's free or its antecedent is in an A-position with an independent θ-role, the Functional Determination Algorithm will still determine *e* as PRO. This means that Binding Theory alone won't tell us everything we need to know about PRO. We need some additional theory about how PRO determines its antecedent.

8.6.4   The Functional Determination of *pro* and Free Assignment of [+/−a]

We've left until last discussion of the null pronominal, *pro*, which we introduced in Section 8.3 above. The eagle-eyed among you will have already noticed why: unfortunately, there's no way to get [−a, +p] out of the Functional Determination Algorithm as we've given it in (24) above.

EXERCISE 3

Convince yourself that this is true. Follow every single possible path through the algorithm and check the resulting possible feature combinations.

The only source for the feature [−a] is by (24a), but that automatically gives you [−a, −p]. By (24b), anything that isn't [−a, −p] is going to be [+a] (either [+a, +p] or [+a, −p]). For this reason, Chomsky (1982) later modifies the Functional Determination Algorithm so that the feature [+/−a] is *freely* assigned. That is, for a given empty category *e*, you can give it either the feature [+a] or the feature [−a], whichever you feel like, and delete part (b) of the algorithm. Doing this, we'll be able to get *pro* in those places where we want it.

To start with, let's consider (38):

(38)   Juan$_i$ dijo que e$_i$ va   a Madrid.
       Juan said that e goes to Madrid
       'Juan said that he is going to Madrid.'

As ever, the first thing to check is whether our empty category has a binder and, if so, whether that binder is in an A-position or an A′-position. We do have a binder (*Juan*) and that binder is in an A-position. Now let's begin by freely assigning the [+/−a] feature. We'll pick [−a], the 'right' choice, first. Since *Juan* is not in an A′-position, part (a) will not cause it to be determined as a variable [−a, −p]. Therefore, part (c) will assign it the feature [+p], since *Juan* has an independent θ-role from the empty category (agent of *say* vs. agent of *go*), and we get what we want. The empty category ends up being [−a, +p], a null pronominal.

Notice that, just as we've seen with other examples above, the 'wrong' choice leads to ungrammaticality. If we freely assign the empty category the feature [+a], then it will be determined as [+a, +p] (i.e., PRO and not *pro*), and we'll end up with a violation of the PRO Theorem on our hands.

Just to be thorough, we need to make sure that we don't lose any of our previous results because of the changes we've made. Clearly, variables won't be affected. We've still got part (a) of the algorithm, so anything that would have been determined as a variable before will continue to be. That leaves anaphors and PRO:

(39)   Mary$_i$ seems e$_i$ to be the best candidate.

(40)   John$_i$ promised e$_i$ to go home early.

In both cases, freely assigning [+a] presents no problem. That's the one we want. And it looks like freely assigning [−a] is no problem either. In (39) if we choose to assign [−a], the empty category will end up being [−a, −p] and we'll have a Principle C violation. So that option looks blocked, as desired. In (40), we'll end up with [−a, +p], which is *pro*. In a non-null subject like English, that option is blocked by the fact that English doesn't have *pro*. However, notice also that Spec IP of an infinitive is not a position where Case is assigned. Since, by hypothesis, *pro* has no other properties other than being unpronounced, it should require Case just like any other pronoun. Therefore freely assigning the feature [−a] in (40) will be ruled out by the Case Filter, whether we're talking about a null subject language or a non-null subject one.

8.7   THE FREE DETERMINATION OF EMPTY CATEGORIES

In the previous section, we came to the conclusion that we needed to modify the Functional Determination Algorithm in (24) in order to allow for null non-anaphoric pronominals, that is, an element with features [−a, +p]. Following the later discussion in Chomsky (1982), we decided to do this by freely assigning the feature [±a] and getting rid of part (b) of the algorithm. Something that might have occurred to you is whether or not we now need the algorithm in (24) at all.

The reason for moving from *intrinsically* determined empty categories to a *functional* determination approach was to reduce stipulations in our theory. Rather than four separate, in principle unrelated statements ('A-movement leaves a [+a, −p] empty category', etc.), we could reduce it to one three-step algorithm. Plus we were able to incorporate the idea that the context of an empty category determines the feature that it has, which seems nice.

However, once it's been decided that the [±a] feature can be freely assigned, a logical next question is whether we can freely assign *both* the [±a] feature *and* the [±p] feature and thereby get rid of the Functional Determination Algorithm altogether. That would mean even fewer stipulations in the theory. This is the path essentially taken by Brody (1984). Let's see whether it can be made to work.

First, let's consider a standard Raising structure again, where [+a, −p] is the feature combination we want:

(41)   Mary$_i$ seems [$_{IP}$ e$_i$ to be the best candidate].

All of the other possibilities seem to be correctly excluded here. [−a, −p] will be excluded by Principle C; [−a, +p] will be ruled out by Principle B; and [+a, +p] will violate the PRO theorem. (PRO would be governed by *seems.)*

EXERCISE 4

Show that [+a, −p] is the only possible combination for the trace of Passive.

For variables, free determination also seems to work well:

(42)   Who$_i$ e$_i$ left?

Since the binder of the empty category is in an A′-position, [+a, −p] is out. So is [+a, +p], since Spec IP of a tensed clause is governed by I. [−a, +p] can be ruled out by the fact that *pro* doesn't exist in subject position in English. So, again, we're OK.

There's a slight hitch about PRO in (43), which we'll in fact clear up in the next chapter:

(43)   John$_i$ promised [$_{CP}$ e$_i$ to go].

[−a, −p] would violate Principle C. [−a, +p] isn't possible for English, and there's no Case available anyway. The problem is that [+a, −p] isn't ruled out by anything we've said so far. In Section 8.4 we went to great lengths to persuade ourselves that Principle A was *satisfied* in configurations like (43) because an element in subject position of a CP infinitival clause has no governing category. That should make [+a, −p] a possible combination. However, we'll put that to one side here, because in the next chapter we're going to argue that null anaphors *must* have a governor. That would leave [+a, +p] as the only possibility.

Last, we have null pronouns. Let's take a look at our standard Spanish case again.

(44)   Juan$_i$ dijo que e$_i$ va   a Madrid.
        Juan said that e goes to Madrid
        'Juan said that he is going to Madrid.'

Anything [+a] will be ruled out. e_i has a governing category, and is free in it. [−a, −p] will result in a Principle C violation. That leaves [−a, +p] as the only possibility of the four which doesn't violate something.

So far so good. It looks as though free determination of empty categories works pretty well. There is, however, a potential problem with the other kind of null subject case, where the empty category is entirely free, as in (45):

(45) e_i Dijiste   que Juan va   a Madrid.
      e said-2sg that Juan goes to Madrid
      'You said that Juan is going to Madrid.'

Just as before, anything [+a] is ruled out, but this time there's nothing obviously wrong with the choice of [−a, −p]. The only constraint on variables we've seen so far is Principle C. But that isn't violated in (45) since e_i is free. We need to say something else to rule out the possibility that e_i could be [−a, −p]. One possibility which has a certain degree of initial plausibility is to impose a *no free variables* condition. That is to say, while a variable cannot have an A-binder (Principle C), it *must* have an A′-binder. We've seen in the previous chapter that operators and variables seem to come in pairs, whether the operator is a wh-word or a quantifier, and this would correctly rule out [−a, −p] in (45). We'd therefore correctly predict that e_i in (45) can only be [−a, +p].

If it's any consolation, it also looks like we need a 'no free variables' condition to account for another problematic case, this time from English, which is noted in Lasnik and Uriagereka (1988:87). Consider (46):

(46)   *$John_i$ likes e_j

This one is kind of a problem, because using the Functional Determination Algorithm gets you the right result here. The empty category would be determined as [+a, +p], which would violate the PRO Theorem. However, if the features are freely determined, we need to make sure that all possibilities are ruled out. That's the only way we'd correctly predict that (46) should be ungrammatical. First, anything [+a] is obviously out again. e_j is governed by *likes* (and therefore has a governing category), but it's free. We can rule out [−a, +p] on the grounds that English doesn't have *pro*, but we have a problem again with [−a, −p], the variable. *John* isn't coindexed with e_j, and therefore doesn't bind it. However, if we adopt a 'no free variables' condition for (45), we account for (46) as well.

8.8   SUMMARY

In this chapter, we've reopened the books on traces, and found that traces aren't a separate kind of DP from the anaphors, pronouns, and R-expressions that we saw in Chapter 5. Instead, following Chomsky (1982), what we've argued is that traces are just a part of a wider group of empty categories, which include our old friend PRO from Chapter 4, and a new kind of empty category, *pro*, which doesn't exist in English, but which is found in null subject languages like Spanish and Italian.

Having discovered these four different kinds of empty categories and their properties, we then tried to tighten up our theory a little bit. Rather than simply defining A-movement as leaving a [+a, −p] trace, or A'-movement as leaving a [−a, −p] trace, we argued that there is only one kind of empty category, e, which has no features at all. The question then becomes, how does this empty category get its features? The first possibility that we looked at was that the featureless empty category has its features defined contextually, by the Functional Determination Algorithm of Chomsky (1982):

(47) *Functional Determination Algorithm*
    a.   An empty category is [−a, −p] if it is in an A-position and its nearest binder is an operator in an A'-position.
    b.   An empty category in an A-position that is not a variable has the feature [+a].
    c.   An empty category in an A-position that is not a variable has the feature [+p] if it is free or its nearest binder is in an A-position and has an independent θ-role. Otherwise, it has [−p].

However, we saw a couple of problems with (47), which led us to revise things further. First, the algorithm needs to be modified in order to make it possible to get the feature combination [−a, +p], which we need for *pro*. Chomsky's solution, which we adopted, was to allow the feature [±a] to be freely assigned. But once we did that, it opened up the possibility of simplifying our theory further by allowing both the [±a] and the [±p] features to be freely assigned. This is a very tempting move, as having a single featureless empty category to which you can assign whatever features you want would seem to be the simplest theory possible. Fortunately, it seemed to work reasonably well, the only complication being the necessary incorporation of a 'no free variables' condition.

OPEN ISSUE: DOES *pro* EXIST IN ENGLISH?

Throughout this Chapter, we've been assuming that the feature combination [−a, +p], that is, *pro*, was automatically excluded in a non-null subject language like English. It seemed pretty straightforward. We assumed that *pro* wasn't possible in English because of the ungrammaticality of sentences like (48), which are perfect in languages like Italian, Spanish or Turkish.

(48) *is going to the store.

However, Epstein (1984) presents some very interesting evidence to suggest that English *does* have *pro*, just not in subject position.

Consider (49), a sentence which up until now we might have analyzed as containing arbitrary PRO:

(49)   It is fun [$_{CP}$ [$_{IP}$ PRO$_{arb}$ to play baseball]].

PRO, the subject of *play* is interpreted in (49) as 'anyone' or 'people in general', which is exactly the interpretation that we've seen for other cases of arbitrary PRO, like (50):

(50)   PRO$_{arb}$ to return early from vacation is unpleasant.

Given that interpretation, it would seem clear that PRO$_{arb}$ should be identified as some kind of universal quantifier, and should therefore undergo Quantifier Raising just like other quantifiers that we saw in Chapter 7.

However, there's a problem. We saw in Chapter 7 that QR was strictly clause bounded. That is, the quantifier can be adjoined at LF only to the 'nearest' IP node. That would seem to conflict with the interpretational facts in (49), in which it appears that QR is not clause bounded.

To see this, we need to take a closer look at what (49) means and the implications that the meaning has for what the structure is at Logical Form. All other things being equal, we'd expect (49) to have the (partial) LF in (51), in which the subject, PRO$_{arb}$, has been QRed to the closest IP that dominates it:

(51)   [$_{CP}$ [$_{IP}$ it is fun [$_{CP}$ [$_{IP}$ ($\forall$x) [$_{IP}$ x to play baseball]]]]]

Unfortunately, this LF is of a sentence which asserts (52):

(52)   If everyone plays baseball, it is fun.

This is not what (49) means. What (49) means is that for any person, it is fun for that person to play baseball. *That* meaning would be associated with the LF in (53), in which the universal quantifier has scope over the matrix clause:[6]

(53) [$_{CP}$ ($\forall$x) [$_{IP}$ it is fun [$_{CP}$ [$_{IP}$ x to play baseball]]]]

This is a problem. The only way to derive this LF at the moment is to say that QR is always clause-bounded, except when we're dealing with PRO$_{arb}$.

And things just get worse, as Epstein notes. It's not just that QR is not clause bounded when dealing with PRO$_{arb}$. It's looks like PRO$_{arb}$ can be QRed exactly one clause higher and no further. Consider (54):

(54)   Josh said it is fun PRO to play baseball.

PRO can have a controlled interpretation here (where Josh asserted that it is fun *for him* to play baseball), but let's focus on the PRO_{arb} interpretation, where Josh is trying to assert something general. What we see is that the LF associated with (54) has to be (55), and not (56) or (57):

(55) $[_{CP} [_{IP}$ Josh said $[_{CP} (\forall x) [_{IP}$ it is fun $[_{CP} [_{IP}$ x to play baseball]]]]]].

(56) $[_{CP} [_{IP}$ Josh said $[_{CP} [_{IP}$ it is fun $[_{CP} [_{IP} (\forall x) [_{IP}$ x to play baseball]]]]]]].

(57) $[_{CP} (\forall x) [_{IP}$ Josh said $[_{CP} [_{IP}$ it is fun $[_{CP} [_{IP}$ x to play baseball]]]]]].

Just as with (51) above, (56) is the Logical Form of a statement which asserts that Josh said 'if everyone plays baseball, it is fun', which is clearly not what (54) means. (57) on the other hand asserts not that Josh made some universal claim, but rather that Josh made a claim or claims which just happen to be true of everyone. For example, suppose that the only people in the universe are Josh and Erich. If Josh at one point says 'It is fun for Erich to play baseball' and then later says 'It is fun for me to play baseball', then (57) would be true. But that doesn't seem like a circumstance under which we would want to say that the sentence in (54) was true. Our intuition is that (54) is only true if Josh said 'it is fun [for everyone] to play baseball'. *That's* the interpretation in (55), in which PRO_{arb} is QRed *exactly one clause higher* than that one it's in, and no more. This is a very, very strange state of affairs indeed.

However, Epstein notices that there's another aspect to the interpretation of (49) which we haven't considered yet, and therein lies a possible way out. Notice that you can have an expressed DP in the place of PRO_{arb}:

(58) It is fun $[_{CP}$ for $[_{IP}$ Babe Ruth to play baseball]].

This is a little hard to see, for reasons which will become clear momentarily, but (58) can mean something like 'it is fun for everyone for Babe Ruth to play baseball'. It gets even better if you make the context a little more plausible, something like *it is good business sense for Babe Ruth to play baseball*. However, notice that we seem to have an extra argument there – a complement of the adjective *fun* – as indicated by the translation of (58). We can even put that second argument in by adding another prepositional phrase:

(59) It is fun for the spectators $[_{CP}$ for $[_{IP}$ Babe Ruth to play baseball]].

Therefore, going back to (49), it looks like there's not just PRO_{arb}, but also a *second* unexpressed argument which is the complement of *fun* and which is coindexed with PRO. What (49) really means is 'for any x: if x plays baseball, it is fun *for x*'. (49) doesn't mean that 'for any x: if x plays baseball, then it is fun for y' (where y is maybe some sadist who likes watching other people run around). This suggests that the logical form that we gave for (49) was wrong. It's not (53), but rather (60), with a variable in the matrix clause and a *controlled* PRO:

(60) $[_{CP} [_{IP} (\forall x) [_{IP}$ it is fun (for) $x_i [_{CP} [_{IP} PRO_i$ to play baseball]]]]]

This suggests that the S-Structure of (49) is really (61), where e_i is a null universal quantifier which undergoes QR:

(61) $[_{CP} [_{IP}$ it is fun $e_i [_{CP} [_{IP} PRO_i$ to play baseball]]]]

This would seem to solve all of our problems about scope. If it's not PRO_{arb}, but rather some null complement of *fun* which is the universal quantifier which undergoes QR, we explain immediately the interpretational facts of (54) above. No modifications are necessary at all. The universal quantifier has exactly the scope it has because it's in the same clause as *fun*, and is moving to take scope over the minimal IP in which it appears.

The question now is what kind of empty category e_i can be. Since e_i itself has no antecedent, [+a, −p] is ruled out. Assuming that e_i is in the same position that the benefactive phrase would be located (as in (59)), it would be governed by *fun*, which rules out [+a, +p]. [−a, −p] is a possibility, but that would run foul of the *no free variables* condition that we proposed in Section 8.7 above. (e_i does need to *create* a variable when it undergoes QR, but remember we're looking into what kind of empty category e itself is.) That just about leaves [−a, +p] as the only choice.

However, what are we now going to do about sentences like (48), which seemed to show that null pronouns aren't allowed in English? Epstein offers a solution, which, conveniently enough, also accounts for the ungrammaticality of (62):

(62) *It is fun for *pro* to play baseball.

He proposes that a crucial feature of *pro* in English is that it cannot be Case marked. This way, *pro* in English will be correctly barred from subject position of a tensed clause (like in (48)), as that will always receive Nominative Case from I. In (62), *pro* will be inappropriately Case marked by the preposition *for*.

Epstein's proposal is extremely interesting, although it does come slightly at a cost, not the least of which is the weakening of the link between *pro* and overt pronominals. If the four featural possibilities for empty categories are truly nothing more than unpronounced versions of their overt counterparts, then we would expect not only that *pro can* bear Case, but that it *must*, in line with other overt pronominals. This seems to be true for *pro* in true null subject languages, but would need to be modified for English.

Also, as Epstein himself notes, there are an additional class of cases which seem to be interpreted in the same way as (49) and (54), but where there is no syntactically expressible argument position:

(63)   John knows [CP how [IP PRO to solve the problem]].

(63) seems to have the logical form in (64):

(64)   [CP [IP (∀xi) [IP Johnj knows [CP how [IP PROi to solve the problem]]]]].

Unlike *fun* however, *know* does not have a position in its argument structure where a null *pro* might be lurking:

(65)   *John knows for/to Bill how PRO to solve the problem.

For these reasons, we'll have to take Epstein's arguments as tentative, rather than conclusive. It is a radical and interesting possibility though.

BIBLIOGRAPHY

The typology of empty categories as we've laid it out in this chapter is originally due to Chomsky's (1982) *Some Concepts and Consequences of the Theory of Government and Binding*, but there are antecedents in Chomsky (1981). It's in the (1981) book, for example, that Chomsky sets out the PRO Theorem, although *pro* doesn't get invented until *Concepts and Consequences*. (Chomsky (1981) says that PRO is the unexpressed subject of null subject languages.) Section 5 of Harbert (1995) also has a discussion of these issues at a slightly more advanced level but with lots of interesting additional data. It's also in Chomsky (1982) that he proposes the functional determination of empty categories, and there's some excellent discussion in Lasnik and Uriagereka (1988).

ANSWERS TO IN-TEXT EXERCISES

Exercise 1

Using the same logic, show that the traces of Passive must also be [+a, −p]. (e.g., Johni was killed ti)

What we need to do is find the governing category for the trace t_i, and then see where *John* falls inside it or outside it. The element is the trace, its governor is the past participle *killed*, but, going up the tree, the first category which has a subject is IP. The subject is accessible, and therefore the governing category for the trace is IP. *John* falls within IP, and therefore the trace of Passive must be anaphoric and not pronominal [+a, −p]. Any other combination would result in either Principle A or Principle B being violated.

Exercise 2

Show that the wh-trace in (5) is not bound in its governing category.

(5)   *Who$_i$ does he$_i$ think [$_{CP}$ t$'_i$ that Mary likes t$_i$]?

This is very similar to the previous question, actually. The governing category for t_i is the IP *Mary likes t_i*. The element is t_i, its governor is *likes*, and the first category which has a subject is the IP *Mary likes t_i*. Coindexation between *Mary* and t_i does not create an i-within-i violation. Therefore *Mary* is an accessible subject for the trace and *Mary likes t_i* is the governing category for the trace. *He* is outside of that IP, and therefore the trace is not bound in its governing category.

Exercise 3

Convince yourself that [the functional determination algorithm cannot generate [−a, +p]]. Follow every single possible path through the algorithm and check the resulting possible feature combinations.

By part (i) of the algorithm, any element in an A-position whose nearest binder is in an A'-position is [−a, −p]. But then part (ii) of the algorithm says that if you're not [−a, −p], then you must be [+a], either [+a, −p] or [+a, +p]. This clearly leaves no way to generate [−a, +p].

Exercise 4

Show that [+a, −p] is the only possible combination for the trace of Passive.

Since the trace of a Passive will be bound in its governing category (see the answer above to Exercise 1), it must be [+a]. However, it can't be [+a, +p], because that's PRO, which would require that the trace have no governing category. But it does. That leaves [+a, −p] as the only possible combination.

ADDITIONAL EXERCISES

Exercise 1

Put empty categories in the correct places in the following sentences. Using the Functional Determination Algorithm, what kinds of empty categories are they predicted to be?

1. Mary tried to fight the system.
2. Bill seems to like books about UFOs.
3. What did John believe Bill said that Mary had written?
4. John is likely to have left.
5. Who promised to leave?
6. What seems to have been taken?

Exercise 2

Redo the sentences in Exercise 1 now assuming that empty categories are determined freely. What problems, if any, do you encounter?

Exercise 3

In addition to freely determining [a] and [p] features, we could also try to make things even more free by allowing *indices* to be freely assigned. Which, if any, of the sentences in Exercise 1 would pose a problem for that? (Remember that now, in addition to checking all feature combinations, you need to check all coreference possibilities as well.)

Exercise 4

Epstein (1983) notes a potential problem for functional determination with sentences like (1):

(1)   *$[_{CP}$ Who$_i$ $[_{IP}$ did he$_i$ try $[_{CP}$ (t_i) $[_{IP}$ e$_i$ to go]]]]?

Compare the free determination, functional determination, and intrinsic determination hypotheses. Does any one of them correctly predict the ungrammaticality of (1)?

Exercise 5

One really nice thing about Chomsky's Functional Determination Algorithm is that it gives you an instant account of so-called 'parasitic gap' constructions, like (1):

(1)   This is [the kind of food]$_i$ which$_i$ you must cook e$_i$ before you eat e$_i$.

What features do the two empty categories possess, using the Functional Determination Algorithm?

9 The Empty Category Principle

Topics: government requirement on traces, that-trace effects, the Empty Category Principle, LF movement and the ECP.

Open Issue: introduction to Relativized Minimality.

9.0 Introduction

In this chapter, we're continuing our exploration of movement, focusing here on the conditions and constraints on movement. We've already seen a number of such conditions and constraints in the last couple of chapters. In Chapter 6, we discussed the Subjacency Condition, which prevents a single movement operation from crossing more than one bounding node. In the previous chapter, we saw how Binding Theory can act as an indirect constraint on movement. Because traces of A-movement are anaphors, for example, the antecedent of the trace must bind the trace within its governing category. In this chapter, though, we're going to see that more is needed. By the end, we'll have developed a very important principle that constrains movement, called the Empty Category Principle.

9.1 A BEGINNING: THE GOVERNMENT REQUIREMENT ON TRACES

As we just mentioned, we've seen that Subjacency and Principle A act as constraints on movement, but it turns out that we need more. Consider the following D-Structure:

(1) e is crucial John to see this
     (cf. e seems John to see this)

The first question we need to ask ourselves is 'what's the structure?'. In particular, does *crucial* take an IP or a CP complement? In order to help decide this, let's take a look at the contrasts in (2):

(2)a. It is crucial PRO$_{arb}$ to understand that change is needed.
   b. It is crucial for Mary to attend the meeting.

Since we appear to get PRO and *for/to* infinitives, it looks as though government by the adjective *crucial* is blocked. Therefore, *crucial* must take a full CP complement as opposed to an IP complement.

We can see this more clearly if we compare *be crucial* in (2) with *be likely* in (3), which, as a raising predicate, we know takes a 'bare' IP complement:

(3)a.   *It is likely PRO$_{arb}$ to understand that change is needed.
   b.   *It is likely for Mary to attend the meeting.

In (3a), the 'defective' IP allows PRO$_{arb}$ to be governed by the adjective *likely*, in violation of the PRO theorem. In (3b), there's no CP, and therefore no C^0 position to host *for*. The grammaticality of (2a) and (b) as compared with (3a) and (b) would seem to confirm that *crucial* takes CP, rather than an IP complement.

Now as (1) stands, the matrix predicate *is crucial* needs a subject, and *John* needs Case, but we could solve both these problems by treating (1) like a Raising structure, and doing A-movement from the embedded subject position to the matrix subject position. If we do this, the result is (4):

(4)   *John$_i$ is crucial [$_{CP}$ t$_i$ to see this]]

There's nothing incoherent about the thought that (4) expresses. It could just mean something like *it is crucial for John to see this*, on analogy with other Raising structures that we saw in Chapter 6. However, instantaneously and without prior instruction, native speakers of English know that (4) is ungrammatical. And that's a problem, because nothing that we've got so far predicts that (4) is ungrammatical.

Before Continuing: Draw the tree for (4). Verify that neither Subjacency nor Principle A is violated.

If we were to try to rule (4) out, we'd have to appeal either to Subjacency or to Principle A, but neither one of those is violated here. Consider first Subjacency:

(5)

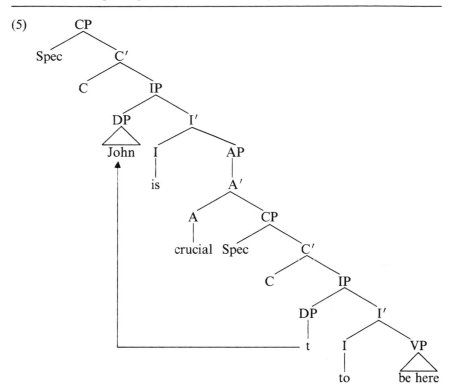

As you can see, the movement in question crosses only one bounding node (the embedded IP), so there's no Subjacency violation. You might think that maybe we can change Subjacency so that AP counts as a bounding node. NPs are bounding nodes, after all. However, that solution's not going to work. If we included AP among the bounding nodes, we'd end up ruling out standard Raising sentences like (6):

(6)   John$_i$ is [$_{AP}$ likely [$_{IP}$ t$_i$ to be here]].

The movement in (6) would hypothetically end up crossing two bounding nodes (IP and AP) and we'd predict that (6) has the same ungrammatical status as (4). So it doesn't look like changing Subjacency is the right move to make.

What about Principle A then? That seems at first glance like it might be a better alternative. Surely the movement in (5), which crosses a CP barrier must result in a trace which isn't bound in its governing category.

In order to see if this is true, we need to find the trace's governing category. Remember that that's the minimal XP containing the trace, a governor for the trace, and a subject which is accessible to the trace. It's obvious where the trace is, but notice what happens when we come to look for a governor. I can't serve as a governor because only *finite* I is a member of the class of governors. C is empty and so isn't a possible governor. And government from outside CP is blocked because the maximal projection CP is a barrier. Therefore, the trace has no governor and therefore has no governing category. (This result shouldn't really be too surprising, by the way. We saw earlier that PRO can appear in the position that the trace is in (subject of a CP infinitival). Remember from the last chapter that PRO cannot have a governing category, and therefore can only appear in positions which are ungoverned.)

But look at the problem that's created by the lack of a governing category for the trace: we had to say in the last chapter that things which have no governing category don't violate *either* Principle A or Principle B. That's how PRO can be both [+a] and [+p]. Therefore, the trace in Spec IP of the embedded clause in (5) must *satisfy* Principle A! And that means that there's no possible Binding Theory violation.

So what can we do about this? It looks as though there's some condition on movement/traces that we need to add over and above Subjacency and Principle A. Given the data that we've looked at so far, it seems as though the easiest thing to say would be that traces of A-movement have to be governed:

(7)   *Government Requirement on A-movement*
       Traces of A-movement must be governed.

A government requirement on traces would be sufficient to rule out sentences like (4). Non-finite I doesn't govern, and government from outside is blocked by the CP. Other adjectives which are going to cause a similar problem are *vital, probable,* and *necessary.*

Let's now take a look at A'-movement to see whether (7) is more general, or something specific to A-movement. If we try to do A'-movement from the subject of the embedded IP in (6), we get (8):

(8)   *[$_{CP}$ Who$_i$ is it crucial [$_{CP}$ t$'_i$ [$_{IP}$ t$_i$ to be here]]]?

Just like (4), it's not that the thought expressed by (8) is incoherent. It should mean 'who is the person x such that it is crucial for x to be here'. However, like (4), (8) is simply ungrammatical. The fact that (8) is just as bad as (4) suggests that the government requirement *should* be extended to traces of A'-movement as well, giving us (9):

(9)   *Government Requirement on Traces*
       Traces must be governed.

A government requirement on traces mean that traces and PRO will be in complementary distribution. Traces must be governed, but PRO must not be governed (the PRO Theorem). That looks like a valid generalization. Examples in the last chapter, where we said that PRO cannot appear because the positions are governed, include things like subject of a finite verb, direct object, and ECM object, as illustrated by (10):

(10)a. *PRO goes to the market every Sunday.
   b. *I hit PRO.
   c. *I believe PRO to be here.

These are all positions in which traces can appear:

(11)a. Who$_i$ t$_i$ goes to the market every Sunday (trace of A′-movement).
   b. John$_i$ was hit t$_i$ (trace of A-movement).
   c. John$_i$ is believed t$_i$ to be here (trace of A-movement).

9.2 FROM GOVERNMENT TO PROPER GOVERNMENT

However, it looks as though just adding the government requirement on traces in (9) to the list of constraints on movement won't be sufficient by itself. To see why, consider the following contrast:

(12)a. Which suspect do you think [$_{CP}$ t$'_i$ [$_{IP}$ t$_i$ committed the crime]]?
   b. *Which suspect do you think [$_{CP}$ t$'_i$ that [$_{IP}$ t$_i$ committed the crime]]?

This illustrates the so-called 'that-trace' effect. Normally in English, complementizer *that* is completely optional. You can put it in, or leave it out, and there's no change in interpretation or grammaticality:

(13)a. I think ø the police arrested Bill.
   b. I think that the police arrested Bill.

(14)a. Which suspect do you think [$_{CP}$ t$'_i$ ø [$_{IP}$ the police arrested t$_i$]]?
   b. Which suspect do you think [$_{CP}$ t$'_i$ that [$_{IP}$ the police arrested t$_i$]]?

However, when you do Wh-movement from the *subject* position of an embedded clause, complementizer *that* must be left out, as in (12a). There's some problem caused by a sequence of *that* followed by a trace (12b).[1] In this section we will focus on the 'that-trace' paradigm, particularly on the ungrammatical (12b), and the contrast between (14b) and (12a).

Before Continuing: Show that Subjacency, Principle C, and the Government Requirement on Traces are satisfied in (12b).

To start with, notice that nothing we've said so far explains why (12b) is ungrammatical Since the movement proceeds in a successive cyclic fashion, Subjacency is never violated. Movement from the embedded subject to Spec CP crosses only one bounding node, the embedded IP, and subsequent movement from the embedded Spec CP to the matrix Spec CP crosses only one bounding node, the matrix IP. As we saw in the last chapter, the trace of Wh-movement is an R-expression, but there is no Principle C violation. The only elements in (12b) which are potential Binding Theory antecedents of the trace are the wh-phrase itself and its intermediate trace. However, both of these elements are in Spec CP, which is an A'-position, and all elements in A'-positions are invisible for Binding Theory purposes. Therefore neither the wh-phrase nor the intermediate trace binds the trace as far as Binding Theory is concerned. Finally, the government requirement on traces is also satisfied. The embedded I is tensed (i.e., it's not infinitival), and so assigns Nominative Case to the embedded subject position. Since we have Case assignment, we have government to that position as well. Therefore, nothing we have so far predicts the ungrammaticality of (12b).

Clearly, we need to modify our theory in order to explain why (12b) is ungrammatical. However, in doing so we need to steer a course between the devil and the deep blue sea, as represented by the grammatical (12a) and (14b). The only difference between (12a) and (12b) is the presence of complementizer *that*. So that must be relevant for the solution. But comparing (12b) and (14b) suggests that the difference between subjects and objects is relevant as well. Movement of the embedded subject over the complementizer *that* causes a problem, but movement of the embedded direct object doesn't. We'll see that *proper government*, a stronger variety of government, will allow us to account for 'that-trace' effects. We'll be able to predict that (12b) is ungrammatical, while still allowing (12a) and (14b).

9.2.1   (12b) vs. (14b)

Let's begin by comparing the ungrammatical (12b) with the grammatical (14b):

(12)b.   *Which suspect do you think [$_{CP}$ t_i' that [$_{IP}$ t_i committed the crime]]?

(14)b.   Which suspect do you think [$_{CP}$ t_i' that [$_{IP}$ the police arrested t_i]]?

Both sentences have an overt complementizer *that*. The difference between the two is that in (12b) you have extraction of a subject and in (14b) you have extraction of a direct object. What we see is a *subject/object asymmetry*. Subjects and objects are not being treated in the same way.

As usual, in order to figure out where we should modify our theory, we should think about what principles are relevant and what the structure of the relevant sentences is. The principles that we have at the moment which govern movement and traces are (1) Subjacency, (2) Binding Theory, and (3) the Government Requirement on Traces. It doesn't look like modifying Subjacency will work. There are actually *fewer* nodes in total crossed in the ungrammatical (12b). Modifying Binding Theory looks hopeless too.

Since traces of A'-movement are R-expressions and must be free, there would have to be a c-commanding antecedent somewhere in (12b) that wasn't in (14b), but that looks impossible. All of the elements which c-command the trace in (12b) also c-command the trace in (14b). Again, if anything, (14b) should be the ungrammatical one!

The last principle we have to check is the government requirement on traces. Is there some government-related difference that we can exploit to explain what's going on? If not, we're out of luck. However, there does seem to be a small sliver of light. In (12b), the governor of the subject position is I, a functional category. On the other hand, the governor of the direct object position in (14b) is V, a lexical category.

That seems to be the only difference we've got, but it does turn out to be the right one. Let's then incorporate that difference into our theory. Anticipating the discussion a little bit, and bringing ourselves into line with standard terminology, let's say that the requirement isn't just that traces have to be governed, but rather that they must be *properly* governed, and that being governed by a *lexical* category is one way to be properly governed. This requirement that traces be properly governed is referred to in the literature as the *Empty Category Principle* (usually abbreviated ECP):

(15) *The Empty Category Principle*
      Traces must be properly governed.

(16) α properly governs β if and only if
      (i) α governs β, where α is a lexical category (usually referred to as 'lexical proper government').

Using (15) and (16), we can explain the difference between (12b) and (14b) in terms of proper government. The trace in (14b) is properly governed by the verb *arrested*. The trace in (12b) on the other hand is not properly governed, and therefore violates the ECP. We therefore predict that (14b) is grammatical but (12b) is not.

9.2.2 (12b) vs. (12a): A Second Kind of Proper Government

Lexical proper government accounts for the difference between (12b) and (14b), but notice that we've gone too far. We correctly predict that (14b) is grammatical and that (12b) is ungrammatical, but we now predict that (12a) is *also* ungrammatical:

(12)a.   Which suspect do you think [$_{CP}$ t$'_i$ [$_{IP}$ t$_i$ committed the crime]]?

    b.   *Which suspect do you think [$_{CP}$ t$'_i$ that [$_{IP}$ t$_i$ committed the crime]]?

In both (12a) and (12b), the trace in subject position is not governed by a lexical category. When the complementizer is absent (as in (12a)), the only governor is I, a functional category. When the complementizer is present (as in (12b)), both I and C are potential governors (since IP is not a barrier), but, again, both are functional categories. Therefore, both (12a) and (12b) violate the Empty Category Principle as we have it in (15) and both are predicted to be ungrammatical.

In order to solve this problem, we've got to pull back somehow. If the grammaticality of (12a) doesn't follow from lexical proper government, perhaps there's some other path to proper government. Is there some government-related reason why (12a) is grammatical, but (12b) is not?

Maybe there is. Notice that in both (12a) and (12b) the intermediate trace m-commands the trace in subject position (the first maximal projection dominating the intermediate trace is CP). The maximal projection IP intervenes, but as we saw before, IP is the one maximal projection which doesn't act as a barrier. Therefore, if we expanded the list of governors to include intermediate traces, the intermediate trace in the embedded Spec CP would govern the trace in subject position. (Only heads govern the way we have the rule at the moment.)

Let's assume that this is the second path to proper government that we were looking for. Even if you're not governed by a lexical category, you can still be properly governed provided that you're governed by an antecedent. This other type of proper government is referred to in the literature, not too surprisingly, as *antecedent government*. So, we need to keep the Empty Category Principle in (15), but modify the definition of proper government in (16):

(17)   α properly governs β if and only if

      (i)   α governs β, where α is a lexical category (lexical proper government), or

      (ii)   α governs β, where α is an antecedent of β (antecedent government).

Adding antecedent government to lexical proper government as the two ways traces can be properly governed, we'll correctly predict the grammaticality of (14b) and (12a). In (14b), the trace in direct object position is properly governed because it's lexically properly governed by the verb *arrested*. It couldn't be antecedent governed because, for example, the barrier

VP intervenes. In (12a), the trace in subject position is properly governed in virtue of being antecedent governed by the intermediate trace. It can't be lexically properly governed because the trace is only governed by I, which is not a lexical category.

But now the pendulum has swung too far in the *other* direction. We've explained the grammaticality of (12a) by saying that the trace is antecedent governed, but that explanation should carry over to (12b). We've gone from predicting that (12a) and (12b) are both ungrammatical to predicting that they're both grammatical. However, with one more little push, we can get the three-way distinction that we need.

9.2.3   A Minimality Requirement

As usual, let's take a look at what's different about (12b), and see if there's a government-related difference that we can appeal to. However, we want to make sure that (12a) and (14b) aren't once again (wrongly) predicted to be ungrammatical! Notice that the overt complementizer is a head, and, since again IP is not a barrier, the complementizer will govern the subject position just as much as the intermediate trace antecedent in Spec CP does. This means that, although both the complementizer and the antecedent will govern the trace in subject position, in (12b) the antecedent is not the *closest* governor. Instead, the complementizer is the closest governor. In the grammatical (12a), by contrast, there is no closer governor than the antecedent.

If we impose a *minimality* requirement on government, we can explain the difference between (12a) and (12b). If you're governed by some element, then that element blocks government by any other element which is further away. This idea is already present in our definition of government via the notion 'barrier'. Something inside VP, for example, can only be governed by V, the closest head, and not by a head from outside, because the maximal projection VP blocks government from anything outside. However, we need to make sure that minimality is respected for *all* forms of government, both government by heads and antecedent government.

So, not only do you need to be either lexically properly governed or antecedent governed, but the governor involved must also be the closest governor to you. This has the effect of blocking antecedent government by the intermediate trace in (12b), because the intermediate trace is not the closest governor. The closest governor is C, which is not a lexical head, and we thereby correctly predict that (12b) is ungrammatical. In the grammatical (12a) on the other hand, the C position is not filled. Therefore the closest governor is the intermediate trace in Spec CP, and the trace can be antecedent governed.

(14b) is unaffected by this. We continue to (correctly) predict that it should be grammatical. When extracting from a direct object, the trace will always be lexically properly governed by the verb. This means that the complementizer *that* may be either present or absent because the verb will always be there to provide lexical proper government. We therefore predict that both (14a) and (14b) are grammatical.

So, by way of summary, let's put together all the definitions that we have so far, including the changes that we've needed to make to the definition of *government*:

(15)   *The Empty Category Principle*
       Traces must be properly governed.

(17) α properly governs β if and only if
       (i) α governs β, where α is a lexical category (lexical proper government), or
       (ii) α governs β, where α is an antecedent of β (antecedent government).

(18) α governs β if and only if
       (a) α is a head or α is coindexed with β (this covers the antecedent government cases), and
       (b) α m-commands β, and
       (c)   no barrier intervenes (where any maximal projection except IP is a barrier), and
       (d)   minimality is respected.

With these definitions, we can now explain the 'that-trace' paradigm that we started the section with. When extracting from a subject, you rely on antecedent government to satisfy the ECP, since the subject position is not lexically properly governed. But the presence of an overt complementizer blocks antecedent government because the antecedent is not then the *closest* governor (a minimality violation). We thus predict that (12a) is grammatical but (12b) is not. On the other hand, since direct objects don't rely on antecedent government, the complementizer has no effect on grammaticality. It can either be present (14b) or absent (14a) because the verb will always be there to provide lexical proper government.

9.3   SUBJACENCY VS. THE ECP

Having motivated the Empty Category Principle in the last section, I want to show how it interacts with one of the other principles of movement that we've been talking about: The Subjacency Principle. As we discussed in the Open Issue in Chapter 4, we can use degrees of ungrammaticality to argue for the existence of separate grammatical principles. We can explain why sentence A feels more ungrammatical than sentence B by saying that sentence B violates more principles than sentence A. This provides a way of showing the reality of the principles that we're proposing – by showing that they correspond with our intuitions about degrees of ungrammaticality. In the particular cases under discussion, if a sentence which contains both a Subjacency violation and an ECP violation feels more ungrammatical than a sentence with either one alone, then we'll have good evidence for the existence of these as separate principles. If, on the other hand, the violations don't feel different, then we'll have evidence that Subjacency and the ECP shouldn't exist as separate principles of grammar, and we should look for ways to collapse them, or reduce one to the other.

With this in mind, let's remind ourselves of what constitutes a standard Subjacency violation:

(19)   *What$_i$ were [$_{IP}$ you wondering [$_{CP}$ who$_j$ [$_{IP}$ t$_j$ read t$_i$]]]?

In (19) we have a typical Subjacency violation. *Who* is filling the embedded Spec CP, forcing *what* to move in one fell swoop to the matrix Spec CP. In doing so it crosses the embedded IP and the matrix IP, resulting in a Subjacency violation.

Before Continuing: Does (19) violate the ECP? Explain why or why not.

Let's see what we've got in (19) with respect to the ECP. The trace t$_i$ in direct object position is properly governed, as it is governed by the verb *read*. The trace in subject position t$_j$ is antecedent governed by *who*. Therefore, (19) satisfies the ECP and only Subjacency is violated. As a way of getting a handle on our intuitions, notice these mere Subjacency violations have a vaguely comprehensible feel to them. On the other hand, if we change the wh-phrases around, we get almost a 'word salad' effect:

(20)   **Who$_j$ were [$_{IP}$ you wondering [$_{CP}$ what$_i$ [$_{IP}$ t$_j$ read t$_i$]]]?

Intuitively, (20) feels much worse than (19). We're in a position to explain this fact under the assumption that the ECP and Subjacency are separate principles.

Before Continuing: Are t$_i$ and t$_j$ properly governed in (20)?

First of all, in (20) there's a Subjacency violation, just as there is in (19). *Who* has to be moved in one fell swoop to the matrix Spec CP, crossing two bounding nodes, the embedded IP and the matrix IP (remember that we cannot fill a single Spec CP position twice). However, (20) also contains an

ECP violation. The trace of the subject, t_j, fails to be lexically properly governed. The only governor is the functional element I. But, unlike (19) the subject trace in (20) also fails to be antecedent governed. *What* in the embedded Spec CP can't antecedent govern t_j, because it's not coindexed with t_j. However, by minimality, what it does do is block antecedent government by anything further away, including t_j's 'real' antecedent *who*. That leaves the subject trace stranded, and unable to satisfy the ECP either by lexical proper government or by antecedent government. Therefore, while (19) violates one principle, Subjacency, (20) violates both that principle and a second principle, the ECP. And the fact that (20) is significantly worse than (19) provides us with an argument for keeping the two principles independent and separate. In the literature, violations like (19) are usually referred to as 'weak' violations (or 'mere Subjacency violations'), whereas (20) is a 'strong' (Subjacency plus ECP) violation.

9.4 THE STATUS OF INTERMEDIATE TRACES

In the last chapter, we didn't say much about intermediate traces. Binding Theory only concerns elements in A-positions and Spec CP is an A'-position. Therefore, the Binding Theory applying to empty categories won't 'see' intermediate traces (which are always in Spec CP). However, since we've now introduced the ECP, which makes reference to traces, we should take a moment and look specifically at intermediate traces and see whether the ECP applies to them or not.

Notice first that the examples that we've been talking about so far won't tell us anything about the status of intermediate traces. Consider a sentence like (14a), mentioned in Section 9.2:

(14)a.   Which suspect$_i$ do you think [$_{CP}$ t_i' ø [$_{IP}$ the police arrested t_i]]?

As normal, t_i is lexically properly governed by *arrested*. Now you might be tempted to think along the following lines: since t_i is properly governed, the only violation that there could be would have to be from t_i', the intermediate trace. Since there isn't a violation, that must mean that t_i' is properly governed. Since lexical proper government of t_i' by *think* is blocked by the barrier CP, it must be the case that t_i' is antecedent governed by *which suspect*.

Now it turns out that this *is* the conclusion that we'll reach, but it's important to see that this example doesn't show it. What's wrong with that argument is that it builds into its assumptions the answer to the question that it's asking. (For you Classics fans, it's technically called the fallacy of *petitio principii*, also known as 'begging the question'.) We want to know 'are intermediate traces relevant for the ECP?' But the above argument *assumes* that they are. (14a) is also compatible with the hypothesis that intermediate traces are just ignored by the grammar for ECP purposes, just as they're ignored for Binding Theory purposes.

So what do we need to do in order to answer the question properly? Looking at grammatical sentences won't help. What we need to do is construct an example where the only potential *violation* would come from an intermediate trace, and see what happens. If we don't see any ECP effects, then we'd conclude that the ECP doesn't apply to intermediate traces. If, on the other hand, we get an ECP violation, then we'd conclude that intermediate traces *do* need to satisfy the ECP.

So what's the right example? It's:

(21) **Who$_i$ were you wondering [$_{CP1}$ why$_j$ John said [$_{CP2}$ t$'_i$ [$_{IP}$ t$_i$ fixed the car]] t$_j$]?

(21) is strongly ungrammatical, and seems to have the 'word salad' feel of a strong ECP + Subjacency violation. The violation can't be coming from t$_i$, though. That trace is antecedent governed by the intermediate trace t$'_i$. It's also not coming from t$_j$. That trace is also properly governed. (We'll see in Section 9.5 that it is antecedent governed by *why*.) Therefore, whatever's wrong with (21) must stem from a problem with the intermediate trace t$'_i$. The movement which leaves the intermediate trace t$'_i$ violates Subjacency, but the violation is stronger than that. That suggests that t$'_i$ also violates the ECP. Now since the sentence is *ungrammatical*, we have evidence that intermediate traces *aren't* ignored. They *do* count.

9.4.1 Antecedent Government or Lexical Proper Government?

Having reached the conclusion that intermediate traces need to satisfy the ECP, we should now turn to the question of how exactly they do so. Consider (14a) again:

(14)a. Which suspect$_i$ do you think [$_{CP}$ t$'_i$ ø [$_{IP}$ the police arrested t$_i$]]?

We've just finished arguing that the intermediate trace t$'_i$ is subject to the ECP, and if that's true, then, unlike (21), the intermediate trace in (14a) must be properly governed. But how is this happening? CP is a barrier to government. Since *proper government* is a kind of government, CP should block that as well, and (14a) should be ungrammatical. What are we going to do?

Well, as usual, let's take a step back and consider the possibilities. First, we could say that there's not really a CP in (14a), just an IP. If there's no CP then there's no barrier. But that can't be right for all sorts of reasons. You can put an overt complementizer into (14a):

(22)　Which suspect$_i$ do you think [$_{CP}$ t$'_i$ that [$_{IP}$ the police arrested t$_i$]]?

So there must be a CP there, because *that* is its head. So that's out.

What looks like a better approach is to assume that we have the right structure, but just not quite the right definition of proper government. If that's right, then somehow in (14a) the intermediate trace is either lexically properly governed or antecedent governed. Let's take the two possibilities in turn, bearing in mind the key problematic fact: (21) is ungrammatical but (14a) isn't. What happens if we modify our assumptions so that t$'_i$ can be lexically properly governed? (Perhaps CP is there, but we were wrong to think that it's a barrier to lexical proper government, for example.) Well, that doesn't look like it's going to capture the difference that we want between (14a) and (21). They look the same in this respect. If we were to modify things somehow so that t$'_i$ was lexically properly governed in (14a), it's hard to see how whatever logic we use wouldn't carry over to (21), giving us the wrong prediction that (21) is also grammatical.

Antecedent government on the other hand looks a lot more promising. In the grammatical (14a), the antecedent of the intermediate trace t$'_i$ (*which suspect*) is right in the next higher CP. In the ungrammatical (21), that's not the case. The next higher CP up from t$'_i$ is filled by *why*, which isn't a potential antecedent governor because it's not coindexed with t$'_i$. (It has index 'j'.) The antecedent of t$'_i$ is *who*, which is *two* CPs higher. This looks very much like the difference we're seeing between (14a) and (21) is caused by a minimality effect. In (14a), *which suspect* is able to antecedent govern the intermediate trace because there is no closer governor. In (21), on the other hand, the nearest governor for the intermediate trace is *why*, which can't antecedent govern the trace. By minimality, though, what it does do is block antecedent government by anything further away, like *who*. As a result, the intermediate trace in (21) is stranded with no way to satisfy the ECP. So, putting aside for the moment the problem about why CP (and VP) aren't barriers to antecedent government, it seems as though appealing to antecedent government, rather than lexical government, is the right way to explain how intermediate traces are properly governed.

Just to put everything together, let's consider the grammatical (22) again:

(22)　Which suspect$_i$ do you think [$_{CP}$ t$'_i$ that [$_{IP}$ the police arrested t$_i$]]?

Both t$_i$ and t$'_i$ need to be properly governed in order to satisfy the ECP. t$_i$ is unproblematic. That's lexically properly governed by *arrested*. t$'_i$, on the other hand, satisfies the ECP by being antecedent governed by *which suspect* in Spec CP of the matrix clause.

Unfortunately, though, we're still left with this nagging problem about how exactly antecedent government works. It seems as though the right thing to say is that an element in one Spec CP can antecedent govern something which is as far away as the next lower down Spec CP. But this means that antecedent government isn't blocked by things like CP and VP, which *are* barriers to lexical proper government. For the moment, we'll just have to stipulate the definition in (23), which removes the 'barriers' requirement. In the Open Issue, we'll be in a slightly better position to explain why things should be this way.

(23) α antecedent governs β if and only if
   (i) α c-commands β,
   (ii) α and β are coindexed, and
   (iii)   minimality is respected.

9.5   ADJUNCTS AND ANTECEDENT GOVERNMENT

In motivating the ECP so far, we've looked particularly at two phenomena: that-trace effects (Section 9.2), and weak vs. strong 'island' violations (Section 9.3). In doing so, we've been focusing on the ways in which subjects are different from direct objects. We've seen that subjects trigger 'that-trace' violations when the complementizer is present and they also cause strong violations when extracted from a wh-island. Direct objects, on the other hand, *can* be extracted over an overt complementizer, and they trigger *weak* violations when extracted out of a wh-island. In this section, we'll take a look at VP-adjuncts, and see that they'll require us to modify our assumptions about lexical proper government.

The problem in a nutshell is that, unlike direct objects and subjects, VP-adjuncts don't behave in the same way with respect to these two phenomena. They act like direct objects in that they don't show that-trace effects. However, they act like subjects in that they seem to trigger strong wh-island violations. Consider first (24):

(24)   How$_i$ do you think [$_{CP}$ t$'_i$ that [$_{IP}$ John fixed the car t$_i$]]?

The string of words in (24) can be (and probably most naturally is) interpreted as having the structure indicated. That is, it's a question about how John fixed the car, as opposed to a question about how you think. An appropriate answer is 'by replacing the manifold'. So if the structure in (24) is a possible one, then following the logic that we used in Section 9.2, t$_i$ must be lexically properly governed by *fixed*. Since (24) is grammatical, t$_i$ must satisfy the ECP. Antecedent government is presumably blocked both for minimality reasons (the complementizer *that* intervenes) and because the barrier VP intervenes. That leaves lexical proper government. This doesn't look like a problem, though, since the structure of the VP is (25):

(25)

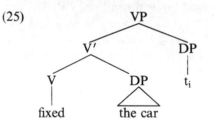

Fixed m-commands the trace, no barrier intervenes, and there's no closer governor to present a minimality problem.

However, this reasonable-looking conclusion starts to unravel when we consider sentences like (26):

(26)   **How$_i$ were you wondering [$_{CP}$ who$_j$ [$_{IP}$ t$_j$ fixed the car t$_i$]]?

(26) seems to represent a strong wh-island violation, on a par with the subject extraction that we saw in (20) above. The only possible interpretation for the string of words in (26) is as a question about how you were wondering. It just can't be interpreted as a question about how someone fixed the car. If you were to respond to the question in (26) with the answer 'by replacing the manifold', it would sound impossibly odd (because people don't wonder by replacing the manifold). Compare (26) with (24). What in (24) is the most natural interpretation for the string of words is just not possible for (26).

But now we've got a problem. Using the logic that we developed in Section 9.3, the strong ungrammaticality of (26) would lead us to conclude that the ECP (as well as Subjacency of course) is violated. But if VP-adjuncts satisfy the ECP by being lexically properly governed, (26) should be only a weak Subjacency violation like (24). t$_i$ is governed by *fixed* in (26) just like it is in (24). The relevant structure (in (25)) is identical. (Clearly, there's no problem with t$_j$. That's antecedent governed by *who* in the expected way.)

So, it seems as though what we *really* need is a three-way distinction between subjects, direct objects, and VP-adjuncts rather than just a two-way distinction between subjects and everything else. In particular, there's a difference between direct objects and adjuncts that we're not capturing. As usual, what we need to do is think about what the difference is between the two, and see if that can form the basis for a way forward.

9.5.1   θ-Marking, Case Marking, and Lexical Proper Government

The main difference between direct objects and adjuncts is that the verb doesn't θ-mark adjuncts. In a sentence like *John fixed the car with a wrench*, the verb assigns the Patient θ-role to *the car*, but it's the preposition *with* which assigns the Instrument θ-role to *a wrench*, leading to the interpretation that *a wrench* is the instrument of the fixing. Had the prepositional phrase been *in Valencia* instead of *with a wrench* then *Valencia* would have been assigned the Location θ-role by *in*. If we restrict lexical proper government so that you only lexically properly govern something if you θ-mark it, then we predict that adjuncts must be antecedent governed.

That would explain why (26) is an ECP violation: t_i fails to be antecedent governed. *Who* is in the embedded Spec CP, but it has a different index from t_i, and so can't antecedent govern t_i. However, by minimality, it blocks antecedent government from *how*.

So, it looks like introducing a θ-marking requirement into the definition of lexical proper government will explain why (26) is strongly ungrammatical. But before we do anything else we should double-check Exceptional Case Marking contexts. ECM subjects, remember, are Case marked as though they were direct objects of the verb, but are θ-marked as if they were the subjects of the infinitival clause. So tying θ-marking to lexical proper government is going to have the knock-on effect that ECM subjects should *not* be lexically properly governed. Does that look like the right result? Well, no actually. Consider (27):

(27) *Who$_i$ were you wondering [$_{CP}$ why$_j$ John believed [$_{IP}$ t_i to be the best candidate] t_j]?

(27) seems to have the vaguely comprehensible feel to it which characterizes violations of Subjacency only, and not the 'word salad' feel of an ECP violation. t_i must therefore be properly governed. Notice that it couldn't be *antecedent* governed. The nearest antecedent governor for t_i is *why*, but that has the wrong index, and also by minimality blocks antecedent government from anything farther away. Therefore, the subject position of an ECM infinitive must be *lexically* properly governed, which contradicts what we would have predicted.

Fortunately, the solution to this problem isn't too difficult. What we need to do is have lexical proper government depend not just on θ-marking, but on *either* θ-marking *or* Case assignment. In the standard case of direct objects, it won't make any difference because they're both assigned a θ-role and assigned Case. However, in order to correctly account for the fact that ECM subjects also seem to be properly governed, we need to allow for just Case assignment being sufficient. Just to be concrete about everything, let's work this discussion that we've had into a revised definition of *lexical proper government* (I've put the new material in bold):

(15) *The Empty Category Principle*
       Traces must be properly governed.

(28) α properly governs β if and only if
    (i)   α lexically properly governs β, or
    (ii) α antecedent governs β.

(29) α lexically properly governs β if and only if
    α governs β, where α is a lexical category **and α assigns either Case or a θ-role to β**.

Let's summarize where we are at this point: contrary to what we thought initially, adjuncts satisfy the ECP by being antecedent governed, rather than by being lexically properly governed. We wanted to say that in order to account for the strong ECP ungrammaticality of (26), where an adjunct has been extracted from a wh-island. (Otherwise we would have predicted just a weak Subjacency violation.) But that meant that we needed to modify our definition of lexical proper government. We made sure that adjuncts wouldn't be lexically properly governed by tying lexical proper government to either Case or θ-role assignment. Direct objects and ECM subjects will therefore be lexically properly governed, while adjuncts won't be. However, we've got one loose end that needs to be tied up.

9.5.2   Levels of Application and a Solution to the Problem of Adjuncts

We've explained why adjuncts pattern with subjects in triggering strong violations when extracted from a wh-island – both subjects and adjuncts are antecedent governed. And the wh-word in the embedded Spec CP, which creates the wh-island, will always present a minimality barrier to antecedent government. However, what we *haven't* explained is why adjuncts don't trigger that-trace violations. In other words, in correctly predicting that (26) is ungrammatical, we predict that (30) is also ungrammatical, which it isn't:

(30) How$_i$ do you think [$_{CP}$ t$_i'$ that [$_{IP}$ John fixed the car t$_i$]]?

If adjuncts are antecedent governed like subjects, then the presence of the complementizer *that* should, by minimality, prevent antecedent government of the trace t$_i$, just like it does for subject extraction. In other words, (30) should be just like (31):

(31) *Who$_i$ do you think [$_{CP}$ t$_i'$ that [$_{IP}$ t$_i$ fixed the car]]?

Lasnik and Saito (1984) suggested that the difference between (30) and (31) lies in the fact that subjects are arguments, whereas adjuncts are just that – adjuncts, not arguments. They are not required by the syntax or semantics of the verb. What Lasnik and Saito propose is that the ECP applies at different levels for arguments as opposed to adjuncts. For arguments, the ECP has to be satisfied both at S-Structure and at LF. For adjuncts, on the other hand, the ECP only needs to be satisfied at LF.[2]

How does this help us with the (30)/(31) contrast? Well, as Lasnik and Saito note, one operation that you can carry out between S-Structure and LF is the deletion of the complementizer *that*. Normally, of course, you can't delete things between S-Structure and LF. Otherwise you'd end up predicting that 'John left yesterday at 3pm' can mean just 'John left', with deletion of the rest of the material between S-Structure and LF.

However, complementizer *that* differs from *yesterday at 3pm* in that *that* has no semantic content. It contributes nothing to the interpretation of the sentence, and LF is the level at which those aspects of the syntax which are relevant for interpretation are represented. Since it contributes nothing at LF, there's no information lost if you delete it. (Arguably, one is even *forced* to delete it, if things which aren't relevant for the interpretation *must not* be present.) In this respect, complementizer *that* is similar to the expletive *there* which we discussed in Chapter 7 which also gets deleted between S-Structure and LF.

But if we're allowed (or forced) to delete complementizer *that* between S-Structure and LF, then we get rid of the minimality problem that it presents. If the ECP then checks adjuncts only at LF, we predict that there should be no that-trace problems.

Let's step through it, sticking with (30) as our example. At S-Structure, we have (32):

(32) How$_i$ do you think [$_{CP}$ t$_i'$ that [$_{IP}$ John fixed the car t$_i$]]?

Both t$_i$ and t$_i'$ need to be properly governed in order to satisfy the ECP. Complementizer *that* is blocking t$_i'$ from antecedent governing t$_i$, but at this stage that doesn't matter. Since we're talking about an adjunct chain, the ECP doesn't care about what's going on at S-Structure.

At LF, what we have is (33):

(33) How$_i$ do you think [$_{CP}$ t$_i'$ ø [$_{IP}$ John fixed the car t$_i$]]?

Now we need to check what the proper government situation is. t$_i'$ presents no problem. It's antecedent governed in the usual way by *how* in the matrix Spec CP. t$_i$ also now presents no problem. It is antecedent governed by t$_i'$. Deletion of complementizer *that* has removed it as a potential closer governor, and the intermediate trace t$_i'$ is thus able to antecedent govern the original trace t$_i$. Therefore, both traces are properly governed, and (32) is therefore correctly predicted to be grammatical.

9.6 SUMMARY OF THE ECP

So, at last, it looks as though we have the three-way distinction that we needed. Direct objects do not trigger that-trace violations, and they result in only a weak Subjacency violation when extracted from inside a wh-island. Subjects, on the other hand, behave in exactly the opposite fashion. They trigger both that-trace violations and strong ECP violations, when extracted from a wh-island. Adjuncts behave in a third, different way. They do not trigger that-trace violations, but they do trigger strong ECP violations when extracted from a wh-island.

We achieved this by assuming that direct objects satisfy the ECP via lexical proper government by the verb. Being arguments, direct objects must satisfy the ECP both at S-Structure and LF, but this raises no problem. Therefore any trace in direct object position will always satisfy the ECP. The presence or absence of a complementizer will not therefore trigger any ECP violations, and, in the case of extraction from a wh-island, the violation will always be weak.

Subjects, on the other hand, are not lexically properly governed, and are therefore dependent on antecedent government to satisfy the ECP. The presence or absence of the complementizer is therefore crucial, because the complementizer represents a closer governor than the intermediate trace. If the complementizer is present, it will block antecedent government, generating the 'that-trace' effect. The possibility of escaping a 'that-trace' violation through complementizer deletion isn't an option for subjects. Since subjects are arguments, they must satisfy the ECP both at S-Structure and LF, and at S-Structure the complementizer is present. When antecedent government fails for some other reason, for example because the antecedent governor is too far away as a result of one-fell-swoop long-distance movement, then a strong ECP + Subjacency violation is triggered.

The fact that adjuncts behave in certain respects like direct objects and in other respects like subjects is explained by the fact that, like subjects, they satisfy the ECP by being antecedent governed rather than by being lexically properly governed. This means that they too trigger a strong ECP + Subjacency violation when antecedent government fails (as in the case of extraction from a wh-island). However, because they are adjuncts and not arguments, they are able to escape the that-trace violations which subjects trigger. At S-Structure, the complementizer blocks antecedent government from the intermediate trace, but the ECP does not check adjuncts at S-Structure. By the time LF is reached, complementizer *that* has been deleted, and therefore no longer presents a minimality barrier to antecedent government. The trace of the adjunct is therefore properly governed at LF, and the ECP is satisfied.

9.7 THE EMPTY CATEGORY PRINCIPLE AND LF MOVEMENT

In Chapter 7, I tried to persuade you that LF movement really existed. One of the central arguments was that LF movement seemed to obey the same principles that overt movement obeyed. We've seen that the Empty Category Principle seems to constrain overt movement. We've also seen that the ECP is checked at LF for traces of A'-movement. In this subsection, we'll give arguments from English and other languages that the ECP constrains LF (covert) movement in addition to S-Structure (overt) movement.

9.7.1 LF Wh-Movement in English

As we saw in Chapter 7, in addition to S-Structure Wh-movement, English also has LF Wh-movement when there are multiple wh-elements. At S-Structure, only one wh-word can move to Spec CP. At LF, however, all other *in situ* wh-words move as well:

(34)　$[_{CP}$ who$_i$ $[_{IP}$ t$_i$ bought what$_j$]]? (S-Structure)
　　　$[_{CP}$ what$_j$ who$_i$ $[_{IP}$ t$_i$ bought t$_j$]]? (LF)

If we can show that the ECP constrains LF Wh-movement as well, then we'll have strong interlocking evidence both for the ECP and for the idea of LF movement in general.

It turns out that this is the moment to repay the promissory note from the Open Issue of Chapter 7. In that section, we were talking in a descriptive way about so-called 'superiority' effects, as illustrated by the contrast between (34 (repeated)) and (35):

(34)　$[_{CP}$ Who$_i$ $[_{IP}$ t$_i$ bought what$_j$]]?

(35)　*$[_{CP}$ What$_j$ did $[_{IP}$ who$_i$ buy t$_j$]]?

The correct description seems to be that when you have two wh-phrases in English, one of which c-commands the other, you have to move the 'higher' or 'superior' one at S-Structure and leave the other one to move covertly at LF.

There's a natural explanation for the contrast between (34) and (35) in terms of the ECP. Subject–object asymmetries are the characteristic mark of ECP effects, and that's precisely what we've got here. In (33) LF Wh-movement would take place from direct object position, which is a lexically properly governed position. On the other hand, in (35), LF Wh-movement would take place from subject position, a position which is not properly governed.

Let's look at (34) and (35) in more detail and see if we can give some substance to this intuition that the ECP is relevant. Consider first (34). At S-Structure, the only trace we have is t_i. This trace is in an argument chain (it's the trace of the subject), and so the ECP will check t_i at S-Structure. It's antecedent governed by *who*, and therefore presents no problem. At LF, however, we have (36):

(36) $[_{CP}$ what$_j$ who$_i$ $[_{IP}$ t_i bought $t_j]]$?

t_i has already been checked, but we now have the trace of LF Wh-movement t_j. This trace presents no problems though. As the trace of a direct object, it is lexically properly governed by the verb. (It's governed by the verb and assigned, in this case, both a θ-role and Case.) Therefore, t_j also satisfies the ECP at LF. Since there are no ECP violations either at S-Structure or LF, we predict that the sentence in (34) is grammatical.

Now let's turn to the ungrammatical (35). At S-Structure, we have:

(37)   *$[_{CP}$ What$_j$ did $[_{IP}$ who$_i$ buy $t_j]]$?

Here, the only trace is t_j. Being the trace of an argument, the ECP will check it at S-Structure. However, this satisfies the ECP as it is again lexically properly governed.

At LF, we have (38):

(38) $[_{CP}$ who$_i$ what$_j$ did $[_{IP}$ t_i buy $t_j]]$?

t_j has already been checked, but LF Wh-movement of *who* creates the trace t_i, which must also be checked. This trace presents a problem, however. Being the trace of a subject, it is not lexically properly governed. But it's not antecedent governed in (38) either. The wh-word *what* is the closest governor, but it does not have the same index as the trace, and therefore cannot antecedent govern it. But by minimality its presence blocks antecedent government from *who*, which does have the same index. Therefore, since the trace t_i is neither lexically properly governed nor antecedent governed, the ECP at LF is violated.

We therefore predict that (37) is ungrammatical. Although the ECP is satisfied as S-Structure, a violation is triggered at LF when the *in situ* wh-word moves to Spec CP. In its essence, the configuration is identical to a 'that-trace' violation configuration, in which necessary antecedent government is blocked by minimality, owing to the presence of a closer governor.

9.7.2   LF Wh-Movement in Chinese

Back in Chapter 7 we argued for the existence of LF Wh-movement in languages like Chinese and Japanese. Remember that, in these languages, all wh-words appear overtly in their D-Structure position. None move to the matrix Spec CP in the overt syntax.

(39)   Zhangsan yiwei Lisi mai-le shenme?   [Chinese]
       Zhangsan think Lisi bought what
       'What does Zhangsan think that Lisi bought?'

However, at LF *shenme* moves to the specifier of the matrix CP, and at that level the question is identical in all relevant respects to its English counterpart.

(40)   [$_{CP}$ shenme$_i$ [$_{IP}$ Zhangsan yiwei [$_{CP}$ t$_i'$ [$_{IP}$ Lisi mai-le t$_i$]]]]?

Again, this is expected if Logical Form is the level which represents those aspects of the syntax which are relevant for interpretation. Presumably there is no difference between Chinese and English questions in this respect.

     However, the relevant question here is: can we show that LF Wh-movement in Chinese and Japanese is also subject to the ECP? Consider the Chinese sentence in (41), from Huang (1995):

(41)   [$_{CP}$ [$_{IP}$ Ni xiang-zhidao [$_{CP}$ [$_{IP}$ wo weishenme mai shenme]]]]?
       You wonder   I   why   buy what
    (a)   'What is the x such that you wonder why I bought x?'
    (b)   *'What is the reason x such that you wonder what I bought for x reason?'

Crucially, the Chinese sentence in (41) only has the interpretation in (a) and *cannot* have the interpretation in (b). This shows that the ECP constrains LF movement in Chinese. It may require a little explanation to see how. Since we're talking about Chinese, we know that all wh-words will be *in situ* at S-Structure. In this case, we've got two of them: *what* and *why*. Where do they need to go at LF? Well, *wonder* is a verb which takes a +wh CP, so one of the wh-words will have to move to the specifier of the embedded CP. That leaves the other wh-word to move at LF to the matrix Spec CP. But which goes where?

Before continuing: Consider the two possibilities for LF movement: (1) *why* moves to the embedded Spec CP and *what* to the matrix Spec CP and (2) *what* moves to the embedded Spec CP and *why* to the matrix Spec CP. Under which cases is there an ECP violation and why?

Well, let's take the two possibilities in turn. First, let's assume that at LF *why* moves to the embedded Spec CP and *what* moves to the matrix Spec CP. That would give us the representation in (42) at LF:

(42)   [$_{CP}$ shenme$_i$ [$_{IP}$ ni xiang-zhidao [$_{CP}$ weishenme$_j$ [$_{IP}$ wo t$_j$ mai t$_i$]]]]
       what   you wonder   why   I   buy

We have two traces, t_i and t_j. How do they fare with respect to the ECP? t_i is the trace of the direct object, and is therefore lexically properly governed by the verb. t_j is the trace of an adjunct, and so will need to be antecedent governed. There's no problem here either, as the antecedent *weishenme* is in the embedded Spec CP. Therefore, neither trace violates the ECP. Interestingly, this is the LF which corresponds to the only possible interpretation for the question in (41): 'what is the x such that you wonder why I bought x'. (There is a question about why the Subjacency violation doesn't seem to trigger much in the way of ungrammaticality here, but the reasons for that are unclear and we'll put it off to the side.)

If we try to do things the other way, and move *what* to the embedded Spec CP and *why* to the matrix Spec CP, we get the LF in (43):

(43) $[_{CP}$ weishenme$_j$ $[_{IP}$ ni xiang-zhidao $[_{CP}$ shenme$_i$ $[_{IP}$ wo t_j mai $t_i]]]]$
         why   you wonder   what   I   buy

In this case, the trace t_i is still lexically properly governed as before. However, there's a problem with t_j. Being an adjunct, it must be antecedent governed. But the nearest governor is *shenme*, which doesn't have the same index. It therefore blocks antecedent government from anything farther away, in particular *wieshenme* in the matrix Spec CP. As a result, in the LF in (43), t_j violates the ECP. And the LF in (43) corresponds to the interpretation of (41) which is *not* possible: 'what is the reason x such that you wonder what I bought for x reason'. This strongly confirms that LF (covert) movement actually takes place in Chinese. Whether overt or covert, Wh-movement is still constrained by the ECP.

9.7.3   Quantifier Raising and the ECP

In addition to Wh-movement of various kinds, we also argued in Chapter 7 that quantifiers in English underwent A'-movement at LF, as illustrated by (44):

(44)a.   S-Structure $[_{CP}$ $[_{IP}$ I like everyone]].
    b.   LF $[_{CP}$ $[_{IP}$ Everyone$_i$ $[_{IP}$ I like $t_i]]]$.

If everything that we've said so far is correct, then we should be able to see ECP effects arising from QR.

At about the same time, Aoun and Hornstein (1985) and May (1985) independently noticed that the ECP gave an account of the following interpretational fact:

(45)a.   At least one voter expects every candidate to win.
    b.   At least one voter expects that every candidate will win.

In (45a), it's possible for the universal quantifier *every candidate* to have wider scope than the quantifier *at least one voter*. In other words, in (45a), for every candidate, there is at least one voter who expects that that candidate will win. This reading is not possible in (45b). (45b) can only mean that there is at least one voter who expects that all the candidates will win.

(46)   *One Possible Interpretation of (45a)*
         At least one voter → Candidate A
         At least one voter → Candidate B
         At least one voter → Candidate C
         And so on

     The Only Interpretation for (45b)
                     Candidate A
                     Candidate B
    At least one voter → Candidate C
                     And so on

The ECP predicts this contrast in readings. Given the S-Structure in (44a), if we try to derive the LF in which *every candidate* has wider scope than *at least one person*, we would have the LF in (47) after the application of QR:

(47)   [$_{CP}$ [$_{IP}$ every candidate$_j$ [$_{IP}$ at least one person$_i$ [$_{IP}$ t$_i$ [$_{VP}$ expects [$_{IP}$ t$_j$ to win]]]]]]

In this LF, all traces are properly governed. The trace t$_i$ is in the subject position of the matrix clause, and it is antecedent governed by the quantifier phrase *at least one person*. The trace t$_j$ is in the subject position of the ECM infinitive, and, since IP is not a barrier, it is lexically properly governed by the verb *expects*.

If we try to derive the same wide-scope reading for *every candidate* in (45b), we end up with a trace which fails to be properly governed, in violation of the ECP:

(48)   [$_{CP}$ [$_{IP}$ every candidate$_j$ [$_{IP}$ at least one person$_i$ [$_{IP}$ t$_i$ [$_{VP}$ expects [$_{CP}$ that [$_{IP}$ t$_j$ will win]]]]]]]

Both lexical proper government of t$_j$ by *expects* and antecedent government by *every candidate* will now be blocked by the intervening CP and by minimality (*that* is a closer governor). Therefore, the trace t$_j$ in subject position of the embedded clause will not be properly governed, and the ECP will be violated. Therefore, the wide-scope reading for *every candidate* in (45b) is correctly blocked, and we predict that it can only have the interpretation given in (46). This would seem to confirm both that QR represents covert movement and that it is constrained by the ECP.

9.7.4 Quantifier Raising in Other Languages

We haven't talked much about QR in other languages so far simply because there's not a lot interesting to say. Most languages work in exactly the same way as English. QR is strictly clause bounded, and occurs between S-Structure and LF. However, there's a famous example from French involving the negative quantifier *personne* 'no one', first discussed by Kayne (1981).

As you may know, French is like other Romance languages in requiring 'double' negation in the standard dialect of the language. In addition to the negative quantifier *personne*, there is also an associated negative marker *ne*, which indicates the clause over which the quantifier has scope:

(49)   Jean n'aime   personne.
       Jean not-likes 3sg no one
       'Jean doesn't like anyone.'

At LF, according to Kayne, *personne* adjoins to the IP of the matrix clause, and (50) results:

(50) $[_{CP} [_{IP}$ personne$_i$ $[_{IP}$ Jean n'aime t$_i$]]]

What's interesting about *personne* is that under certain circumstances it can associate with a *ne* which is in a higher clause. (Moving to a higher clause is something that quantifiers usually can't do, being strictly clause bounded.) However, in French, we can have (51) at S-Structure, which means we must have (52) at LF:

(51) $[_{CP} [_{IP}$ Jean n'exige $[_{CP}$ que $[_{IP}$ Marie a vu   personne]]]].
       Jean not-insist 3sg that   Marie has seen no one
       'Jean didn't insist that Marie saw anyone.'

(52) $[_{CP} [_{IP}$ personne$_i$ $[_{IP}$ Jean n'exige $[_{CP}$ que $[_{IP}$ Marie a vu t$_i$]]]]]

Under the assumption that the ECP is relevant, there won't be any problem. t$_i$ is in direct object position, and will be therefore be lexically properly governed by *seen*.

What Kayne noticed is that ungrammaticality results if *personne* is in the subject of the embedded clause as opposed to the direct object. The grammatical (51) contrasts with the ungrammatical (53):

(53)   *Jean n'exige   que personne est venue.
       Jean not-insist 3sg that no one is come
       'Jean didn't insist that anybody come.'

(54) $[_{CP} [_{IP}$ personne$_i$ $[_{IP}$ Jean n'exige $[_{CP}$ que $[_{IP}$ t$_i$ est venue]]]]]

Once again we have a subject/object asymmetry, suggesting that the ECP may be at work. Taking a look at the relevant LF in (54), it's not hard to see what the problem might be. The subject trace t_i isn't lexically properly governed, but the intervening complementizer blocks antecedent government from the antecedent *personne*. Therefore, the subject trace at LF will fail to be properly governed, and we predict that (53) is ungrammatical. A nice result, predicted by the assumption that QR at LF is subject to the ECP.

9.8 SUMMARY

In this chapter, we began by considering constraints on the movement operation. We observed that traces needed to be governed, but saw that a stronger principle was needed, which we called the *Empty Category Principle*.

(15)   *The Empty Category Principle*
       Traces must be *properly* governed.

Consideration of that-trace violations and the existence of weak vs. strong wh-islands led us to the conclusion that there were two paths to proper government: lexical proper government (for direct objects and ECM objects) and antecedent government (for subjects):

(28) α properly governs β if and only if
       (i) α lexically properly governs β
       (ii) α antecedent governs β.

(29) α lexically properly governs β if and only if
       α governs β, where α is a lexical category and α assigns either Case or a θ-role to β.

(23) α antecedent governs β if and only if
       (i) α c-commands β,
       (ii) α and β are coindexed, and
       (iii) minimality is respected.

The ECP predicts a difference between subjects, which are antecedent governed, and objects which are lexically properly governed. However, in order to explain the behavior of adjuncts, which are antecedent governed, but pattern with direct objects in not showing that-trace effects, we needed to assume, following Lasnik and Saito (1984), that the ECP applied at different levels, depending on whether the trace in question is in an A-position or an A'-position:

(55) *Levels of Application of the ECP*
The ECP applies:
(a) at S-Structure to traces in A-positions;
(b) at LF to traces in A'-positions.

In introducing the ECP, we've also found some support for the idea of covert movement at Logical Form, which we discussed in the last chapter. It appears as though LF movement in English, LF movement in languages like Chinese and Japanese, and Quantifier Raising all behave as if they obey the ECP.

OPEN ISSUE: INTRODUCTION TO RELATIVIZED MINIMALITY

In this chapter's 'Open Issue' we're going to look at an important modification that has been made to the ECP, particularly in order to address the conceptual problem with antecedent government that came up in Section 9.4.1. The essential problem is that the way the ECP is formulated looks to be a bit of a trick. It says that traces need to be 'properly governed', with the two paths to proper government being lexical proper government or antecedent government. Although we've called these two kinds of government 'proper government', implying that they're really the same thing, in reality they look quite different. Lexical proper government, on the one hand, does look plausibly like a variety of the kind of government that we saw in Chapter 4. It involves heads and seems sensitive to the same kinds of barriers (especially CP) which block 'regular' government. Antecedent government, on the other hand, really doesn't look like a variety of 'regular' government. The elements that antecedent govern are not heads, but instead maximal projections, and, crucially, you can antecedent govern through maximal projections like CP and VP. This makes it look like we're talking about two different things, and that's being obscured because we're calling them both 'government'.

There's also a question about the nature of antecedent government when we consider in more detail the question of elements which block it. Rizzi (1990) raises an important question which we've swept under the carpet until now: why doesn't the subject block antecedent government of adjunct traces? Consider (56):

(56) *[CP how$_i$ did [IP John say [CP what$_j$ [IP Bill fixed t$_j$ t$_i$]]]]?

Just like in the other cases that we discussed in this chapter, the problematic trace is t$_i$, the trace of *how*. t$_i$, being an adjunct, needs to be antecedent governed. However, the closest governor is *what*, which doesn't have the same index as *how*. Therefore, it both fails to antecedent govern t_i itself and also blocks antecedent government from *how*, which is further away.

But consider the implications of this explanation for a simple sentence like (57):

(57) [$_{CP}$ Why$_i$ did [$_{IP}$ John leave t_i]]?

(57) is grammatical, and with respect to the trace t_i, we would say that it satisfies the ECP in virtue of being antecedent governed by *why*. (In this case, there's no difference between the S-Structure and the LF representations, although technically, being an adjunct trace, it wouldn't be checked until LF.)

But Rizzi points out that we need to answer a crucial question about (57). Why doesn't the subject *John* block antecedent government by *why*? *John* is a DP which c-commands the trace t_i, and *John* doesn't have the same index as the trace. (It's not clear what it would mean for *John* and an adjunct *why*-phrase to be coindexed anyway.) Therefore, *John* (or any other subject) should, by minimality, always block antecedent government, and we therefore predict that any adjunct Wh-movement should be ungrammatical.

It's clear that we don't want this result. But now what's the difference between the ungrammatical (56) and the grammatical (57)? There's an obvious possibility – in (56), the element which blocks antecedent government is a wh-word in Spec CP. In (57) on the other hand, the subject (which we want not to be a blocker) isn't in Spec CP. Subject position isn't even an A′-position, it's an A-position.

Rizzi (1990) sees this as the key difference. He proposes changing the conception of minimality. As we've discussed it in the chapter, the concept of minimality in the ECP is a *rigid* one. That is to say, if a given element has a closer governor *of any kind*, it blocks government from *any* other governors which are further away. What Rizzi proposes we do is change to a *relative*, rather than a rigid, conception of minimality. We've got different kinds of government – government by heads (lexical proper government) and government by phrases (antecedent government), and the idea behind relativized minimality is that different kinds of governors are only blocked by closer governors *of the same type*.

According to Rizzi, we actually need to differentiate between not just *two*, but *three* different types of government. First, in order to explain the difference between (56) and (57), we need to break antecedent government down into two separate sub-cases, depending on whether the potential governor is in an A-position or an A′-position. The basic idea is that we've got two kinds of chains: A-chains and A′-chains (that is, chains formed by movement to an A-position and to A′-positions), and, under the *relativized* minimality approach, antecedent government from one type of position won't be blocked by an element in the other type of position.

In (56), we need to see if the trace t_i is antecedent governed. *How* is the trace's antecedent, but *what* is a closer governor. However, does *what* count as a blocker under relativized minimality? Yes, it does. It is, in Rizzi's terminology, a 'typical potential governor' for the trace. It's in an A′-position – the embedded Spec CP, and it's closer to t_i than *how* is. It therefore blocks antecedent government, and we still correctly predict that (56) violates the ECP.

But look how the situation changes now with respect to (57) under relativized minimality. We again are looking at t_i, and we need to see whether antecedent government by *why* is blocked. In this case, the potential intervenor is *John*. However, *John* is in an A-position, not an A′-position. It therefore isn't a 'typical potential governor' for a wh-trace, and therefore doesn't block antecedent government from Spec CP. We therefore avoid the prediction that we seemed to be stuck with under rigid minimality, in which *John* should count as a blocker and (57) should be ungrammatical.

Rizzi's relativized approach to minimality can also explain the other question which we raised initially in Section 9.4.1, and came back to at the beginning of this Open Issue: why does antecedent government seem able to pass right through supposed barriers like CP and VP when lexical proper government can't? Under relativized minimality, it's not that VP and CP are barriers in themselves. Rather it's the fact that CP or VP indicate the presence of a closer head, namely C or V, and those C or V heads will block government by any head which is further away (for example, if we're talking about Case assignment or lexical proper government). On the other hand, what's relevant for antecedent government is XPs (full phrases) in A- or A′-positions, not heads. So antecedent government will only be blocked by XPs in the relevant positions. Therefore, while a C head might block a verb from lexically properly governing a trace in Spec CP (as it would constitute a closer governor), that same trace could be successfully antecedent governed by something in the higher Spec CP (provided of course that there are no other intervening XPs in A′-positions) because antecedent government doesn't care about heads.

So, as you can see just from this introduction, it looks like Rizzi's concept of *relativized,* as opposed to *rigid,* minimality has a lot going for it. However, rather like the ending of *Star Trek II: The Wrath of Khan*, the price of success in the mission is the life of an old friend. In moving from rigid to relativized minimality, we lose the ECP analysis of 'that-trace' effects, which crucially depends on rigid minimality. Consider the familiar contrast in (58):

(58)a.　*Which suspect do you think [$_{CP}$ t_i' that [$_{IP}$ t_i committed the murder]]?
　　b.　　Which suspect do you think [$_{CP}$ t_i' [$_{IP}$ t_i committed the murder]]?

Since t_i is the trace of a subject, and therefore the trace of an argument, its status with respect to the ECP is checked at S-Structure. At this level, though, the intervention of the complementizer blocks antecedent government, and (58a) is ungrammatical. Under relativized minimality, however, it's not clear why complementizer *that*, which is a head, should be a blocker of antecedent government by a wh-trace in the embedded Spec CP. Being a head, we expect it to block lexical proper government, but not antecedent government. Rizzi is not unaware of this problem, however, and devotes a significant portion of his (1990) book to coming up with a new analysis of that-trace effects compatible with relativized minimality.

BIBLIOGRAPHY

Next to Binding Theory, the Empty Category Principle is probably the topic with more written about it than any other in Chomskyian generative grammar. There are all manner of permutations and formulations, and what we've presented here is only a basic, vanilla version. Like a lot of things, the original proposal can be found in Chomsky (1981). One of the first big revisions/expansions of the idea was mentioned back in Section 9.5.2, Lasnik and Saito (1984). It has a (deserved) reputation for being extremely difficult to read, though, and I definitely wouldn't recommend that you start there. I'd start with Lasnik and Uriagereka (1988), which is an intermediate/advanced textbook which covers the ECP. There's also some excellent discussion in Webelhuth (1995a), which you should be able to follow at this stage. Both Lasnik and Uriagereka and Webelhuth have a lot of references to the primary literature which you can follow up on.

EXERCISES

Exercise 1

Give the S-Structure and LF representations for the following sentences, being sure to insert all appropriate traces. (You may use labeled brackets rather than trees.) Show how the ECP accounts for the indicated judgement.

1. What did John buy?
2. I know who John likes.
3. Everyone believes John to be a fool.
4. Who does John believe to be a fool?
5. Who said that John left when?
6. *Why did who leave?
7. John seems to be here.
8. How did John see the man who bought the book? (Answer: with a telescope)

9. *How did John see the man who bought the book? (Answer: with a credit card)
10. Who seems to be seen every day?

Exercise 2

Do extracted objects of prepositions, as in 1, satisfy the ECP by being lexically properly governed or antecedent governed?

1. Who$_i$ did John give the book to t$_i$?

What does that predict about the following sentences? Is that prediction confirmed?

2. Who did John say that Bill gave the book to?
3. Who did John wonder whether Bill gave the book to?

What's the problem posed by the following sentence?

4. *Who did you get angry after Bill showed the photograph to?

Exercise 3

We didn't mention this in the text, but intermediate traces can also be antecedent governed by other intermediate traces. Construct the relevant example and show that this conclusion is correct.

Exercise 4

In addition to deletion of complementizer *that*, there are also situations where we want to say that intermediate traces can be deleted prior to LF. (This is presumably allowed because the *intermediate* traces themselves have no semantic content.) Discuss the relevance of this issue to the following example, under the assumption that *whether*, unlike *that*, may not delete at LF:

1. ?Who were you wondering [$_{CP}$ whether John said [$_{CP}$ t$_i'$ [$_{IP}$ ti left]]]?

Exercise 5

Discuss the problem posed for the ECP by the following example. Be sure to draw the S-Structure and LF trees and include all traces (including intermediate ones):

1. Who said that who left?

10 Verb Raising and the Analysis of Infl

Topics: verb raising, the functional category AgrOP, the 'split' Infl hypothesis.

Open Issue: more evidence for AgrOP in English.

10.0 INTRODUCTION

Since introducing phrase structure and X'-Theory way back in Chapter 2, we haven't seen any reason to modify the basic structure of the clause. As it stands, in addition to whatever *lexical* categories are needed (VP, DP, PP, etc.), the clause contains the *functional* categories IP and CP, giving us the basic structure of the clause in (1):

(1)

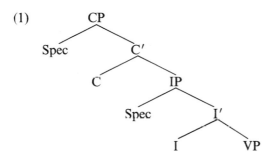

In this chapter, we examine the region between CP and VP in a little more detail. We'll see that we need more than just the single functional category IP between CP and VP. We'll in fact see that we have *three* functional categories there.

We'll first see that we need an additional functional category between IP and VP, called AgrO (which is the head of AgrOP). (The 'Agr' part is to make you think of 'agreement' and the 'O' stands for 'object.) We'll reanalyze accusative Case assignment as movement of the direct object to the specifier of AgrOP. We'll then see that 'I' itself needs to be broken up. When we introduced 'I' in Chapter 2, we said that it contains two kinds of information: subject-verb agreement and tense. We'll see that subject-verb agreement and tense each need their own functional category, AgrS ('S' for 'subject') and T respectively. Therefore, instead of the functional category IP between CP and VP, we actually have three: AgrSP, TP, and AgrOP:

(2)

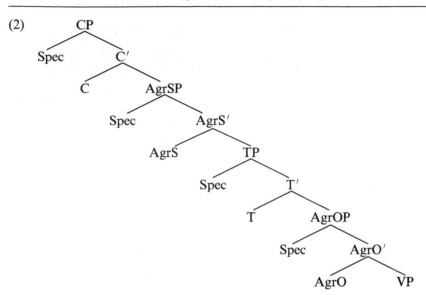

A central diagnostic that we'll be using to establish the existence of AgrSP, TP, and AgrOP will involve *verb raising*. We ignored verb raising in Chapter 6 when we observed that there was I-to-C movement in yes/no questions (*Has* John hit the ball?). We'll now come back to that. The position of the verb relative to other DPs in the sentence will be an important piece of our arguments for these three functional categories.

In Section 10.1, we'll discuss verb raising in some detail. In Section 10.2, we'll examine the arguments for AgrOP as a functional category which sits between IP and VP. In Section 10.3, we'll explore the arguments for breaking up IP into AgrSP and TP.

10.1 VERB PHRASES AND VERB RAISING: AN INTRODUCTION

Before we can begin giving arguments for AgrSP, TP, and AgrOP, we need to discuss a topic that we only mentioned in passing back in Chapter 6. Since the introduction of the concept of movement in that chapter, we've seen many different kinds of movement taking place both between D-Structure and S-Structure (overt) and between S-Structure and LF (covert). Now all of these movements had something in common. They consisted of XP movement; that is to say, movement of maximal projections. I now want to come back and say a little more about the movement of *heads*, also known as X^0-movement. Head movement, and verb movement in particular, plays a crucial role in the main arguments that we'll be giving in this chapter.

10.1.1   A Review: Raising from I-to-C

The most frequent type of head movement, and the one which we'll be entirely concerned with here, is verb movement. We saw our first instance of verb movement briefly back in Chapter 6, when we introduced Wh-movement in English. In English there are S-Structure word order alternations between a wh-question and its corresponding declarative, as illustrated in (3):

(3)a.   What can John buy?
   b.   John can buy a book.

We know that the wh-word in (3a) must be in Spec CP, and we also know the subject *John* must be in Spec IP (the structural position for subjects). Based on this information, we can feel pretty confident in saying that the auxiliary has moved from I to C, as illustrated by the tree in (4):

(4)

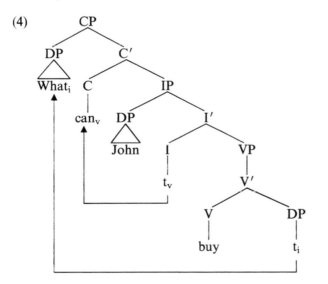

The word order tells us that the auxiliary must be somewhere between Spec CP and Spec IP, and the only available position is the empty head of the CP, C^0. Since C^0 is a head position and the auxiliary *can* is a head (it's an I), there's no phrase-structure incompatibility in moving it from I to C.[1]

The logic is pretty obvious, but it's worth making it explicit because it illustrates a standard procedure for figuring out where an element has moved. Rather like navigating across the ocean, what you need to do is figure out where your fixed points of reference are and then triangulate based on them. So, in the above example, our fixed reference points are the wh-word in Spec CP and the subject in Spec IP. We know that those elements are in those positions. Therefore, based on the word order, the position of the auxiliary *can* in the phrase-structure tree must be somewhere where it can end up between *what* and *John*. And, because we're talking about the movement of a head, the position that it's moving to must be a head position. In this case, there's only one position which fits the requirements, and that's C.

10.1.2   Raising from V to I

In addition to raising from I to C (in questions, for example), we also have instances where verbs raise from V to I. French is a language which is commonly used to illustrate this kind of verb movement. In French, main verbs obligatorily appear to the left of both VP-oriented adverbs and sentential negation. They may not appear to the right of either. (The analysis of negation in French is complicated slightly by the fact that the standard dialect contains two negative elements *ne* and *pas*. Following normal practice, we'll assume that it's *pas* which represents the sentential negation. We'll take *ne* to be a part of the verb.[2])

(5)a.   Jean *va* souvent à l'école.
         Jean goes often to the school
         'Jean often goes to school.'
   b.   *Jean souvent *va*   à l'école.
         Jean often   goes to the school.

(6)a.   Jean ne va pas au magasin.
         Jean *ne* go not to the store
         'Jean isn't going to the store.'
   b.   *Jean ne pas va à la magasin.

Like Spec CP and Spec IP, adverbs and negation are often used as fixed points of reference to help us navigate in the wide-open seas of movement and word order. It's standardly assumed that so-called 'VP-oriented' adverbs (which we'll discuss in more detail below) establish the left-hand boundary of the VP. (The usual assumption, which we'll adopt here, is that these adverbs are adjoined to VP. Negation, on the other hand, is normally assumed to head its own function projection between IP and VP.) Therefore, the fact that the verb in French must appear to the left of these adverbs and *pas* (as (5) and (6) illustrate) is taken to show that they've raised out of the VP to some higher position. In this subsection, we'll examine this issue in detail, and look at some similarities and differences between French and English with respect to verb movement.

10.1.2.1   Adverbs and Negation: Two More Reference Points
Let's start by looking at *VP-oriented* adverbs. These are adverbs which specifically modify the verb phrase, as opposed to the entire sentence. A canonical VP-oriented adverb is *completely*. VP-oriented adverbs are one of the key reference points when looking at V Raising to I because they're usually assumed to be adjoined to VP. Therefore, the sentence in (7) has the tree in (8):

(7)   John will completely destroy the town.

(8)
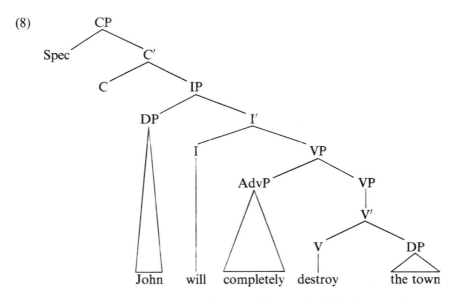

Completely is serving as an adverbial modifier to the VP *destroy the town*. We would therefore expect it to be a sister to the VP, which it is under the VP-adjoined analysis. With respect to the linear order, it comes to the right of the auxiliary in I and to the left of the verb in VP, which is also as expected. (VP-oriented adverbs are different from *sentential* adverbials such as *probably*, which modify the entire sentence and are not always adjoined to VP.)

   Sentential negation is also standardly used as a diagnostic for the left edge of VP. The only difference between negation and adverbs is that negation is standardly assumed to have its own functional projection NegP, rather than being simply adjoined to VP. So the tree for a sentence like (9) would be (10):

(9) John will not destroy the town.

(10)

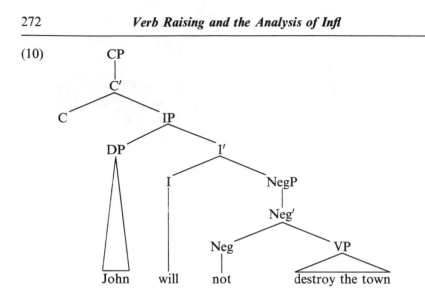

So in the context of the question of whether a verb has raised from V to I, VP-oriented adverbs and negation play a key role. If the verb appears to the left of the adverb/negation, then we assume that it is in a higher position like I. On the other hand, if the verb is appearing to the right of the adverb/negation, then we assume that it is within the VP.

10.1.2.2 V-to-I Raising in English and French

Let's now take a look at some facts about French and English verbs, and where they appear relative to the fixed points that we've been discussing. Compare the following English sentence with its French translation:

(11)a.   John is *seldom* greedy.
    b.   Jean est *rarement* avide.
       J. is seldom greedy.

If *seldom* is adjoined to VP both in French and in English, and *John/Jean* is in Spec IP, then the verb *is/est* must therefore be in I. But could it have been base-generated there at D-Structure? That would be unlikely. If it were, we would be left with a verb phrase with no verb head – not possible. So we must assume that *is* was base-generated at D-Structure as the V head of VP, and then moved to I at S-Structure. That gives us the representations in (12) for D-Structure and S-Structure (which are the same for French and for English, aside from the words of course).

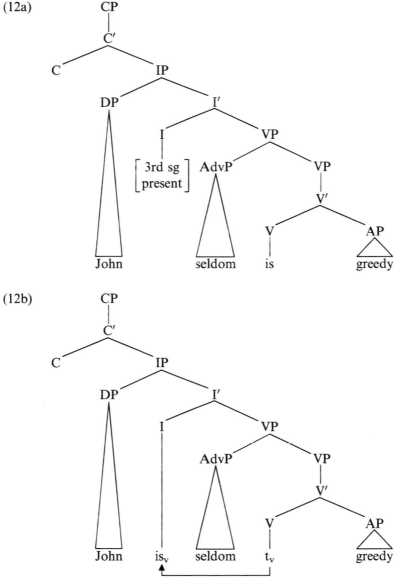

(12a)

(12b)

So (12) shows the raising of *be* from V to I both in English and in French. In a yes/no question, V to I raising combines with I to C raising, resulting in V-to-I-to-C raising:

(13)   [CP Is_v [IP John t'_v [VP seldom [VP t_v greedy]]]]?

Given the situation in (12), we'd expect the same facts to obtain when we turn from adverbs to negation, and our prediction seems to be borne out. In English, auxiliaries in I appear to the left of negation and not to the right:

(14)a.   John is *not* greedy.
   b.   *John *not* is greedy.

The only difference in the structure between adverbs and negation is that negation is assumed to head its own functional projection, NegP. So instead of a tree as in (12), we have (15):

(15)

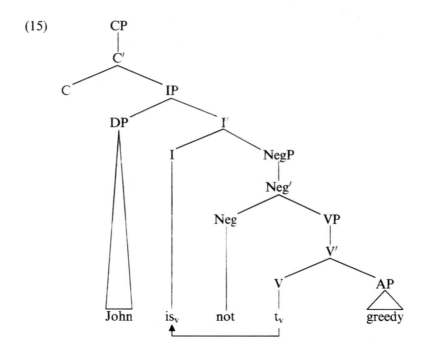

In French, the grammatical translation of (14a) is (16):

(16)   Jean n'est *pas* avide.
       Jean *ne* is not greedy

As expected, the verb *to be* appears to the left of negation, suggesting again that it has raised from V to I, as illustrated by (17):

(17)

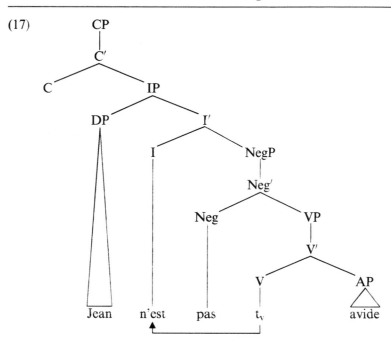

Again, this raising is obligatory, as illustrated by (18):

(18)   *Jean ne *pas* est avide.

It therefore seems that, with respect to the verb *to be*, both English and French behave identically. The adverb and negation placement tests suggest that in both cases the verb obligatorily raises from V to I.

The situation is similar with respect to the verb that behaves like an auxiliary, *have*, at least in British dialects of English. Like the verb *be*, *have* raises from V to I in the syntax, appearing to the left of both VP-adjoined adverbs and negation:

(19)a.   John has seldom enough money.
   b.   John hasn't enough money.

In most American dialects of English, on the other hand, the verb *to have* patterns with 'main' verbs, whose behavior we'll talk about now.

French and English differ with respect to the behavior of 'main' verbs. Main verbs in English do *not* raise to Infl, but in French they do. Consider first the adverb placement situation, this time using another VP-oriented adverb *completely*:

(20)a.   John *completely* answered the question.
   b.   *John answered *completely* the question.

(21)a.   Jean répondait   *complètement* à la question.
         Jean answered (imperf) completely   the question
         'Jean completely answered the question.'
   b.   *Jean *complètement* répondait à la question.

In (20), we see that the English main verb appears to the right of the adverb
and may not appear to its left. In French, we have the reverse situation. This
seems to show that the main verb in French must raise to Infl, but cannot in
English. Just as we'd expect, French main verbs can also undergo further
raising to C if there is a yes/no question, but English main verbs do not.

(22)a.   Répondait-il à la question?
   b.   *Answered he the question?

(Interestingly, the fact that (22b) may feel 'Shakespearian' to you is a
reflection of the fact that, at an earlier stage of its history, English was like
French in allowing main verbs to raise from V-to-I and from I-to-C.)
   Turning now to negation, the word order facts with respect to verb raising
are identical to what we've seen with adverbs. As expected, English main
verbs may not raise to I past the NegP:

(23)a.   *John goes *not* to the store.
   b.   John does *not* go to the store.

Precisely here we see the 'dummy' verb *do*, which we saw in Chapter 6,
which is needed because the full verb is not raising from V to I. French
verbs, on the other hand, not only *can* appear to the left of NegP, they *must*
appear there:

(24)a.   Jean ne va *pas* au magasin.
         Jean ne goes not to the store
         'Jean doesn't go to the store.'
   b.   *Jean ne *pas* va au magasin.

From this, we conclude that French main verbs must be raising past the
NegP from V to I.
   The copula verb *to be* in both French and in English appears to the left of
adverbs and negation, corresponding to raising from V to I. However, there
appears to be a difference with respect to main verbs. In English they may
not raise from V to I, but in French they must.

10.1.3 LF V-Raising and a 'Checking' Theory of Morphology

In comparing French and English verb raising, we've seen that French verbs
raise from V to I, but full verbs in English do not. But we need to qualify

this statement. English main verbs don't raise from V to I at S-Structure, but they do at LF.

Remember that back in Chapter 7 we saw instances of XP movement which took place between S-Structure and LF – that is, (covert) XP movement that you don't 'see'. There's no *a priori* reason why the same shouldn't be true of head movement. The possibility should exist that there are head movements that you don't 'see' because they take place between S-Structure and LF. English verb raising is such a case.

First, there are good conceptual reasons for thinking that English verbs *do* raise at LF from V to I. Throughout the book, we've been assuming that I contained two important items: the subject-verb agreement information and the tense information. One reason we mentioned back in Chapter 3 was that this information seems to be left behind in VP deletion/ellipsis constructions – (25), for example:

(25)   John practices for three hours every day and Bill does too.

In (25), the VP *practice for three hours every day* has been elided, but the agreement and tense information seem to have been left behind. They're not deleted, but instead are realized on the 'dummy' verb *do*. It shows third person singular agreement (it's *does* and not *do*) and it's in the present tense (*does* and not *did*). We took this as an argument that this agreement and tense information was in Infl, not V, and therefore did not get elided.

But at the same time, this information *is* realized on the verb when there's no auxiliary. In the first conjunct of the above sentence, the verb *practices* is also third person singular and present tense. If that verb is in V and the agreement and tense information is in I, how do the two things ever get hooked up together? In French, you have V-to-I raising in the syntax, so it's not really a problem. But how does English work?

There's an obvious answer. It's not that what comes out of the lexicon is *practice*, which then merges somehow with the agreement and tense information to give you *practices*, *practiced*, or whatever. Instead, the verb is selected from the lexicon 'fully formed', for example, as *practices*, and then after V-to-I raising, it checks its tense and agreement features with the features in Infl. If they match, everything's OK. If they don't match, then the sentence is ungrammatical. In French, this happens overtly between D-Structure and S-Structure, because we see the effects of V-to-I in the overt linear order of the words. But in English this checking process happens at LF. So therefore, an English sentence like (26) really has (27) as its LF:

(26) John [$_{VP}$ often [$_{VP}$ sees Bill]].

(27)

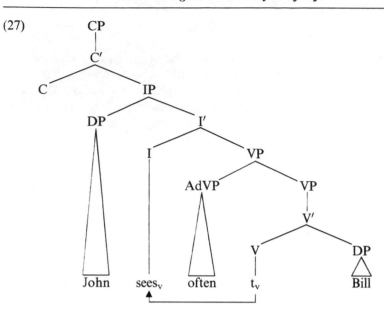

This is a nice conclusion because it dovetails perfectly with some of the arguments that we gave for LF movement of XPs back in Chapter 7. Logical Form encodes those aspects of the syntax which are relevant for interpretation. But it's hard to imagine that there's any difference with respect to LF between a simple English declarative sentence and its French translation. But if we don't postulate LF raising, then the LFs *will* be different. For example, negation would have wide scope relative to the verb in English because negation c-commands the verb. In French on the other hand, the verb would have wider scope than negation (because the c-command relations are reversed). We don't expect to see LF differences like this, and they don't seem to exist. By positing LF V-to-I raising in English, we then make the claim that French and English *are* the same at LF, which looks like the right thing to say.

EXERCISE 1

Which of the following languages have overt V-raising?

(a) **Gianna non parla più/*Gianni non ancora più.**
     Gianni not speaks anymore
     'Gianni is not speaking anymore.'

                                                    (Italian, from Belletti (1994))

(b)   ... at me ikke kjøpæ bokje/* ... at me kjøpæ ikke bokje
    that we not buy(pl) the.book
    '... that we didn't buy the book'
                (Hallingdalen dialect of Norwegian, cited in Vikner (1994))

10.2   AgrO: A NEW FUNCTIONAL PROJECTION

In the rest of this chapter, we'll be giving arguments, often using verb raising as a diagnostic, for revising the structure of the clause. The first functional projection that we'll be looking at is called AgrOP. As mentioned, the 'Agr' part is to remind you of 'agreement', and the 'O' for 'object'. The main function of this functional category is to serve as a mediator for accusative Case assignment. It lies between IP and VP, as illustrated in (28):

(28)

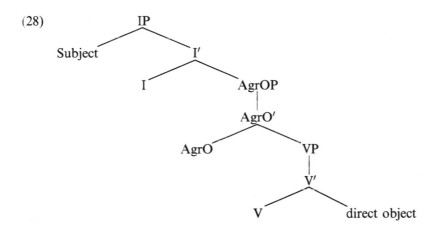

Up until this point, we've been assuming that accusative Case is assigned to an object under government from the verb. Under the AgrOP analysis, it works a little differently (and hopefully better!). Recall that nominative Case is assigned in a *specifier-head* relationship: the *head* of (finite) I assigns nominative Case to the DP which is in the *specifier* of IP. Under the AgrO analysis, accusative Case is essentially the same. Accusative Case is assigned in a specifier-head relationship by having the direct object raise to the specifier of AgrOP. As before, V raises to I, but in the AgrO analysis it passes through AgrO on its way to I:

(29)

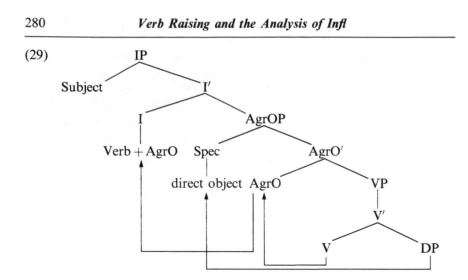

This can sometimes happen in the overt syntax, and we'll see an example of this in Icelandic. However, it is more common for it to happen at LF, which is the way it happens in English. Let's now look at the arguments for this new AgrO analysis.

10.2.1 A Conceptual Argument

The first argument for AgrOP that we'll consider is one that I have just alluded to. It's a conceptual argument regarding Case assignment, first discussed by Chomsky in joint work with Howard Lasnik (published as Chapter 1 of Chomsky (1995)). In Chapter 3 we argued that government provided the unifying concept for Case assignment. I and V are both governors. With respect to nominative Case, I m-commands the subject in Spec IP, no barrier intervenes. It is therefore able to assign nominative Case to the subject. For accusative Case, the verb m-commands the direct object and again no barrier intervenes.

However, Chomsky and Lasnik note that, despite the fact that government allows us to provide a unified analysis of nominative and accusative Case assignment, true unity is still lacking because Case assignment takes place in two different structural configurations. Nominative Case is assigned in a specifier-head relationship (between I and Spec IP), but accusative Case assignment takes place in a head-complement relationship (between V and its sister DP). Chomsky and Lasnik believe that we would have a better theory if we could make nominative and accusative Case assignment more unified, specifying a single configuration in which Case assignment takes place.

It's, of course, possible that the single unified configuration we're looking for is neither of the ones we have at the moment, neither specifier-head nor head-complement. However, the easier approach would be to try to collapse one into the other. Perhaps nominative Case assignment 'really' happens in a head-complement configuration. Or perhaps it's the other way around: accusative Case assignment 'really' happens in a specifier-head configuration.

Chomsky and Lasnik suggest that it's accusative Case assignment which is the one that is 'out of step', so to speak, and that Case assignment should be unified as a specifier-head relationship with a functional category. For nominative Case assignment, we already have the functional category IP, with the subject in the specifier of IP. For accusative Case assignment, Chomsky and Lasnik introduce the functional category AgrO.

So, it's because of general considerations of theory neatness that we would prefer to have one configuration for Case assignment rather than two. These are the kinds of considerations that I've been calling 'conceptual'. However, as mentioned in the Introduction, we can be more sure of our conclusions when we find *empirical* motivation. In other words, conceptual considerations are most useful when they serve to predict concrete facts especially ones that we had not noticed before. In the remaining parts of this section, we'll examine some empirical arguments for the correctness of Chomsky and Lasnik's hypothesis.

10.2.2 Object Shift

Some empirical support for the idea that direct objects move to the specifier of a VP-external functional category (AgrO) in order to get accusative Case comes from a phenomenon seen in Germanic languages which goes under the general name of 'object shift'. To take Modern Icelandic as an example, it appears that full DP direct objects may optionally move to a position which precedes the VP but follows IP. A natural assumption is that this movement represents *overt* movement of the object to the specifier of AgrOP.

To begin, let's look at a standard Icelandic sentence like (30):

(30) Jólasveinninn   borðaði ekki hattinni.
      the Christmas troll ate   not the hat
      'The Christmas troll didn't eat the hat.'

First, we need to figure out what the correct structure for (30) is. Icelandic is a head-initial language, so heads precede their complements. Like English, the subject is in Spec IP. One minor difference is that in Icelandic the sentential negation, *ekki*, is standardly assumed to be just another VP-adverb. It is therefore adjoined to VP rather than having its own projection, as in French or English. Given this information, it seems clear that the Icelandic verb in (30) has raised from V to I, giving us (31):

(31)

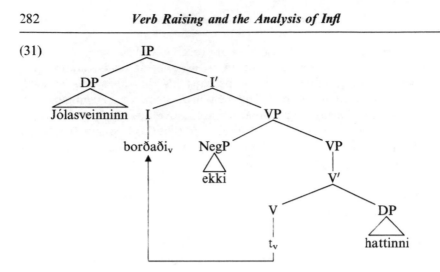

However, consider now (32) (from Bobaljik and Jonas (1996)), which is equivalent in meaning to (30):

(32)   Jólasveinninn   borðaði₍ᵢ₎ hattinni₍ⱼ₎ [ᵥₚ ekki [ᵥₚ tᵢ tⱼ]].
       the.Christmas.troll ate   the.hat   not
       'The Christmas troll didn't eat the hat.'

In (32), *ekki* is still marking the left edge of VP and the verb has again raised from V to I. Given that this is the case, we are left in something of a quandary as to where the direct object *the hat* could be. There is no position which corresponds to where *the hat* seems to have moved to.

(33)

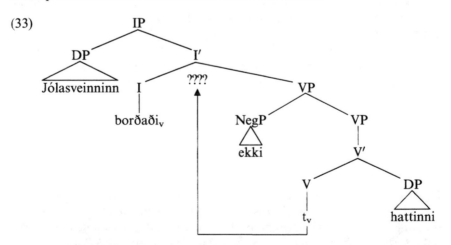

You might wonder why we don't analyze *ekki* as being VP-*final* in (32). That way, there would be no reason to assume that *the hat* is anywhere other than it its base-generated direct object position, giving us the analysis in (34):

(34)   Jólasveinninn   borðaði_i [_{VP} [_{VP} t_i hattinni] ekki].
       the.Christmas.troll ate   the.hat   not
       'The Christmas troll didn't eat the hat.'

However, as (35) shows, *ekki* must appear VP-initially, and cannot appear VP-finally:

(35)a.   *Jólasveinnin hafa [_{VP} borðað   hattinni ekki].
         the.Christmas.troll   has eaten the.hat not
   b.   Jolasveinnin hafa [_{VP} ekki borðað hattinni].

In (35a) and (b), we can be sure that that past participle *borðað* is still within the VP because the obligatory V-to-I raising is taken care of by the auxiliary *hafa*. This in turn means that *hattinni* must be in its base-generated direct object position. The fact that (35a) is ungrammatical shows that *ekki* simply may not appear VP-finally. It may only appear VP-initially. Therefore, back in (32) *ekki* must still be VP-initial, with both the verb and the direct object having moved out of the VP.

But if that's correct, then we appear to need another category between IP and VP in order for there to be a place for the direct object to move to in (32). The functional category, AgrOP, between IP and VP, would seem to provide exactly what we're looking for. The direct object is simply moving to the specifier of AgrOP:

(36)

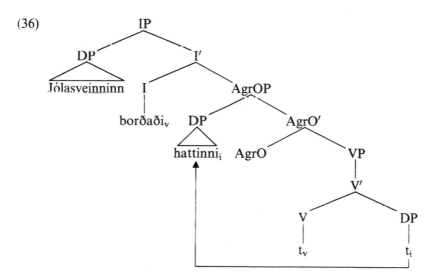

So it seems that in Icelandic, we see overt movement to Spec AgrOP, corresponding to the covert movement that we postulated in the case of English.

10.2.3   V-Raising of Infinitives in French

Having seen the need with Object Shift in Icelandic for an XP position between IP and VP, in this section I want to turn to some evidence that suggests that we need a *head* position between IP and VP as well. To do this, we need to return to the issue of verb raising in French, we we discussed earlier in the chapter.

We saw evidence back in Section 10.1.2.2 that main verbs in French obligatorily raise from V to I. We concluded this because they obligatorily appear to the left of negation and VP-oriented adverbs. However, when we turn to the behavior of main verb *infinitives* in French, we see a problem. Although main verbs infinitives in French must appear to the right of negation, they *can* appear to the left of VP adverbials. The problem is that, under our current assumptions, there's no head-position corresponding to that place in the linear order. Put another way, without AgrO, there's nowhere for them to move to.

Let's start by looking at infinitives of the verb *be*, which are basically unproblematic. The verb *be* in its finite form is required to raise from V to I, as we saw above. However, when it's in the infinitive form, it may optionally raise from V to I in the syntax, but is not required to.[3] Consider first the word order relative to VP-oriented adverbs:[4]

(37)a.   Être *complètement* malhereux est dangereux.
        to be completely   unhappy   is   dangerous
        'Being completely unhappy is dangerous.'

     b.   *Complètement* être   malhereux est dangereux.
        completely   to be unhappy   is   dangerous
        'Being completely unhappy is dangerous.'

Since the infinitive may either precede or follow the adverb adjoined to VP, we conclude that 'auxiliary' infinitives like *être* may optionally raise from V to I.

This conclusion is reinforced by the evidence from negation, as illustrated in (38):

(38)a.   N'être   *pas* heureux est une condition pour écrire.
        Ne to be not happy   is   a condition   for   to write
        'Not being happy is a condition for writing.'

     b.   Ne *pas* être heureux   est une condition pour écrire.
        Ne not to   be happy is   a condition   for   to write
        'Not being happy is a condition for writing.'

The infinitive again may appear either to the left or to the right of negation, suggesting again that it may raise from V to I in the syntax, but it is not required to.

Turning now to main verb infinitives, they initially seem unproblematic. If we take a look at the word orders relative to VP-adjoined adverbs, we have (39):

(39)a.   Perdre *complètement* la tête   est dangereux.
         to lose completely   the head is dangerous
         'To completely lose one's head is dangerous.'

   b.   *Complètement* perdre la tête   est dangereux.
         completely   to lose the head is dangerous
         'To completely lose one's head is dangerous.'

On the evidence of adverb placement, it would seem that main verb infinitives pattern together with the infintive of *être* just discussed. These infinitives may raise from V to I in the syntax, but are not required to.

(40)

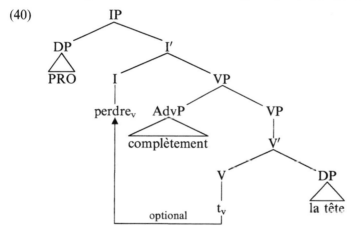

However, the facts regarding *negative* placement tell a different story. On the basis of adverb placement, we'd expect that, since main verb infinitives can optionally appear to the left of VP-adjoined adverbs, they should be able to appear to the left of negation. But this prediction is not borne out:

(41)a.   *Ne sembler *pas* heureux est une condition pour écrire.
         Ne to seem not happy   is a condition   for   to write
         'Not to seem happy is a condition for writing.'

   b.   Ne *pas* sembler heureux est une condition pour écrire.
         Ne not to be   happy   is a condition   for   to write
         'Not to seem happy is a condition for writing.'

This is a problem. (39) suggests that main verb infinitives *can* move from V to I, but (41) suggests that they can't. However, the problem is in reality even worse. If we put negation plus an adverb together, what we find is that the infinitive can optionally move to a position *between the adverb and negation*. Pollock himself doesn't actually supply the relevant example, but we have the following from Haegeman (1994):

(42) Ne *pas* arriver *souvent* en retard, c'est triste.
     Ne not to.arrive often   late   that's sad
     'Not often arriving late is sad.'

(42) corresponds with the unproblematic (43), in which raising does *not* take place:

(43) Ne pas souvent arriver en retard, c'est triste.

What the contrast between (39) and (41) suggests, and what (42) seems to show explicitly, is that there's a head position somewhere between VP and NegP which main verb infinitives in French can optionally move to. It can't be moving all the way to I, because then otherwise we'd expect that it could appear to the left of negation, which is lower than I, and (41a) should be grammatical. But the phrase-structure system with just IP and VP can't accommodate this. Just as with object shift in the previous section, an element appears to be moving into a position that doesn't exist:

(44)

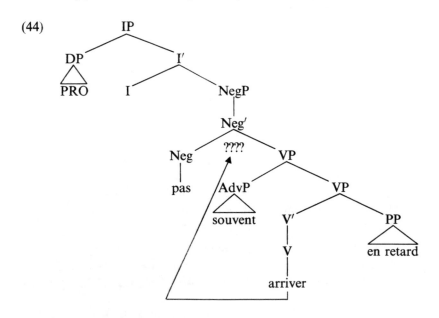

What we seem forced into assuming is that there is a functional projection of some kind which lies between NegP and VP, and the verb may optionally raise from V to this intermediate head position. Fortunately, this intermediate position is precisely where AgrO is hypothesized to be:

(45)

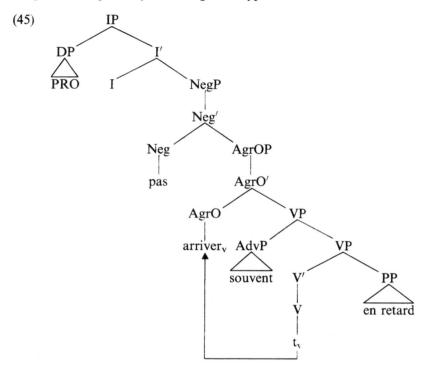

Under the assumption that main verb infinitives in French may optionally raise from V to AgrO, but not any further, all of the facts seem to be explained.

10.2.4 Antecedent Contained Deletion in English

We've seen data from Icelandic and French suggesting that we need a functional projection between IP and VP, but what evidence is there from English? Well, Hornstein (1995) provides an empirical argument from English for the claim that accusative Case is assigned by moving to the specifier of AgrO.

In this case, the argument comes from a phenomenon referred to as *antecedent contained deletion*, which is a subpart of a more general process called *ellipsis*. (46) illustrates ellipsis:

(46)   John has gone to the store and Bill has ... too.

Clearly, the second conjunct is missing some information, indicated by the ellipsis. Specifically, it seems to be missing its VP. However, (46) is not ungrammatical. Instead, the VP for the second conjunct is interpreted as identical to the VP in the first conjunct. So, as far as the interpretation is concerned, we have (47):

(47)   John has gone to the store and Bill has [gone to the store] too.

There are various ways in which such ellipsis is accounted for, but one standard assumption is that the whole VP from the first conjunct is copied into the VP of the second conjunct at LF. That will ensure that *Bill has too* gets the correct interpretation. The predicate of which Bill is the subject isn't just *gone*. It's *gone to the store*. (46) doesn't mean that John has gone to the store and Bill has just gone somewhere. It seems that it's the whole VP *gone to the store* which gets copied.

There are cases, however, where the VP gap that we're trying to fill in is *inside* the VP that we're trying to copy. These are instances of *antecedent contained deletion*. It turns out that the VP-copying explanation for ellipsis runs into some potentially serious problems when we look at sentences with antecedent contained deletion. Take a look at (48):

(48)   John kissed everyone that Sally did [e].

Just as we did above, in order to recover the 'missing' material, and figure out what the meaning of (48) as a whole is, we need to copy a VP into the place of the gap. However, watch what happens when we try to apply our VP-copying rule. The only VP around is the matrix VP *kissed everyone that Sally did [e]*. And what happens when we copy that VP? We get (49):

(49)   John kissed everyone that Sally did kiss everyone that Sally did [e].

And this doesn't solve our problem. We still don't know what the sentence as a whole means, because we've still got elided material. In other words, we've still got a gap to fill in. Just as before, there's no VP to copy into the gap other than *kissed everyone that Sally did [e]*, but that contains another gap. As you can see, we can continue this procedure for as long as we want to, but we'll never get to the end. It seems that no matter what we do, we'll never be able to figure out what (48) means, because we'll always have missing material that needs filling in.

May (1985) realized that this problem of the interpretational infinite regress with antecedent contained deletion could be solved by Quantifier

Raising (and in fact gave this as an argument for QR). Let's look at (48) not at S-Structure, but at LF:

(50) [$_{IP}$ everyone that Sally did [e]$_i$ [$_{IP}$ John [$_{VP}$ kissed t$_i$]]]

At LF, the entire quantified phrase *everyone that Sally did [e]* undergoes QR and adjoins to IP. Notice how this changes the picture. At LF, the matrix VP no longer contains a gap. It contains a trace, which is crucially different. If we take the VP *kissed t$_i$* and paste it into the gap, we get (51):

(51) [$_{IP}$ everyone that Sally did [$_{VP}$ kissed t$_i$]$_i$ [$_{IP}$ John [$_{VP}$ kissed t$_i$]]]

There's no elided material anywhere in (51), so we've managed to avoid the infinite regress problem. And we've also managed to get exactly the interpretation that (48) has. The LF in (51) is interpreted as 'for every x such that Sally kissed x, John kissed x'. And that seems to be exactly what (48) means.

It turns out that we can use antecedent contained deletion in Exceptional Case Marking contexts to construct an argument for AgrOP in English. Consider the contrast in (52):

(52)a. ?I expect everyone you do to visit Mary.
  b. *I expect everyone you do will visit Mary.

Clearly, what (52a) and (52b) are trying to convey is mutual expectation. You have some number of people who you expect will visit Mary, and I want to assert that I have the same people in mind.

Let's take these back to front and start with (52b). What we find in (52b) is that we run into another infinite regress problem, even with Quantifier Raising. The LF of (52b) is (53), with the quantified phrase *everyone you do [e]* adjoined to the embedded IP:

(53) [$_{CP}$ [$_{IP}$ I [$_{VP}$ expect [$_{CP}$ [$_{IP}$ everyone you do [e]$_i$ [$_{IP}$ t$_i$ will visit Mary]]]]]].

We need to find a VP to plug into the gap [e]$_i$, but there isn't one that works. We could try the VP *visit Mary*, but that's not what (52b) means. The gapped VP has to do with expectation, not with visiting Mary. But the VP which is headed by *expect* is *expect everyone you do[e]$_i$ t$_i$ will visit Mary*, and this VP has another [e] gap. If we plug this VP into the gap in the LF in (53), we'll get another gap and so on and so on.

Look how this changes with (52a), which feels a little clumsy, but which is much better than (52b). In (52a), the gap is in the Exceptionally Case Marked object. Under the hypothesis that we're advancing here, even though it's the subject of the lower clause, it must move at LF to Spec AgrOP in order to be assigned accusative Case:

(54) [$_{CP}$ [$_{IP}$ I [$_{AgrOP}$ everyone you do [e]$_i$ [$_{VP}$ expect [$_{IP}$ t$_i$ to visit Mary]]]]]

It will then undergo QR and adjoin to the matrix IP:

(55) [$_{CP}$ [$_{IP}$ everyone you do [e]$_i$ [$_{IP}$ I [$_{AgrOP}$ t$_i'$ [$_{VP}$ expect [$_{IP}$ t$_i$ to visit Mary]]]]]]

With the LF in (55), we've solved our infinite regress problem. We've got a VP *expect t$_i$ to visit Mary* which we can copy into the position of the gap:

(56) [$_{CP}$ [$_{IP}$ everyone you do [$_{VP}$ expect [$_{IP}$ t$_i$ to visit Mary]]$_i$ [$_{IP}$ I [$_{AgrOP}$ t$_i'$ [$_{VP}$ expect [$_{IP}$ t$_i$ to visit Mary]]]]]]

This also results in the correct interpretation: for every person x such that you expect x to visit Mary, I expect x to visit Mary.

This is a good argument for movement to AgrOP at LF, because it's the move to Spec AgrOP which allows the quantifier to escape from the VP. If we didn't have movement to AgrOP, then when the quantified phrase underwent QR, it would adjoin to the embedded IP, and we'd have (57) at LF:

(57) [$_{CP}$ [$_{IP}$ I [$_{VP}$ expect [$_{IP}$ everyone you do [e]$_i$ [$_{IP}$ t$_i$ to visit Mary]]]]]

When we then tried to look around for a VP to fill the gap in [e], we'd have the same problem we had when we were looking at (52b). There are only two VPs around: *visit Mary* and *expect everyone you do [e]$_i$ t$_i$ to visit Mary*. We don't want the first one, because that doesn't get the right meaning, and we don't want the second one because that has elided material in it, and we'll get into an infinite regress.

The fact that we get the right meaning without an infinite regress suggests that the ECM subject is raising to a position outside the VP, something which is already predicted under the assumption that it must move, for Case reasons, to the specifier of AgrOP. Notice that this has the effect of making Exceptional Case Marking less 'exceptional'. Both direct objects and ECM objects receive accusative Case because both move to the specifier of AgrOP.

EXERCISE 2

Use the following sentence to argue for Object Shift in Danish. (Assume that *ikke* behaves similarly to Icelandic *ekki*.):

(a) Í går   læste Peter den uden tvivl   ikke.
     yesterday read Peter it   without doubt not
     'Peter without doubt didn't read it yesterday.'

10.3   EVIDENCE FOR A 'SPLIT' INFL: TRANSITIVE EXPLETIVE CONSTRUCTIONS IN ICELANDIC

In discussing AgrOP in the previous sections, we've been assuming that it lies between IP and VP. However, in this section, we're going to examine some evidence that IP itself must be split into two different functional categories, AgrSP and TP, corresponding to the two pieces of information that I contains: subject-verb agreement and tense. We'll be using essentially the same logic we've been using all along though. Elements seem to be moving to and attached to positions that, under our current assumptions, don't exist. By splitting Infl into two different categories, we can explain the various word orders that we find.

Some of the most compelling evidence for the need to split Infl into parts is seen in some Germanic languages (most notably Icelandic, but also German, Dutch, and Yiddish, among others). These languages possess a construction known in the literature as the *Transitive Expletive Construction (TEC)*. These constructions are similar to the expletive constructions found in languages like English, which we took a look at in Chapter 7:

(58)   There is a book on the floor.

What gives transitive expletive constructions their name is the fact that, unlike in English, for example, expletive constructions can be used with transitive verbs, as illustrated by the Icelandic sentence in (59):[5]

(59)   það hafa   margir jólasveinar   borðað búðing.
      There have many Christmas trolls eaten   the pudding.
      'Many Christmas trolls have eaten the pudding.'

The corresponding English sentence is of course completely ungrammatical:

(60)   *There have many Christmas trolls eaten the pudding.

The problem that the sentence in (59) raises for our theory of phrase structure should be obvious. *There* seems to be in Spec IP, the subject position, and *have* has presumably raised from V to I. (We saw in discussing object shift that Icelandic verbs always raise from V to I in the syntax.) But where does that leave the 'logical' subject *many Christmas trolls*?

Well, as usual, we need to think about what kind of diagnostic tools we have and see what we can do with them. The first thing we ought to try to determine is whether *many Christmas trolls* is inside or outside the VP. To do that, we'll be calling on our old friends, adverbs. Beginning with Ottósson (1989), the standard view was that the adverb tests showed that subjects of transitive expletive constructions were in Spec VP:

(61) það hafa [VP sennilega [VP *margir stúdentar* lesið bókina]].
There have   probably   many students read the book
'Many students have probably read the book.'

The assumption was that the adverb *probably* was adjoined to the matrix VP, and therefore *many students* must be inside the VP since it appears to the adverb's right.

However, Bobaljik and Jonas (1996) suggest that the position of *probably* has been misconstrued. *Probably* seems to modify the whole sentence, rather than just the VP. In other words, it's a sentence adverb rather than just a VP adverb. Because of this it's possible that it's adjoined not to VP, but to some category higher up in the tree. This view seems to be confirmed when we look at what happens when we have two adverbs:

(62) það luku   sennilega *einhverjir stúdentar* alveg
There finished probably some students   completely
verkefninu.
the assignment.
'Some students probably completely finished the assignment.'

Here we see the subject of the TEC, *some students*, appearing between the sentence-modifying adverb *probably* and the VP-modifying adverb *completely*. Since *completely* is undoubtedly adjoined to VP, this suggests very strongly that the subject has moved to a position outside the VP and that the sentence-modifying adverb *probably* is indeed adjoined somewhere higher in the tree.

(62) in particular raises two problems. The first is the one we've been discussing: where is *some students*? There's now a second problem, though. Where is *probably*? Under standard theories of adverb placement, adverbs can only be adjoined to XPs. We've just argued that *probably* isn't adjoined to VP, but it can't be adjoined to IP either. If it were, we'd expect it to precede the expletive in Spec IP. It looks as though we need another XP somewhere between IP and VP for *probably* to be adjoined to. This might sound at first glance like a job for our old friend from the previous section: AgrOP. It seems on the surface to have the right properties. The subject of the TEC could be in Spec AgrO and the adverb *probably* could be adjoined to AgrOP. That would certainly get us the right word order.

I'm sure you've already spotted the problem, though. Because this is a *transitive* expletive construction, we've got a direct object (*the assignment* in (62) and *the book* in (61)). It will presumably need to move at LF to Spec AgrO in order to be assigned accusative Case. If the subject of the TEC is in Spec AgrOP, we'd predict that *it* rather than the object would be assigned accusative Case, and we'd have to come up with some other mechanism for assigning Case to the direct object. Otherwise the direct object would never be assigned Case and we'd wrongly predict that TECs are ungrammatical.

So, it looks like, in addition to AgrOP, we need yet another functional category in order to provide a space for the subject of the TEC to be and also for the adverb *probably* to be adjoined to.

We could simply add in another functional category between AgrOP and IP, but what's traditionally done is to break up Infl into its two constituent parts. Recall from our first discussion of Infl back in Chapter 2 that Infl contains two pieces of information. Infl is first the repository of agreement information for the subject of the sentence. The specifier-head relationship between I and Spec IP allows subject-verb agreement to take place. However, in addition Infl also contains the information about the Tense of the sentence (present, past, etc.). If we split these two pieces of information into two functional categories, which are usually called AgrSP and TP, we'll have the landing sites that we need. The expletive can be in Spec AgrSP, the adverb *probably* can be adjoined to TP, and the TEC subject can be in Spec TP.

(63)

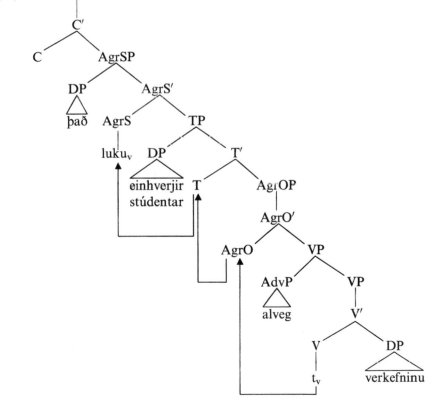

This leaves the specifier of AgrOP free for the direct object to use at LF.

(64)

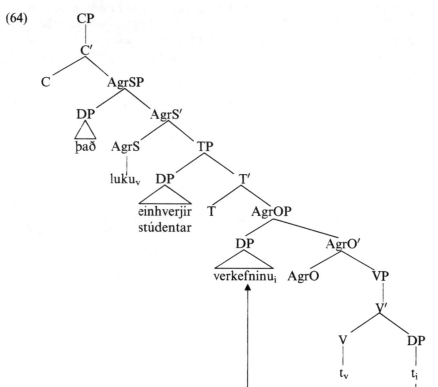

We can see conclusive evidence that splitting IP into AgrSP and TP is the right approach by taking a look at what happens when we have overt object shift in TECs. When we were looking at (61) and (62), we said that AgrOP couldn't be the functional category we needed because it had to stay free for the direct object to move to at LF. Since, as you'll recall from Section 10.2, Icelandic allows overt object shift of a DP direct object, we can test this hypothesis about AgrOP needing to be free. Conveniently enough, Icelandic allows object shift in TECs, as (65) indicates:

(65) það lauk$_v$ einhver [$_{AgrOP}$ verkefninu$_i$ [$_{VP}$ alveg [$_{VP}$ t$_v$ t$_i$]]].
      There finished somebody   the assignment completely.
      'Somebody completely finished the assignment.'

Now we can be pretty sure that our argument for breaking up IP was a good one. We know that the shifted object *the assignment* must be in Spec AgrOP and the subject of the TEC is to the left of that. That seems to indicate that the TEC subject can't be in Spec AgrOP. Just as we've seen before in our arguments for AgrOP, it looks as though we need another position *between*

AgrOP and IP to serve as the position for the subject of the TEC. The structure of (65) should therefore be (66):

(66)

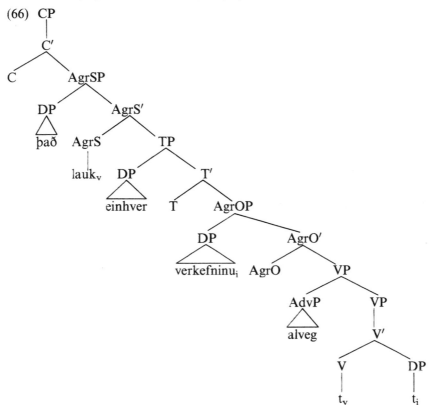

10.4 SUMMARY

Using verb movement as our central diagnostic, we've been arguing in this chapter that the structure of the clause assumed since Chapter 2 was in need of revision. Specifically, when we looked in more detail at English as well as other languages, we saw that the standard model in (67) wasn't sufficient:

(67)

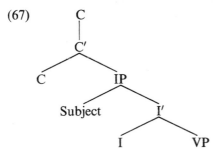

In particular, we saw that the structure in (67) couldn't account for the movement of various heads and XPs. They seemed to be moving into places where no position existed. To provide landing sites for these movements, we first proposed that there is a functional category AgrOP which dominates VP. This also allowed us to revise our theory about accusative Case in line with the proposal by Chomsky and Lasnik, and we saw some evidence that direct objects and ECM subjects (both of which are assigned accusative Case) were moving to the specifier of AgrOP. An added advantage here was that ECM cases are made to appear less 'exceptional' in that accusative Case is assigned to any DP in the specifier of AgrOP.

We saw evidence from Icelandic that we needed to go even further, however. Not only did we need to add AgrOP, but it seemed that IP itself needed to be split. The two pieces of information that the traditional IP contained, subject-verb agreement information and tense information, were given separate functional categories, AgrSP and TP. In this way, we could account for how you could have both an expletive and a subject (the expletive is in Spec AgrSP and the subject is in Spec TP) while at the same time having an object shifted into Spec AgrOP. We were left by the end with the following revised assumptions about the structure of the clause:

(68)

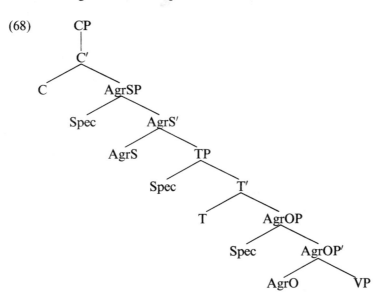

Because we're assuming that something as basic as the structure of the clause will be the same for all languages, we're assuming that other languages like English also have Infl 'split' into AgrSP, TP, and AgrOP. However, there are other possible views, and you'll find the references to some of them in the Bibliography section.

OPEN ISSUE: MORE EVIDENCE FOR AgrOP IN ENGLISH

In the open issue for this chapter, I want to return to an argument for AgrOP from English. I discuss it here in the Open Issue section rather than in the main text because, although the data and the argument are really interesting, the data are, to my ear, a little unclear, and there are some potentially problematic implications.

Lasnik and Saito (1991) suggest that there is further evidence from c-command that subjects in ECM constructions move to a position outside the VP. In a nutshell, Exceptionally Case Marked subjects, which are in the specifier position of the embedded IP, appear to c-command elements in the *higher* VP. This is quite unexpected under the standard analysis of Exceptional Case Marking, in which a sentence like (69) has the tree in (70):

(69)   I believe John to be the best candidate with all my heart.

(70)

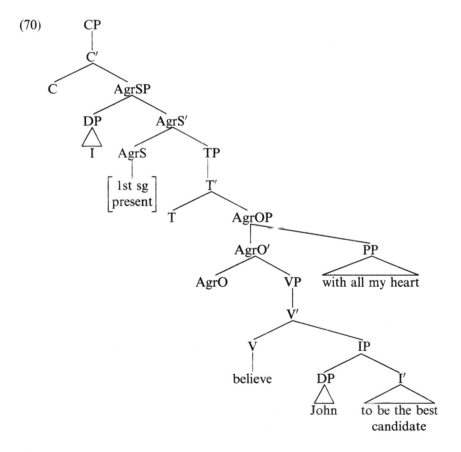

In all of our previous discussions of ECM, we've been assuming that the subject of the ECM infinitive *John* is assigned accusative Case by *believe* without moving from its D-Structure position. However, as you can see from the tree in (70), this makes the clear prediction that it should not be able to c-command any elements which modify the VP, such as a prepositional phrase like *with all my heart*, which in (70) is a sister to the matrix V'. If, on the other hand, it could be shown that the ECM subject *is* able to c-command elements in the matrix VP, that would be quite strong evidence that ECM subjects are moving from their D-Structure position to somewhere outside the VP. The specifier of a hypothetical AgrOP which dominates VP would seem to provide exactly what's needed.

(71)

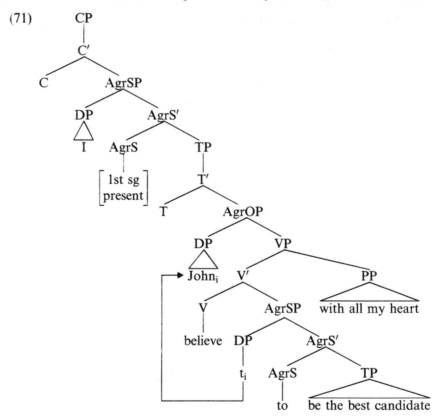

As you can see from the tree in (71), if the ECM subject were to move to the specifier of AgrOP, it would be in a position to c-command other elements in the VP.

To take a first example from Lasnik and Saito's data, let's consider their evidence from Binding Theory. As we've discussed in Chapter 5 and Chapter 8, Principles A, B, and C all use c-command to define the range of possible antecedent relationships. If anything can be said to be the key unifying force in Binding Theory, it's c-command. Principle A, for example, specifically requires, among other things, that the anaphor be c-commanded by its antecedent. This is in order to ensure that sentences like those in (72) are correctly ruled out:

(72)a. *Himself$_i$ likes John$_i$.
   b. *The woman who talked to John$_i$ yesterday hit himself$_i$.

Observations like those in (72) form some of the core facts about Binding Theory.

However, Lasnik and Saito observe contrasts like the following:

(73)a. The District Attorney proved [two men$_i$ to have been at the scene of the crime] during each other$_i$'s trials.
   b. *The District Attorney proved [that two men$_i$ were at the scene of the crime] during each other$_i$'s trials.

Although the contrast in (73) is not as strong for me personally as I'd prefer, Lasnik (1999a) reports that (73a) contrasts significantly with (73b) for most of the speakers that he's interviewed. If ECM subjects did not move to Spec AgrOP, we'd predict that (73a) and (73b) should be identical. The first branching node dominating *two men* in both cases is the embedded AgrSP. Therefore both sentences violate Principle A, since the anaphor *each other* is not c-commanded by its antecedent. On the other hand, if ECM subjects move to Spec AgrOP at LF, then in (73a), but not (73b), *two men* will c-command *each other* – leading to the prediction that only (73b) is ungrammatical.

A related kind of example which Lasnik and Saito discuss concerns Negative Polarity Items (NPIs). DPs with *any* (including things like *anyone* or *anywhere* and also DPs like *any record*) are NPIs. These elements can be interpreted as negatives when they are c-commanded by another negative expression. In this way, you avoid the dreaded 'double negative' that you were warned about in school:

(74)a. No witness saw any suspect.
   b. *No witness saw no suspect.

If the c-command relationship isn't there, then you can't use *any* expressions in this 'negative' way.

(75) *Any witness didn't see the car.

What Lasnik and Saito observe is that ECM subjects appear to license negative polarity expressions in the higher VP, which they shouldn't be able to do under the standard assumptions about ECM and Case.

(76)a.   The District Attorney proved [*no suspect* to be guilty] during *any* of the trials.

    b.   *The District Attorney proved [that *no suspect* was guilty] during *any* of the trials.

(You might be able to get a handle on the intuition by thinking about it this way: (76a) is about how the District Attorney *failed* to prove something. It's a 'negative' sentence. (76b) on the other hand is a 'positive' sentence. The District Attorney proved something, namely that no suspect was guilty.) The negative element has to c-command 'any' in order to get this 'not any/ failure' reading, but if the ECM subject remains in the subject position of the embedded infinitive, it's not clear how that happens, or why there should be a contrast. On the other hand, if ECM subjects raise out of the infinitive VP to the specifier of AgrOP, then they will be in a position to c-command other elements in the VP, and we explain the contrast in (76). In (76a), the ECM subject undergoes Raising, but in (76b) the subject of the *finite* clause cannot. Therefore in (76a) we get the 'failure' reading and in (76b) we don't.

Unfortunately, though, this argument for Spec AgrOP raises an issue which is going to be a little problematic for us. In Hornstein's (1995) antecedent contained deletion argument from the previous section, we concluded that ECM objects moved to Spec AgrOP *at LF*. This was consistent with the general view about English and with everything we've seen so far in this chapter. Main verbs in English don't move out of the V *until LF*. At S-Structure, we expect the verb in English to be in its base-generated position.

The problem is that, in order to account for these contrasts which Lasnik and Saito reveal, you need to assume that the ECM subject is moving to Spec AgrOP at *S-Structure*, not at LF. This is because S-Structure A-movement changes binding relations and negative polarity licensing, but LF A-movement doesn't. Consider (77) and (78). In the (a) sentences, we have S-Structure movement. In the (b) sentences, we have a parallel LF movement as part of expletive replacement:

(77)a.   Two men$_i$ seem to each other$_i$ t$_i$ to be in the room.

    b.   *There seem to each other$_i$ to be two men$_i$ in the room.

(78)a.   No trainee$_i$ seems to any manager t$_i$ to be suitable for the job.

    b.   *There seems to any manager to be no trainee suitable for the job.

The ungrammaticality of the (b) sentences cannot be attributed to any incompatibility between expletive *there* and the intended associate, or some problem with expletive replacement, as (79) shows:

(79)a.   There seem to be two men in the room.

    b.   There seems to be no trainee suitable for the job.

So we seem to be left with a problem. We had evidence in Section 10.1.2.2 that main verbs in English stay in their base-generated position at S-Structure. But we now seem to have evidence that ECM subjects move *in the overt syntax* to Spec AgrOP (i.e., at or before S-Structure). Putting these two things together, you'd expect that the word order that you get in ECM constructions would have the ECM object in Spec AgrOP *preceding* the verb in V:

(80)   *I Mary$_i$ believe t$_i$ to be the best candidate.

This is clearly not a grammatical sentence of English.

Lasnik and Saito's evidence looks really interesting. If we accept it, we've got some nice evidence for the existence of AgrOP in English. The downside is that we're forced into the conclusion that ECM verbs in English are raising from V to AgrO in the overt syntax, rather than at LF, which seems to contradict what we saw earlier.

BIBLIOGRAPHY

Now that we've made it to the last chapter, you're in a position to follow up some of the specific references in the text directly. As you've probably gathered, the first person to explicitly claim that Infl needed to be split up is Pollock (1989). The order that we've given is more or less the standard one, but there are a number of different proposals about how many extra functional heads there are and what their hierarchical relationships are. Webelhuth (1995b) has an excellent overview of a handful of proposals. Lightfoot and Hornstein (1994) is a collection of papers which deal entirely with verb movement and split Infl issues. This is a really interesting book because following most of the papers there are comments on the paper from another linguist. Contrary to what we've been assuming, Thráinsson (1996) argues that not all languages have a split Infl. He claims that Icelandic does, as we've argued, but that English doesn't. Lasnik (1999a) and (1999b) also have some good discussion, particularly with respect to the issues raised in the Open Issue.

ANSWERS TO IN-TEXT EXERCISES

Exercise 1

Which of the following languages have overt verb-raising?

(a) Gianni non parla più/*Gianni non più parla
     Gianni not speaks anymore
     'Gianni is not speaking anymore.'

                                  (Italian, from Belletti (1994))

(b) ... at me ikke kjøpæ bokje/* ... at me kjøpæ ikke bokje
     that we not buy(pl) the.book
     '... that we didn't buy the book'
                  (Hallingdalen dialect of Norwegian, cited in Vikner (1994))

The key question is where the verb appears relative to negation, or any material which is plausibly adjoined to VP. Under the assumption that Italian is like French, then the negative adverb *più* marks NegP. Therefore, Italian does have overt verb Raising, since the verb must precede più and may not follow it. Norwegian, on the other hand, does not have double negation, and therefore *ikke* is marking the position of NegP. The fact that the verb *kjøpæ* must follow *ikke* suggests that this dialect of Norwegian does not have overt verb Raising.

Exercise 2

Use the following sentence to argue for Object Shift in Danish. (Assume that *ikke* behaves similarly to Icelandic *ekki*.):

(a) Í går læste Peter den uden tvivl ikke.
     yesterday read Peter it without doubt not
     'Peter without doubt didn't read it yesterday.'

Under the assumption that Danish *ikke* behaves similarly to Icelandic *ekki*, then it must be adjoined to VP, just as Icelandic *ekki* is. Therefore, it (and the adverbial phrase *uden tvivl*) must be marking the left edge of VP. This suggests that the pronoun *den* has moved to a position outside the VP. Since it is appearing after the subject *Peter*, which is presumably in Spec IP, a logical conclusion is that it has moved to Spec AgrOP.

ADDITIONAL EXERCISES

Exercise 1

Draw the S-Structure and LF trees for the following sentences, being sure to keep in mind verb raising and movement to AgrOP as needed:

1. John can hit the ball.
2. Mary has usually been reading the book.
3. The government may not always be honest.
4. Je ne suis pas arrivé. [French]
   I ne am not arrived
   'I haven't arrived.'
5. Je pensais ne pas pouvoir dormir dans cette chambre. [French]
   I thought ne not to be able to sleep in this room
   'I thought I wouldn't be able to sleep in this room.'

Exercise 2

One of the useful things that a split Infl can do for us is give us more places to adjoin adverbs, since it's assumed that adverbs can only adjoin to maximal projections. What do the following sentences suggest to you about where *probably* is adjoined?

1. John will probably completely destroy the town.
2. það luku sennilega einhverjir stúdentar alveg verkefninu. (Icelandic)
   there finished probably some students completely the.assignment
   'Some students probably completely finished the assignment.'

Exercise 3

Do the following sentences provide evidence for a 'split' Infl? Under what assumptions/analysis would they or would they not? (Keep in mind that both German and Dutch are head final.)

1. Es   essen brave Kinder   grüne Äpfel
   There eat   well-behaved children green apples
   immer sorgfältig. (German)
   always carefully

2. Ele disse existirem muitos candidatos nesta eleição. (Portuguese)
   He said exist-3pl many candidates in this election
   'He said that there are many candidates in this election.'

3. ... dat er veel mensen dat boek gestern gekocht hebben. (Dutch)
   that there many people the book yesterday bought have
   '... that many people have bought the book yesterday.'

Notes

4 θ-THEORY AND CASE THEORY

1. In fact, there's a joke in *Alice in Wonderland* based on precisely this misunderstanding about expletives, where two characters argue about what the thing was that the Archbishop of Canterbury found when he 'found it advisable that ... '.
2. You may be wondering about examples such as *John is likely to be home now* or *John seems to be doing well*. There's something a little different going on in these cases, and we'll discuss them in Chapter 6.

6 MOVEMENT AND CHAINS

1. We will ignore for the moment the transformation that also moves I to C. We will return to this though in Chapter 10.
2. This is a considerable oversimplification. Modern Irish has a lot of different complementizers for different kinds of contexts, but they're not relevant for the present discussion. See Chung and McCloskey (1987), as well as McCloskey (1979) for more details. The examples are from Chung and McCloskey.
3. The capital L does not appear in the orthography, but is merely present to indicate that this is the complementizer *a* which triggers lenition mutation on the following word (as opposed to a different complementizer *a* which does not).
4. We won't concern ourselves here with the mechanism by which the element in the *by*-phrase gets assigned the θ-role that would normally be assigned to the subject.
5. The attentive reader will have noticed that this is not quite true, strictly speaking. We still have things like (51) in the text to account for. There is much disagreement in the literature about how to handle these cases. Some recent accounts are Lasnik (1995), Moro (1997) and my own work (Poole 1996). We'll take a closer look at some of the issues involved in Chapters 7 and 8.

7 LOGICAL FORM

1. Czech (Toman 1981) and Hungarian (Kiss 1994) are other examples.
2. A true semanticist would probably be screaming obscenities at this point, as this is precisely the way that people like Geach (1972) say that you

shouldn't think about quantifiers. However, since we're only interested here in the *syntactic* behavior of quantifiers, this issue, along with much else, will be swept under the rug. For anyone who'd like to take a peek under said rug, there are a number of good textbooks on formal semantics, including Larsen and Segal (1995) and Heim and Kratzer (1998).

3. In fact, what's even more natural in my dialect is to use a *plural* pronoun, even when it's explicit that only one person is involved. So (53) is most natural for me as:

(i)   As for the new employee, their duties will include ...

The problem is that even a plural pronoun doesn't *force* a bound-variable interpretation in the way that 'he/she' does. In (ii) *they* can still be interpreted as referring to some unmentioned group of people:

(ii)   Who thinks that they're smart?

For this reason, I'll continue with 'he/she', even though it's a little less natural.

4. I'm putting aside cases where the verb *be* contracts with *there*. In my dialect, for example, (i) is fine:

(i)   There's three things I need to do.

However, without contraction (i) is impossible.

5. It should be mentioned that although superiority is a topic which received a lot of attention in the literature (Lasnik & Saito 1984 is one of the best known), its effects are not well understood at all, and judgements about sentences like (15b) in particular can vary under different discourse situations. Chomsky (1995: Chapter 4, footnote 69) goes so far as to suggest that the phenomenon doesn't really exist. See particularly Kuno (1987) for some discussion.

6. To my ear, *what on Earth* can't be substituted in this way, so apologies to anyone offended by the profanity. It's all in the name of Science.

8   THE BINDING THEORY AND EMPTY CATEGORIES

1. The sentences usually given as illustrations of strong crossover are a little simpler, something like (i), which cannot by synonymous with (ii):

(i)   *Who$_i$ does he$_i$ like t$_i$?
(ii)   Who$_i$ t$_i$ likes himself?

These simpler sentences don't illustrate the point we need to make about wh-traces, though; hence the need for the more complicated (5) and (7).

2. Dropping the subject is sometimes possible in English. For example, in describing your day in an e-mail message, you might say 'Went to the store. Saw a good movie', etc. This is clearly something different from true null subject languages for several reasons, not the least of which is that the subject can usually only be dropped if it's *I*, or sometimes expletive *it*.

3. But see the 'Open Issue' section of this chapter.

4. See Rizzi's (1986) original article for more extensive argumentation.

5. Notice, though, that this result might not be incredibly exciting for the following reason: *Mary* is in the subject position of *seem*, which is not a θ-position. So, if *Mary* and *e* aren't coindexed in (27) and don't form a chain then *Mary* will end up violating the θ-Criterion since it won't get a θ-role. So the sentence in (27) will be ruled out independently of the Functional Determination Algorithm. We'll return to this issue in Section 8.7 However, we will see in just a minute places where the Functional Determination Algorithm alone does tell us (indirectly) that certain indexations that we don't want are impossible.

6. (53) is deliberately vague about exactly how successive cyclicity for QR would be represented (does it move through Spec CP or just from IP-adjoined position to IP-adjoined position?, etc.) because we won't need it by the time we get finished.

9   THE EMPTY CATEGORY PRINCIPLE

1. As I mentioned way back in Chapter 1, there are some rare dialects of American English which don't have the 'that-trace' effect for reasons which are not clear. If you're a speaker of one of those dialects, I do apologize.

2. In Lasnik and Saito's terminology, when a trace is checked by the ECP, it receives the feature $+\gamma$ if it satisfies the ECP and $-\gamma$ if it does not. We won't adopt that terminology here, but I mention it because you will often see references to 'gamma marking' in the literature on the ECP as another way of saying 'checking to see if a trace satisfies the ECP'.

10   VERB RAISING AND THE ANALYSIS OF INFL

1. This principle of phrase-structure compatibility, which says that only heads can move into head positions and that only XPs can move into XP positions (like specifiers), was first explicitly discussed by Emonds (1976) under the name of the principle of Structure Preservation.

2. See Pollock (1989, footnote 3) for some discussion. Also potentially relevant is the fact that some non-standard dialects of French which have only one negative marker use only *pas* and not *ne*.
3. Just as above when discussing English, we'll continue to assume that if the verb doesn't raise to I in the syntax, then it does so at LF.
4. Unless otherwise indicated, the French examples in this section are from Webelhuth (1995b), which are adapted/simplified from the original data in Pollock (1989). (Some irrelevant detail, such as VP modifiers and other prepositional phrases have been omitted, for example.)
5. Unless otherwise indicated, all Icelandic examples are taken from Bobaljik and Jonas (1996).

References

Abney, S. (1987) *The English Noun Phrase in its Sentential Aspect*, unpublished PhD dissertation, Massachusetts Institute of Technology.

Aoun, J. and N. Hornstein (1985) 'Quantifier Types', *Linguistic Inquiry* **16**, pp. 623–37.

Aoun, J., N. Hornstein and D. Sportiche (1981) 'Some Aspects of Wide Scope Quantification', *Journal of Linguistic Research* **1**, pp. 69–95.

Baker, C. L. (1970) 'Notes on the Description of English Questions: The Role of an Abstract Question Morpheme', *Foundations of Language* **6**, pp. 197–219.

Barss, A. and H. Lasnik (1986) 'A Note on Anaphora and Double Objects', *Linguistic Inquiry* **17**, pp. 347–54.

Belletti, A. (1994) 'Verb Positions: Evidence from Italian', in D. Lightfoot and N. Hornstein, eds, pp. 19–40.

Bobaljik, J. D. and D. Jonas (1996) 'Subject Positions and the Role of TP', *Linguistic Inquiry* **27**, pp. 195–236.

Borsley, R. (1994) 'In Defense of Coordinate Structures', *Linguistic Analysis* **24**, pp. 218–46.

Brody, M. (1984) 'On Contextual Definitions and the Role of Chains', *Linguistic Inquiry* **15**, p. 355–81.

Burzio, L. (1986) *Italian Syntax* (Dordrecht: Foris).

Chomsky, N. (1957) *Syntactic Structures* (The Hague: Mouton).

Chomsky, N. (1965) *Aspects of the Theory of Syntax* (Cambridge, MA: MIT Press).

Chomsky, N. (1970) 'Remarks on Nominalization', in R. A. Jacobs and P. S. Rosenbaum, eds, *Readings in English Transformational Grammar* (Waltham, MA: Ginn), pp. 184–221.

Chomsky, N. (1973) 'Conditions on Transformations', in S. Anderson and P. Kiparsky, eds, *A Festschrift for Morris Halle* (New York: Holt, Reinhart and Winston), pp. 232–86.

Chomsky, N. (1981) *Lectures on Government and Binding* (Dordrecht: Foris).

Chomsky, N. (1982) *Some Concepts and Consequences of the Theory of Government and Binding* (Cambridge, MA: MIT Press).

Chomsky, N. (1986) *Barriers* (Cambridge, MA: MIT Press).

Chomsky, N. (1988) *Language and Problems of Knowledge: The Managua Lectures* (Cambridge, MA: MIT Press).

Chomsky, N. (1995) *The Minimalist Program* (Cambridge, MA: MIT Press).

Chung, S. and J. McCloskey (1987) 'Government, Barriers, and Small Clauses in Modern Irish', *Linguistic Inquiry* **18**, pp. 173–237.

Emonds, J. (1976) *A Transformational Approach to English Syntax* (New York: Academic Press).

Epstein, S. D. (1983) 'A Note on Functional Determination and Strong Crossover', *The Linguistic Review* **3**, pp. 299–305.

Epstein, S. D. (1984) 'Quantifier PRO and the LF Representation of PRO_{arb}', *Linguistic Inquiry* **15**, pp. 499–505.

Epstein, S. D. (1990) 'Differentiation and Reduction in Syntactic Theory: A Case Study', *Natural Language and Linguistic Theory* **8**, pp. 301–13.

Epstein, S. D. and N. Hornstein (1999) *Working Minimalism* (Cambridge, MA: MIT Press).

Freeborn, D. (1992) *From Old English to Standard English* (Basingstoke: Macmillan – now Palgrave).

Geach, P. T. (1972) *Logic Matters* (Berkeley and Los Angeles, CA: University of California Press).

Gregg, K. (1989) 'Second Language Acquisition Theory: The Case for a Generative Perspective', in S. M. Gass and J. Schacter, eds, *Linguistic Perspectives on Second Language Acquisition* (Cambridge: Cambridge University Press), pp. 15–37.

Grimshaw, J. (1990) *Argument Structure* (Cambridge, MA: MIT Press).

Haegeman, L. (1994) *Introduction to Government & Binding Theory* (Oxford: Blackwell).

Harada, K. (1972) 'Constraints on WH-Q Binding', *Studies in Descriptive and Applied Linguistics* **5**, pp. 180–206.

Harbert, W. (1995) 'Binding Theory, Control, and pro', in G. Webelhuth, ed., pp. 177–240.

Heim, I. and A. Kratzer (1998) *Semantics in Generative Grammar* (Oxford: Basil Blackwell Publishers).

Hornstein, N. (1995) *Logical Form* (Cambridge, MA: MIT Press).

Huang, J. (1982) *Logical Relations in Chinese and the Theory of Grammar*, unpublished PhD dissertation, Massachusetts Institute of Technology.

Huang, J. (1983) 'A Note on the Binding Theory', *Linguistic Inquiry* **14**, pp. 554–61.

Huang, J. (1995) 'Logical Form', in G. Webelhuth, ed., pp. 125–77.

Jackendoff, R. S. (1977) *X'-Syntax: A Study of Phrase Structure* (Cambridge, MA: MIT Press).

Jackendoff, R. S. (1984) *Semantics and Cognition* (Cambridge, MA: MIT Press).

Jackendoff, R. S. (1990) *Semantic Structures* (Cambridge, MA: MIT Press).

Jackendoff, R. S., J. Maling and A. Zaenen (1993) 'Home is Subject to Principle A'. *Linguistic Inquiry* **24**, pp. 173–77.

Jaeggli, O. (1982) *Topics in Romance Syntax* (Dordrecht: Foris).

Kayne, R. (1981) 'ECP Extensions', *Linguistic Inquiry* **12**, pp. 93–133. [Reprinted in Kayne (1984) *Connectedness and Binary Branching* (Dordrecht: Foris).]

Kiss, K. (1994) 'Sentence Structure and Word Order', in F. Kiefer and K. Kiss, eds, *Syntax and Semantics 27: The Syntactic Structure of Hungarian* (San Diego, CA: Academic Press).

Koopman, H. and D. Sportiche (1982) 'Variables and the Bijection Principle', *The Linguistic Review* **2**, pp. 139–60.

Kuno, S. (1987) *Functional Syntax*, (Chicago, IL: University of Chicago Press).

Larson, R. K. (1988) 'On the Double Object Construction', *Linguistic Inquiry* **19**, pp. 335–91.

Larson, R. K. and G. Segal (1995) *Knowledge of Meaning* (Cambridge, MA: MIT Press).

Lasnik, H. (1989) *Essays on Anaphora* (Dordrecht: Kluwer Academic Publishers).

Lasnik, H. (1995) 'Case and Expletives Revisited: On Greed and Other Human Failings', *Linguistic Inquiry* **26**, pp. 615–33.

Lasnik, H. (1999a) *Minimalist Analysis* (Oxford: Blackwell).

Lasnik, H. (1999b) 'Chains of Arguments', in Epstein and Hornstein (1999), pp. 187–216.

Lasnik, H. and M. Saito (1984) 'On the Nature of Proper Government', *Linguistic Inquiry* **15**, pp. 235–89.

Lasnik H. and M. Saito (1991) 'On the Subject of Infinitives', in L. M. Dobrin, L. Nichols and R. M. Rodriguez, eds, *CLS Part I, The General Session* (Chicago, IL: Chicago Linguistics Society). [Reprinted in Lasnik (1999a).]

Lasnik, H. and M. Saito (1992) *Move α* (Cambridge, MA: MIT Press).

Lasnik, H. and J. Uriagereka (1988) *A Course in GB Syntax* (Cambridge, MA: MIT Press).

Lightfoot, D. and N. Hornstein (1994) *Verb Movement* (Cambridge: Cambridge University Press).

Martin, R. (1999) 'Case, the Extended Projection Principle, and Minimalism', in Epstein and Hornstein (1999), pp. 1–26.

May, R. (1977) *The Grammar of Quantification*, unpublished PhD dissertation, Massachusetts Institute of Technology [reprinted (1990) New York: Garland].

May, R. (1985) *Logical Form* (Cambridge, MA: MIT Press).

McCloskey, J. (1979) *Transformational Syntax and Model Theoretic Semantics* (Dordrecht: Reidel).

Moro, A. (1997) *The Raising of Predicates* (Cambridge: Cambridge University Press).

Oehrle, R. (1976) *The Grammatical Status of the English Dative Alternation*, unpublished PhD dissertation, Massachusetts Institute of Technology.

Ottóson, K. (1989) 'VP-Specifier Subjects and the CP/IP distinction in Icelandic and Mainland Scandinavian', *Working Papers in Scandinavian Syntax* **44**, pp. 89–100.

Pesetsky, D. (1987) 'Wh-in-situ: Movement and Unselective Binding', in E. Reuland and A. ter Meulen, eds, *The Representation of (In)definiteness* (Cambridge, MA: MIT Press), pp. 98–129.

Pollock, J.-Y. (1989) 'Verb Movement, UG, and the Structure of IP', *Linguistic Inquiry* **20**, pp. 365–424.

Poole, G. (1996) *Transformations Across Components*, unpublished PhD dissertation, Harvard University.

Reinhart, T. (1976) *The Syntactic Domain of Anaphora*, unpublished PhD dissertation, Massachusetts Institute of Technology.

Reinhart, T. (1983) *Anaphora and Semantic Interpretation* (London: Croom Helm).

Rizzi, L. (1982) *Issues in Italian Syntax* (Dordrecht: Foris).

Rizzi, L. (1986) 'Null Objects in Italian and the Theory of pro', *Linguistic Inquiry* **17**, pp. 508–51.

Rizzi, L. (1990) *Relativized Minimality* (Cambridge, MA: MIT Press).

Ross, J. R. (1967) *Constraints on Variables in Syntax*, unpublished PhD dissertation, Massachusetts Institute of Technology.

Russell, B. (1905) 'On Denoting', *Mind* **14**, pp. 479–93.

Saito, M. (1989) 'Scrambling as Semantically Vacuous A'-Movement', in M. Baltin and A. Kroch, eds, *Alternative Conceptions of Phrase Structure* (Chicago, IL; University of Chicago Press).

Smith, N. and I. Tsimpli (1995) *The Mind of a Savant* (Oxford: Blackwell).

Thráinsson, H. (1996) 'On the (Non-)Universality of Functional Categories', in W. Abraham, S. D. Epstein, H. Thráinsson and C. J.-W. Zwart, eds, *Minimal Ideas: Syntactic Studies in the Minimalist Framework* (Amsterdam: John Benjamins), pp. 253–81.

Toman, J. (1981) 'Aspects of Multiple Wh-Movement', in R. May and J. Koster, eds, *Levels of Syntactic Representation* (Dordrecht: Foris), pp. 293–302.

Torrego, E. (1984) 'On Inversion in Spanish and Some of its Effects', *Linguistic Inquiry* **15**, pp. 103–30.

Vikner, S. (1994) 'Finite Verb Movement in Scandinavian Embedded Clauses', in Lightfoot and Hornstein, eds, pp. 117–49.

Webelhuth, G., ed., (1995a) *Government and Binding Theory and the Minimalist Program* (Oxford: Blackwell).

Webelhuth, G. (1995b) 'X′-Theory and Case Theory', in G. Webelhuth, ed., pp. 15–96.

Index

312

LIBRARY, UNIVERSITY OF CHESTER